D0674192

School-Community Relations, Under Reform

SECOND EDITION

ROBERT L. CROWSON
Vanderbilt University

with chapters by
Mary Erina Driscoll and Julius Menacker

McCutchan Publishing Corporation
P.O. Box 774, 2940 San Pablo Ave., Berkeley, CA 94702

ISBN 0-8211-0233-8
Library of Congress Catalog Card Number 97-76281

Printed in the United States of America

CONTENTS

INTRODUCTION

Educators would not be surprised to hear that U.S. schools are under reform. Included in this reform movement are the following initiatives:

- Professionalism in public schooling is being re-thought to offer teachers a greater sense of workplace involvement and empowerment.
- The nationwide concern about the quality of the public schools has led to an abundance of proposals to improve school effectiveness.
- There is experimentation in changing the very structure of public education, including a "chartering of individual schools and the encouragement of greater parental choice through vouchers.
- Serious questions about the quality of teacher and administrator training have led to proposals for fundamental changes in the teacher-training process.
- There is a new press toward parent involvement in education and a strengthening of school-community relations.

This book is about the last of these reform-minded initiatives. Today's reform of school-community relations in public education is not a simply focused initiative; rather, it is richly varied and many sided—an effort full of proposals, experiments, new policies, and state legislation all designed to bring the schools somehow closer to the parent and community clientele. Included are such consumer-sovereignty initiatives as choice and home-schooling, an array of partnership programs between the schools and businesses or universities, a new "outreach" from schools toward parents as supporters of and sharers in effective schooling, a renewed "service-coordination" thrust in public education, and some far-reaching steps toward greater

1

parental involvement in the governance of neighborhood schools.

Whatever the direction—from choice to partnership to shared governance—today's reforms in school-community relations are challenging mightily many accepted assumptions about educational institutions and their environments. Old administrative strategies aimed toward a distancing between educator and parent find changes now in a search for much closer ties and even a sharing of pedagogic responsibilities. An interest-group and a conflict- or difference-oriented politics of school-community relations looks now for greater consensus between school and community. Parents, previously expected to be at best supporters and advisors, are now asked to acquire more vital and more active roles as school site-level policymakers, planners, and partners in instruction. The school as a respondent to its community environment finds a revised role in a notion of the school as the proactive creator of a sense of community and community strengths (or "social capital") within that environment. Parent roles as recipients of communications *from* the schools and as representatives of parental perspectives *to* the schools are changing toward roles as active and fully participative agents *with* the schools.

As is typical of any reform movement, such changes in the assumptions, policies, and practices of school-community relationships are not without controversy or cost. Among the administrative and political problems of magnitude are (a) a search for cooperation between, while simultaneously preserving the independence of, both parent and professional; (b) a challenge to the school to be responsive to parents while simultaneously seeking to change the behaviors of parents; (c) the task of "opening" the school to its community, amid institutional traditions and procedures that emphasize barriers between school and community; and (d) the problem of a broadening of teachers' professional roles toward cooperation and outreach amid historical traditions of teacher isolation and autonomy. In short, warns Seymour Sarason (1990), schools are peculiarly "intractable" institutions.[1]

Although intractability—that is, a unique capacity to remain unchanged by reform—may be a decided feature of the public

---

[1] See Seymour B. Sarason, *The Predictable Failure of Educational Reform.* San Francisco: Jossey-Bass Publishers, 1990, pp. 1–8.

schools, it is the central thesis of this book that something important and fundamental is currently taking place in discussions of school-community relationships. In examining this something, *School-Community Relations, Under Reform* pursues two major objectives. First, the book attempts to convey a political/historical sense of the changing relationships between public schools and their communities—and the policy/administrative implications of these changes. We suggest that the literatures on the community-relations aspects of school administration and the politics of education are currently in need of revision—particularly toward a fuller consideration of linkages between parents and professionals, between community relations and school effectiveness, and between schools generally and their community environments.

Second, the book seeks to provide, in nearly every chapter, a sense of administrative and policy alternatives. There is throughout an examination of differing (both traditional and emergent) theoretical perspectives on school and community—and the administrative insights to be gained from these perspectives. We do suggest in this book that the administrative literature and theory treating community relations is decidedly in transition—moving somewhat away from the "old" politics-of-education topics of interest groups, power structures, needs assessments, and a "PR" approach toward key administrative issues of shared governance, direct parental involvement in instruction, conflict between parents and professionals, strategic planning, and new administrative frontiers in the implementation of children's services and outreach reforms in public schooling.

The book is in two parts. Part I examines school-community relations in historical and theoretical perspective—paying special attention to evolving questions of school administration, the local politics of education, parental-involvement effects on the schools, and the law vis-à-vis school-community relations. Part II turns to more specific questions of administrative practice in the improvement of school-community relations—including school-site planning, strategies of parental involvement, the management of community relations, and school outreach toward the community.

School-Community Relations, Under Reform was first written while efforts to restructure the public schools and to redefine school-community relations were well (indeed furiously) underway, but by no means played out. In this, its second edition, the book builds upon a literature that has strengthened and deepened considerably in the last five years. The ties between and the attention given to schools and their parents/communities have increased, almost geometrically. Some of the early '90's innovations such as home-schooling and service-integration partnerships with the schools now have a bit of history; but many others (e.g., charter-schooling and voucher initiatives) are still in the early stages of experimentation. For this reason, the book has attempted to provide practicing educators and students of school politics or administration with a sense of conceptual alternatives and their possible strengths and weaknesses, rather than with a summary of hard-and-fast findings from the research literature. Even where some valuable findings are beginning to emerge, as on the impact of parental involvement on school achievement (Chapter 6), the message we want to convey is that there are still many more questions than answers about community-relations effects, issues, strategies, and alternatives.

The book will be most useful if the reader approaches it less as a set of prescriptions than as the beginning of a dialogue—as the foundation for a discussion of, and a search for a bit of clarity regarding, the administration of public schools amid traditional and emergent forms of school-community relations. Indeed, many of the exercises and activities at the end of each chapter suggest a careful and critical administrative- or policy-minded weighing of the pros and cons, the competing values, and the alternative forms and effects of community-relations choices in education.

The book and its dialogues also work best if the reader tests many of its ideas against practice. Thus, many of the exercises and activities additionally suggest that the reader conduct interviews, engage in some direct observation in the schools, and otherwise compare for him- or herself the practices of parents and professionals against the book's generalizations and conclusions. It will be obvious to the reader that the authors of this book have a bias toward a richer involvement of parents and the community in the work of the schools and, indeed, even toward a greater outreach of the schools into the community. Nevertheless, it will hopefully also be obvious to the reader that much of our knowledge about "best" practices in reforming school-community relations remains to be developed. Thus the reader is invited to join actively in some initiatives for learning together to improve the schools.

Part I
School-Community
Relations in Perspective

Chapter One

SCHOOL-COMMUNITY RELATIONS UNDER REFORM

Each year the child is coming to belong more to the state, and less and less to the parent.
—Ellwood P. Cubberley, *Changing Conceptions of Education*, 1909

Ellwood Cubberley saw it as a battle finally won in 1909: The century-long effort to create a system of "common" schooling for America had been hugely successful. Compulsory education had become a fact of growing up in all but a few of the states. Unquestioned by this time was the right of government to tax its citizens for the support of elementary education and even, after a struggle, secondary education. The public school was fully accepted as a force for national unity, a hedge against diversity, a source of common loyalties and values, an equalizer (see Spring, 1986; also Glenn, Jr., 1988). For the good of society and for the good of the individual child, it was the school's mission to provide a well-educated and thoroughly socialized citizenry to meet the nation's future needs. Thus a strong public education, a fully developed system of common schooling, was needed. By 1900, the answer to Declaration of Independence signer Benjamin Rush's plea (in 1786) for a system of public education, seen as a necessary act of state authority over the family, finally seemed to be well in place.

But Cubberley was wrong—the battle had just begun. By the third quarter of this century, a determined reform movement found much fault with public education's lack of responsiveness to parental concerns and to questions of local diversity. A reform movement in education has consumed the remainder of the century. The charge, essentially, has been that the schools have become too heavily imbued with a "four-walls-of-the-school" mentality. Attributed to Chicago's 1950s-era Superintendent Ben Willis, the four-walls-of-

7

the-school dictum had stressed a strict separation between parent and pedagogue. Inside the schoolhouse door, the professional educator should be fully in charge of the child—unavailable to and free from the intrusions of "outsiders." A school and a profession separated from the public freed educators to do "what's best" for children, without the encumbrances of neighborhood politics or pressure. Indeed, for years the phone numbers of Chicago's individual schools were not to be found in the city's public telephone directory.

Declining public confidence in schooling, perceptions of a crisis in school quality, and a lessening faith in the inviolability of professional expertise have helped lead to a reform movement that is rediscovering the power of the parent. Among the reforms have been state laws telling local educators to be more communicative with parents on the topic of school quality. Illinois, for example, newly required that an annual "school report card" be mailed to each set of parents; it requires a comparison of the achievement scores in the school their child attends with state achievement averages. Other reforms have gone far beyond communication to the promotion of enhanced parental discretion. An opting out of the public sector into private schooling has long been a viable option. Now, there is much increased stress on choice in the public domain—including a piloting of voucher programs in some cities, permitting the use of public funds for the payment of tuition at private institutions. In addition, Minnesota parents searching for educational quality may cross school district boundaries to choose which public schools their children will attend (Mazzoni, 1987). In a number of states across the nation, there is now a new category of public schooling called charter schools, which permit independent groups of teachers, parents, and other participants considerable freedom in running their own schools. In Chicago, the reform emphasis citywide has been on consumer choice from the perspective of neighborhood-based governance. Indeed, a major restructuring of the city's arguably overcentralized school system has been underway since 1988 toward a decided empowerment of "Local School Councils," which feature majority representation from parents. Another indicator of declining confidence in public schooling, disturbing to many educators, is the increasing numbers of parents in recent years who have opted for "home-schooling" (a removal of their children from formal schooling altogether), thus turning the clock of common schooling back many generations.

America's educators, through experience and training, have tended to be far more comfortable with a "four-walls" approach to community relations than with a "come-join-us" approach. School administrators are often more typically "trustees" than "delegates" in their involvements with parents. As Dale Mann (1977) puts it, trustees see themselves as the embodiment of an authoritative, hierarchical tradition—committed to doing what is best for children and the community as they, the professional experts, see it. Delegates, far fewer in number, choose as a first priority to represent and reflect the needs and wishes of their local constituencies. Educators seldom are trained in, or have opportunities to observe, delegatelike administration. Despite the recent press toward parental involvement and parental discretion in public schooling, the administrative skills necessary to achieve an effective blending of school with parents and community are not part of the ready-repertoire of most practitioners. Consequently, many educators have had difficulty adapting to a new assertiveness among parents in many communities, an assertiveness particularly expressed around topics of discipline, the curriculum, religion/morality, and teacher appointments.

In sum, educators have received little assistance to date in adapting to reform-minded demands for reduced top-down, authoritative administration in favor of enhanced bottom-up, responsive management strategies. Adding to the complexity of it all for the practicing administrator is the rest of a "market basket" of reform that has been sweeping the profession. Parental involvement is just one of a panoply of initiatives. Further, necessary adaptations for local administrators stem from reform-minded moves toward enhanced teacher autonomy and teacher professionalism, school-site management, state-mandated testing and state standards, tightened teacher-preparation and teacher-evaluation guidelines, new administrator-training strategies, and strengthened preparation-for-college curricula in the high schools (Crowson and Hannaway, 1989; Murphy and Hallinger, 1993; Wilson and Daviss, 1994). Understandably, many educators sense a shifting focus to their administrative lives—but without the firmness and stability to be derived from a clear sense of direction and a knowledge of resource alternatives. It is the purpose of this book to assist educators in the development of a new sense of perspective and theory-to-practice awareness in the important domain of school-community relations.

Table 1.1

A Broad Categorization of Community-Relations Alternatives

Community-Relations Purposes	Common Administrative Strategies
Community/parental support	Facilitative
Community/parental involvement	Interactive
Community/parent representation	Negotiative

COMMUNITY-RELATIONS ALTERNATIVES

One of the first difficulties in the development of a sense of direction is deciding just what the term *community relations* means. It is a broadly defined construct, with changing interpretations over the years and marked differences in notions of how to achieve "good" community relations. To some educators, the terms *community relations* and *public relations* are synonymous. The effective communication of school goals, activities, and achievements to a (hopefully) receptive public would be the simple definition of community relations, from a decidedly public-relations (PR) perspective. To others, good community relations occurs when the direction of communications is effectively turned around—when parental needs, viewpoints, and interests are transferred to a (hopefully) receptive school. A third group might define good community relations as something in between, where both community and school are equally receptive and are indeed engaged in a help-one-another-toward-effectiveness form of sharing.

Table 1.1 identifies these three broad categories of community-relations alternatives plus the administrative strategies common to each category. Each alternative is explained in some detail in the remainder of this chapter, with added elaboration throughout the book.

Community and Parental Support

From the onset of public schooling, educators have recognized that the public-service nature of their craft requires the pursuit of support from a surrounding community. Indeed, one of the earliest wars in public education (Ravitch, 1974) involved a loss of support among a large portion of one of New York's religious communities. This group felt that its values had been decidedly left out of the curriculum of the common schools. Later, the public schools were again criticized for a "closed-system" attitude toward their external environments (Campbell et al., 1987). Nevertheless, few educators do not recognize that tax revenues, the construction of new schools, a favorable board majority, and their own jobs fundamentally depend on the maintenance of support from the community and parents. While the public schools are wary of the public and have even battled with the public, they have never been so standoffish as to neglect the need for support (especially financial) from the public.

To maintain support, the most common administrative strategy is the *facilitative* act of opening channels of communication between the school and the home or community. This activity often takes on the flavor of a public-relations perspective, involving careful attention to (and even specialized personnel for) school newsletters, newspaper coverage and news releases, open-house activities, school performances, and fundraisers (e.g., bake sales, Halloween fun nights). Educators realize full well that community support results from multiple, often subtle, sources. Thus, it is not by accident that important support-related initiatives include award-winning marching bands, successful football teams, unusually attractive school buildings, carefully choreographed graduation ceremonies, and even the personal appearance and grooming of the school superintendent. Similarly, the savvy school executive will often be sure to establish him- or herself as a community figure by accepting speaking engagements, attending business-group luncheons, becoming a joiner and a volunteer. Seldom, even in the most "closed" school districts, does the local superintendent focus entirely inward on the schools. His or her focus is much more typically outward, toward supporters and the "powers that be" in the community.

Of late, the search for parental and community support has become decidedly proactive. In recognition of the importance of the home environment to good schooling, educators are now asking parents to support the schools by exercising their *responsibilities* toward the schools. Parent guidelines and handbooks are the typical medium of communication. These usually alert parents to, and ask their assistance in enforcing, the rules of the school but additionally provide parents with extra hints for helping with homework, maintaining their children's health, establishing a "positive" home environment, and promoting good study habits. In some school districts, the responsibilities of parents are enforced. The Chicago Public Schools, for example, have required parents to come in person to school to retrieve their son's or daughter's report card at the end of each marking period.

Beyond facilitating good public relations and communicating parental responsibility, the sense among educators is that well-organized campaigns to garner public support for the schools are vital today to effective schooling. Joleen Cattermole and Norman Robinson (1985) discovered that parents' *second* most preferred means of learning about their children's schools is a now-common PR device—the school newsletter. However, Cattermole and Robinson also discovered that parents' *most* preferred source of information is "what my son or daughter tells me." Furthermore, parents' two other top sources of information were (1) personal visits to the school and (2) conversations with friends and neighbors. In short, parents are effectiveness-minded today; they are prone to check up on the "party line" promoted by their schools. They are additionally prone to rely heavily on direct personal contacts, plus their own observations, as fully reliable insights into "what's really going on" at the local schoolhouse. While the PR approach may be necessary, and may help to raise or stabilize community support, it may not be a sufficient community-relations device unto itself. Parents are looking for something more, for evidence of their own that the schools are doing their job.

Community and Parental Involvement

A 1988 Gallup survey asked public school parents how much effort the local schools made to involve them in school affairs. Table 1.2 summarizes the results of that survey, showing that only 25 percent of the respondents felt the schools made "a great deal" of effort toward encouraging parental participation.

Nevertheless, Cattermole and Robinson (1985) discovered that parents considered participation (or "involvement") the most effective method of communicating with the schools. Far from the one-way communication emphasized in a PR approach, what parents valued most was an *interactive* relationship. Ranked first, second, and third in the list of most-effective communication methods were (1) direct approach by phone or in person, (2) parent-teacher conferences, and

Table 1.2

Parent Participation Survey

"To what degree do the local public schools attempt to attract participation by parents in school affairs?"

	Percentage of Public School Parents Responding
A great deal	25
A fair amount	49
Not very much	20
None at all	2
Don't know	4

Source: "The 20th Annual Gallup Poll of the Public's Attitudes Toward the Public Schools," by Alec Gallup and Stanley Elam, *Phi Delta Kappan* 70(1), September 1988, p. 42, © 1988 Phi Delta Kappan, Inc. Reprinted with permission.

(3) work as a school volunteer. Within the top ten in effectiveness were also the participatory strategies of (a) the PTA, (b) informal social meetings, and (c) participation in a school activity (e.g., fund raising) (Cattermole and Robinson, 1985, p. 49).

Even though parental participation is now mandatory in some programmatic areas (e.g., special education placements), an opening up of the school and a promotion of community involvement do not come easily to many educators, who have legitimate reasons for such reluctance. First, educators and parents often have different and even conflicting interests. Willard Waller (1932) warned of such strains nearly six decades ago. Parents tend to have particularistic concerns about their own children, while teachers need to think about the whole classroom. Furthermore, schools often think of themselves as people-changing institutions—working hard to impart a respect for learning, some character development, and a school-achievement work ethic (often in community environments where such values are not universal).

As a second source of reluctance, educators are understandably wary of inroads into their professional expertise. David Tyack (1981, p. 19) quotes Nicholas Murray Butler's observation in 1906—it is as foolish to talk of "democratization of the treatment of appendicitis" as it is to think of a "democratization of schools." Teachers, no less than physicians, it is felt, should not have to seek a majority vote before plying their trade. To be sure, while teachers and school administrators admit that in the professionalization of their field they are far from the standard represented by physicians, key questions of instructional method, pupil grouping, choice and sequencing of learning materials, and the evaluation of student progress are still considered the special province of the trained educator.

It is therefore remarkable that despite differences in interest and questions of professionalism, the involvement of parents in the ongoing work of the schools has grown quite appreciably. Although just 25 percent of Gallup respondents (Table 1.2) indicated "a great deal" of involvement, an additional 49 percent said their schools now do "a fair amount" to attract participation. Indeed, in a later Gallup Poll (1994), statistics on citizen contact with the schools were compared over time with interesting results (see Table 1.3). In analyzing poll data from 1983 to 1991 and 1994, the discovery was that the frequency of public contact with the schools had nearly doubled. Significant gains were noted in attendance at school events, in meetings with teachers or administrators, in "school situation" meetings, and in attendance at school board sessions.

With greater contact, some of the barriers between professional and parent in education have softened. In public schools across the nation, it is usual for the professional staff to work closely today with community-resident aides serving in a variety of nonprofessional roles. Parental-advisement committees for schools are also becoming common, beyond the traditional relationship with a PTA or that which has been mandated under state or federal controls. Many school districts actively encourage parents to visit the schools, to observe classes in progress, and to volunteer their services. Indeed, volunteerism (e.g., senior citizens as tutors) is decidedly on the upswing and is heavily encouraged in most locales. Furthermore, while retaining their professionalism, many teachers today have gained perspective because they themselves are parents and at the same time serve as full-time teaching professionals. There is more understanding now of the concerns (and more people playing dual roles) on both sides of the "four walls" (Hulsebosch, 1988).

Achieving popularity during the 1980s was a special, formalized approach to community involvement, termed the "school partnership" (Ryan, 1976; Barton, 1983; Meroff, 1983; Jones and Maloy,

Table 1.3

Citizen Contact with the Schools

"Since last September, which of the following, if any, have you yourself done?"

	Percentage of Public School Parent Respondents		
	1994	1991	1983
Attended a school play or concert in any local public school	79	56	42
Attended a local public school athletic event	70	49	42
Met with any teachers or administrators in the local public schools about your own child	87	77	62
Attended any meeting dealing with the local public school situation	51	36*	18
Attended a PTA meeting	49	38	36
Attended a school board meeting	27	13	16

* In 1991 this category was worded: "Attended any meeting dealing with the local public schools."

Source: "The 26th Annual Gallup Poll of the Public's Attitudes Toward the Public Schools," by Stanley M. Elam, Lowell C. Rose, and Alec M. Gallup, *Phi Delta Kappan,* 76(1), September 1994, p. 54, © 1994 Phi Delta Kappan, Inc. Reprinted with permission.

1988). By the early 1980s, thousands of individual schools had established voluntary, help-the-schools agreements with corporations, universities, human service agencies, and community organizations (Jones and Maloy, 1988). The most popular arrangement was an "adopt-a-school" program involving most frequently an infusion of resources into the schools in the form of special expertise, tutors, extra equipment, staff development, program enrichment, and support for the extracurriculum (Mann, 1987). Recently, partnership experiments (particularly in city schools) have been structured around a "linkages" concept, wherein individual schools receive assistance from one or more partners (a university, city social service agencies, private groups) in coordinating an array of education-related services to parents, children, and school staff members. These "co-ordinated-services" projects may range from the provision of added health and nutrition services, to adult literacy programs, to child care, to employment training, to social work and counseling services, to an amalgam of curricular and instructional services to classroom teachers (see Behrman, 1992; Nucci, 1989).

Indeed, a major provision in a 1990 educational reform law for the state of Kentucky called for the establishment of Family Resource Centers at targeted school sites throughout that state. These Centers were charged with connecting families and children with the special services (e.g., health services, parenting education, social services, child care) that would meet basic family needs necessary to children's development and learning (Smrekar, 1994).

Community and Parental Representation

To be sure, the public schools are opening up and are becoming increasingly receptive to community participation and involvement. Yet, there has also been a deep sense in these reform-minded times that something vitally important is still missing in community relations. Although many partnership and coordinated-services experiments remain in place, and others are starting anew, these innovations have often had difficult times. The partners (e.g., businesspeople, educators, social work professionals, and health professionals) typically speak very different workaday languages, have differing traditions of decisionmaking, have competing interests and perspectives, and are suspicious of each other's expertise and commitment (Trubowitz et al., 1984; Jones and Maloy, 1988; Crowson and Boyd, 1993).

Perhaps one indication of the malaise that continues in the arena of community and parent relations is found in John Holt's (1983) suggestion that the schools should even try to form a facilitative partnership with those growing numbers of families who are among those most disenchanted with public schooling—the home-schoolers. In effect, Holt has argued that in the interest of good relations, the supposedly "sick" schools should partner closely with those who wish to leave them. Indeed, in the years since Holt's observation, home schooling has been decidedly on the increase across the nation, and, increasingly, some school systems have explored limited partnerships, wherein home-schooled children can participate in selected public school activities (e.g., team athletics, the science club) (see Mayberry et al., 1995; Page, 1996).

Increasingly, under the press of reform, educators are being asked to go beyond encouraging parental and community involvement to instituting a full-fledged *representation* of the citizenry in the lifeways and decision processes of the school. John Goodlad (1981) developed the essential rationale as this: Human learning is a communal endeavor; schools and their communities buttress one another. However, there has of late been a "withering of community" in America and an accompanying "accelerating erosion of the educative function of the school" (p. 333). In response, continued Goodlad, schools must seek to reestablish a productive balance between home and school—sharing a sense of community and indeed serving themselves as "learning communities" (p. 353). Goodlad quoted Urie Bronfenbrenner (1974, p. 6), who put the point even more forcefully:

The schools have become one of the most potent breeding grounds of alienation in our society. For this reason it is of crucial importance for the welfare and development of school-age children that schools be reintegrated into the life of the community.

A reintegration of the school into the life of the community, from the perspective of many modern-day reformers, means a community-relations strategy leaning heavily toward shared governance in education. From this perspective, parents are not simply the recipients of school-to-home communications in the interest of a supportive environment, nor are they outside participants in the life of a school controlled by a heavily centralized school bureaucracy. They are, rather, coequals in the decisionmaking framework of their schools.

A parallel reform accompanying and aiding this power-to-the-parents movement has been a push toward school-based governance in education—a drive toward decentralizing school district bureaucracies and instituting school-site autonomy. The central benefit for community-relations activists, as Don Davies (1981) has noted, is that decisionmaking can be brought down the educational hierarchy to a level where citizens *can* participate, with a solid chance of seeing some tangible results from their efforts.

The drive toward a representation of community in the governance of the local school is by no means new. It had solid roots in the school decentralization experiments of the late 1960s and early 1970s in New York, Detroit, Chicago, and elsewhere (LaNoue and Smith, 1973). There were prior roots in the maximum feasible participation requirements of much of the welfare, urban renewal, and education legislation of the Great Society. The most far-reaching restructuring of educational governance to date, however, has been the school reform effort initiated in 1989 in Chicago. The centralized authority of the Chicago Public School System was much weakened by legislative mandate in 1989, with considerable authority decentralized to Local School Councils at each of the city's nearly six hundred schools. Each Local School Council (LSC) remains community dominated, composed of a building principal, two teachers, six parents, and two at-large community members. The councils have been vested with broad authority to set policy for their schools, including the power to hire or rehire the building principal.

Showing rather remarkable staying-power (for many such reforms tend to be short-lived), the Chicago effort to emphasize community-level government has remained in place through the 1990s. The Chicago reform has not been without controversy, including charges of community corruption and school-improvement expectations unmet. Furthermore, there has been added reform within the reform, including a mayoral "takeover" of the management of the school system in 1995. While considerable community-level autonomy has continued under the mayor's takeover, there has simultaneously been a tightening of citywide "standards" (Wong, 1996).

Experience thus far would indicate that community relations with a governance flavor takes on a *negotiative* temper (see, again, Table 1.1). While a partnership between home and school would be ideal, the reality is that the individual school building, and certainly the larger school district, represent a congeries of differing (usually competing) interests. The interests tend to "come alive" as groups of individuals meet, discuss, search for consensus, and labor toward agreement. While professional educators typically prefer low-key disagreements and mute or bypass overt conflict, the public school has always displayed the qualities of a "negotiated order" (Strauss, 1979). Under reform-minded structures for a sharing of decisions between profession and laity, these negotiations simply become much more pronounced and more potent—more potent in that the schools must now join the families of their pupils and the neighbors of these families in deciding important matters of school purpose, personnel, program, and performance. Few educators to date have been trained in or have experience in such a governance-minded restructuring of school-community relations.

There are problems aplenty in a blending of professional-based and community-based governance—in a representational approach to school-community relations, with the give and take and negotiation that this approach requires. Many of these problems will be discussed in detail, with accompanying practical suggestions, in the following chapters in this book. Problems of professionalism and power, of organizational design and reward systems, of authority and legality, of what works in pupil achievement and what does not, of history and ideology, of role definition and role preparation—these are just a few of the near-overwhelming issues reformers face in developing changed relationships between public schools and their communities.

SUMMARY

Educational reformers of years past sought increased school authority over the autonomous family. A major element of today's reform movement is the effort to reduce the apparent distancing of the school from the family. The public schools are being asked (indeed frequently required) to be more responsive to parents and the surrounding community, to involve parents in the lifeways of the school, and in some instances, to give parents a direct voice in the governance of the school.

While "community relations" is by no means a new concept in educational administration, the meanings and actions educators attach to this broad term have been undergoing rapid change. One still vital interpretation of community relations finds its central purpose in the maintenance of community support for the schools. No mean task, this effort can require a sophisticated, conscientious, and time-consuming program of public relations—with the need for careful, vigilant attention to keeping channels of communication open and productive. A second interpretation of community relations finds its roots in the direct participation of parents and citizens in the work of the schools. In many communities, volunteerism, paraprofessionalism, and discussions of partnerships between home and school are helping to soften the once impermeable "four-walls" definition of education. Finally, a third interpretation, the newest and least thoroughly investigated to date, finds the essence of community relations in the formal representation of parents and community in the ongoing governance of the local school. Sometimes under state mandate, occasionally voluntarily, school districts are beginning to award significant school-site decisionmaking to local school councils—with equal, or near-equal, representation from parents and professionals.

Each of the community-relations alternatives has its own problems and school-improvement prospects. However, they should not be viewed as mutually exclusive. Much community support for the schools can derive as a side effect from strategies for participation. Participation or involvement, well structured, can offer parents many opportunities for a voice in school governance. Excellent public relations, effectively handled, can give parents a sense of involvement in their schools. As this book proceeds, we will continue to distinguish among the three alternatives, considering the pitfalls and the mechanisms of each, but we will also suggest that a viable community-relations program for public schools in the 1990s includes much from all three.

Exercises
SOME DO MORE THAN OTHERS

1. Consider our three alternative forms of school-community relations.
2. As you think about your own school district, list its many activities and points of contact between school and community.
3. Categorize each of these activities and contacts as mostly emphasizing (a) public relations, (b) involvement, or (c) shared governance
4. Share your answers with classmates from other school districts. What can you conclude after comparing the attention your district gives to community relations with the predominating form of attention in other districts?

Suggested Activities

1. Interview a range of school personnel (e.g., teachers, principals, clerks, central-office administrators, coaches). Ask each to recall, in full detail, at least one story of parent or citizen interaction.
2. Consider the notion of a partnership between school and community. Ideally, what does each partner *bring to* such a relationship and what does each partner *receive from* the relationship?
3. Observe carefully the interactions of parents and school personnel during a typical community-relations forum in a selected school (e.g., a PTA meeting, an open house, an advisory-group meeting, a parent-orientation session). Who does most of the talking and listening? What issues and topics are discussed; what are avoided?
4. Talk with a few parents of children in school. Ask each to recall the details of a memorable communication or meeting with a child's teacher or school staff member (e.g., a principal, a counselor). How are these incidents remembered? With gratitude? Feelings of frustration? A sense of accomplishment? Hostility?
5. Invite a veteran superintendent and a veteran principal to tell the class about the changes in community relations and parent attitudes toward the schools that they have experienced over the course of their careers.

SUGGESTED READINGS

Davies, Don (ed.) (1981). *Communities and Their Schools.* New York: McGraw-Hill.

Greenstein, Jack (1983). *What the Children Taught Me: The Experience of an Educator in the Public Schools.* Chicago: University of Chicago Press.

Peshkin, Alan (1978). *Growing Up American: Schooling and the Survival of Community.* Chicago: University of Chicago Press.

Sarason, Seymour B. (1995). *Parental Involvement and the Political Principle.* San Francisco: Jossey-Bass.

Saxe, Richard W. (1984). *School-Community Relations in Transition.* Berkeley, Calif.: McCutchan Publishing.

Smrekar, Claire (1996). *The Impact of School Choice and Community: In the Interest of Families and Schools.* Albany: State University of New York Press.

Chapter Two

SCHOOLS AND THEIR COMMUNITIES

Only the farmers' realization that they would be in charge of everything, from the building of a schoolhouse to the hiring of a teacher to the raising of money to pay for it all, made free public education acceptable to them.
—Wayne Fuller, *The Old Country School*, 1982, p. 46

There may be some nostalgia in their portrayals, as historians hark back to a time seemingly lost—to a time of "community" in early American education. David Tyack and Elisabeth Hansot (1982) make the point with delightful imagery. It was not by accident that our earliest schools resembled churches, with their steeplelike bell towers. The schools were at the center of the educational, social, political, and even religious activities of their immediate communities. Nor is it by accident that school buildings in the early, industrializing part of the twentieth century resembled factories. Like the factory, these twentieth-century schools were "separate from family and community, hierarchical in organization, planned, purposive, consequential" (Tyack and Hansot, 1982a p. 512). The social and moral togetherness of a church versus the assemblyline and "produce-them" impersonality of a factory—these are continuing, powerful images of a public school transformed in American education.

SCHOOL AND COMMUNITY IN THE NINETEENTH CENTURY

A continuity between home and school, a blending of school and community, and the school as a "focus for people's lives outside the home" (Tyack, 1974, p. 15) are common themes in examinations of nineteenth-century schools. The little red schoolhouse was seldom red and more often unpainted clapboard. It was more likely to be located on swampy land than on good, tillable soil. It was an uncomfortable learning environment, with hard benches and sufficient warmth for only those near the stove. It was likely to be full of children only when farm activities slackened. And it was likely to be a place of little joy, with daily rote memorization, line-by-line recitations, much drilling, and frequent physical punishment (Kaestle, 1983).

Nevertheless, the schoolhouse was controlled by its neighborhood, and especially by its parents. The community chose the textbooks to be used, the subjects to be taught, and the teacher to teach them. The schoolhouse was constructed, provisioned, cleaned, and repaired by the families. Because they were in charge, as Wayne Fuller (1982) notes, they were willing to pay for it (although not lavishly). In a sense, "educators in overalls" (local farmers as part-time school board members) accomplished all that paid, full-time school administrators attend to today—establishing rules, overseeing the conduct of the teacher, accounting for funds spent, maintaining discipline, ordering textbooks and supplies, taking the yearly census of the district's children (Fuller, 1982).

The local farmers who led the schools were people the community knew well and whom the community depended on. They were elected again and again. Fuller (1982, pp. 83–84) writes:

They had no training in school administration, of course, and their philosophy of education was no more involved than that the school's purpose was to teach their children to read, write, figure, and spell. They had never read a textbook on school administration and very likely would have scoffed at the necessity for one.

More than just a schoolhouse, the country school was often the very center of its community. Fourth of July picnics, weekly spelling bees, "hoe downs," pot-luck suppers, Christmas parties, town meetings, corn roastings, travelogues, even Sunday services and the occasional revival were all schoolhouse centered. To be sure, there were divided communities whose factions were fully equipped with long, long memories of slights and disagreements. New schools might be created when feuds would split a community, each faction deciding to create its own place for learning. Much more commonly, however, school and community represented tightly knit groups of people; and, writes Tyack (1974, p. 17), "more often than not, the rural school integrated rather than disintegrated the community."

By no means was the close relationship between school and community limited to rural and small-town America. City schools in the early to mid nineteenth century tended to be heavily "ward-based" organizations (Cronin, 1973). Although a central school committee might serve the entire city, its membership was typically representative of each city ward or local district—with real power lodged not at the central level but at the ward-organization level. Teachers were hired, school sites selected, textbooks purchased, and school programs established separately, ward by ward. Furthermore, as cities grew and added wards, the public schools were often taught in the "old country" language(s) of the surrounding neighborhood. Not until mid-century did cities begin hiring professional educators as general superintendents of schools. Joseph Cronin (1973, p. 53) notes that the board of education's first order to its newly hired superintendent in Buffalo, New York, was to hire a horse and buggy, then set out in the city to "ascertain where the schools were situated."

CENTRALIZATION AND CONSOLIDATION

Many nineteenth-century schools were characterized by broad parental participation, and reflected closely the needs and interests of their communities. However, as the century wore on, they were increasingly criticized for their serious pedagogical deficiencies. The schools in rural areas were usually open for just a few weeks a year, with pupil attendance voluntary and sporadic at best. The teachers were often scarcely more literate than their pupils, and would more likely be hired for their piety or their "fit" with the community than for their training and experience. Although farming communities valued controlling their schools, their preferences did not always extend toward taxing themselves heavily to pay for them. The teachers tended to be woefully underpaid, the buildings in poor repair, the classrooms overcrowded, and the teaching materials decades old as well as in inadequate supply. Parental "involvement" was manifest in a number of communities in (a) their insistence that the children study from books sent with them to school by their families and (b) the practice of sending children as young as two years of age to school "to get them from under foot" at home (Kaestle, 1983, p. 15).

In the cities, with their ward-based schools, the criticism of school inadequacy was much the same, but included charges of misconduct.

Principals and teachers forced to purchase their jobs, a "rake-off" on school construction and maintenance by ward politicians, school budgets gone astray into political coffers, textbook purchases swollen by ward-boss "contributions"—these were admittedly the conditions of local governance in many city schools (Cronin, 1973). Tyack (1974, p. 89) quotes John Philbrick's observation in 1885: "Everywhere there are unscrupulous politicians who do not hesitate to improve every opportunity to sacrifice the interests of the schools to the purposes of the political machine."

An added criticism of the neighborhood-dominated rural school as well as the city schools was that they often tended to be bastions of narrow-minded provincialism and prejudice. The values of close-knit communities will not infrequently include a deep-seated fear of the customs, language patterns, and opinions of a larger, more cosmopolitan America. Keeping children "safe" from outside influences, preserving a way of life that others might consider to be out of touch with changing times, and guarding against rather than embracing modernity can be among the not-so-desirable outcomes of community autonomy. Thus, Horace Mann, one of the earliest and most forceful spokespersons for strong state leadership, argued that public education must build toward common, national values and national unity above narrow, parochial values and community separatism (Glenn, Jr., 1988).

A great crusade of the late nineteenth and early twentieth centuries sought an end to the inadequacies and corruptions of local domination by "taking the schools out of politics" (Tyack, 1981). The consolidation of rural schools and a centralization of the governance of city schools would correct the deficiencies of unfettered local control. Larger, consolidated schools, with up-to-date facilities and well-trained teachers, would help to bring rural and small-town America into an accord with a rapidly industrializing and urbanizing society (Tyack, 1974). Centralized city administration, with school boards appointed or elected at-large and run by professional school administrators, would correct the evils of corruption and partisan politics. The public schools would be simultaneously more efficient and more effective, assisted mightily by state laws for compulsory school attendance and by state standards for the training of professional educators. "The central result," concludes Tyack (1981, p. 19), "was greatly to lessen the influence of citizens over the schools in their neighborhoods. This was deliberate, for the centralizers did not trust the people to run the schools."

A QUESTION OF COMMUNITY

Tyack (1981) suggests that the period of centralization, consolidation, and standardization in American schooling lasted roughly from 1890 to 1950. The consolidation of rural schools was a slower, more difficult task than the centralization of city schools. Fuller (1982, p. 234) writes: "To the farmers consolidation meant not only the loss of the little school down the road to which they were sentimentally attached, but also the loss of their ability to control their children's education for which they had to pay."

In some states, a number of little schools down the road remain unconsolidated today. Many high schools in sparsely populated areas, for example, maintain inadequate enrollments for comprehensive secondary education. Nevertheless, these schools also field football and basketball teams that provide an intense local pride and "togetherness." Consequently, the schools staunchly and emotionally spurn state efforts and incentives toward consolidation. Interestingly, beyond concerns about the capacities of small schools to offer comprehensive curricula, there is now a renewed interest in school "smallness" as an important academic value. Schools-within-schools are particularly on the upswing, representing efforts to provide an enhanced sense of "community" to both students and faculty.

There are other examples of determinedly nineteenth-century relationships between school and community. In *Growing Up American*, Alan Peshkin (1978) describes in rich detail the local control of schooling in the small midwestern agricultural community of "Mansfield." From an overflow crowd at the Friday night football game, to a liberal dosage of religion in the school curriculum, to being certain that an incoming superintendent of schools is suitably "country," the community of Mansfield is fully in possession of its schools; and vice versa.

Although Mansfield-type relationships between school and community can still be found, even in city neighborhoods, James Coleman (1985, 1987) argues that the close-knit, functional communities exemplified by Mansfield are a vanishing breed. As reform-minded efforts toward a reintroduction of "community" into the schools continue today, including the school-within-a-school movement, it is important to examine the key differences in the concept of community in nineteenth-century and in mid-twentieth-century versions of public schooling. More than just a bit of imagery, Tyack's (1982) comparison between church and factory represents two very different approaches to the "community" side of the community-relations construct. The one posits a closeness (almost a oneness) of school *and* community; the other acknowledges a dependency yet simultaneously a separateness *between* school and community. In sociologists' language, the difference is between *gemeinschaft* and *gesellschaft* interpretations of communal relationships—the former focusing on the feelings and traditions that bind people together and the latter noting commonalities but also separate, individual interests among people.

We will examine each of these notions of community in turn, for each has its merits as well as weaknesses. We will begin with the "business" or gesellschaft notion of community and then look at the gemeinschaft interpretation.

School and Community: A Commonality yet Separate

"No school is an island," write John Chubb and Terry Moe (1988, p. 131). Indeed, many educators complain that our modern schools are much too governed by federal requirements, state statutes, administrative rules and regulations, court decisions, standardized tests, and conflicting publics. Furthermore, the schools must contend with strong teachers' unions, a watchful media, college admissions requirements, a litigious society, and inadequate revenues from reluctant-to-tax state legislatures.

Additionally, the surprising connectedness of locally controlled schooling nationwide has been noted (Meyer and Rowan, 1977). A fourth-grader who leaves upstate New York (one day) for a new home in southern California (the next day) will likely discover that she is entering a classroom she recognizes well, reading at much the same place in familiar textbooks, within the same set of subjects taught by the new teacher in an approach much like that of her teacher in New York. For all the talk of local differences in education, we find that public school schedules, structures, curricula, and pedagogies are remarkably the same throughout the land. A theoretical term now used to describe this phenomenon is *institutionalization*. As institutionalized organizations, the public schools display a sameness, a persistence (or resistance to change), and a relationship to society that cuts across all localities (see Crowson, Boyd, and Mawhinney, 1996).

The central point is that the public schools are under the influence of many communities that extend far beyond the limited scope of an adjoining neighborhood; furthermore, as state and national as well as local institutions, they are simultaneously a part of but also separate from the locality. Although public schools may belong to a Mansfield and many share its culture, the schools are also the representatives of a larger commonweal. Joel Spring (1986, p. 165) quotes an 1896 observation in the *Atlantic Monthly*: "The common schoolhouse is in reality the most obvious center of national unity." As rural, as isolated, and as parochial as it may be, the public schoolhouse still binds us together more than any other single American institution. And, of course, they can depend for their very legitimacy as institutions on just how well they do bind us together and represent our collective interests (Crowson, Boyd, and Mawhinney, 1996).

Early debates regarding the purpose of American education stressed this national unity theme. To many of the nation's first proponents of public schooling, it was the creation of a single nation and one people out of an already divided nation and many immigrant peoples that represented the essence of a viable school "system" for America (Spring, 1986; Kaestle, 1983; Glenn, Jr., 1988). Common loyalties and values, and an American community, were to be nurtured within a democracy easily endangered by conflicting loyalties and competing values.

Modern, late-twentieth-century schools have continued much that may still be considered a commonweal interpretation of public education. Examples of the present-day sense of a larger, national good above the interests of each locality include the school desegregation movement, the protection of educational opportunities for physically and mentally handicapped pupils, efforts toward racial and gender equality, protections for language-minority students, and the attainment of national standards in school quality. Furthermore, a sense of self-definition, a frame of reference, for the professional educator in our modern times typically includes the notion that the educator must try to broaden the perspectives of an often insulated or nonworldly clientele. Introducing pupils to the literary classics, creating an appreciation of cultures and races other than one's own, fostering a willingness to consider both sides of controversial issues, and opening new horizons are among the key contributions teachers can make to enlighten their students.

The problem from a community-relations perspective is that the worldly view of the educator can be a source of friction and frustration for the locality. Thus *Catcher in the Rye* may be banned from some high school reading lists; evolution unaccompanied by creation may be disturbing to sizable numbers of parents; Richard Wright's *Native Son* may be too heavily "charged" for some locales; sex education may be a topic some parents prefer to teach themselves; values clarification may be seen as values imposition; and daily prayers, no matter what the Supreme Court says, may be "the way we do things in this town." In the face of such pressures, professional educators often find themselves going "underground"—perhaps, for example, assigning *Fahrenheit 451* (about book burning) in place of *Catcher in the Rye.*

As the representatives of a national community, and indeed as the representatives of many communities beyond the locality, the public schools reflect interests and perspectives that are not always at "one" with their neighborhoods. The public schools are *in* but not completely *of* their immediate environments. They serve a larger, more all-encompassing and more "institutionalized" societal role.

This is the gesellschaft interpretation of communal relationships. The recognition is that school and communities share common interests, but that the institution of the school and the local community may have differing, sometimes conflicting, interests. We have talked already about the larger, professional interests of educators. The individual community, on the other hand, might have concerns about property taxes, school remodeling, community development, provisions for parks and recreation, and school attendance boundaries that are decidedly at odds with the preferences of local educators. During the 1980s and the 1990s, local school superintendents have often been in the thick of controversies over the extension of tax advantages to developers who would benefit the community in the long run but burden the schools in the short run.

A clear, well-argued model of a gesellschaft approach to school-community relations was introduced in 1966 by Sumption and Engstrom. At a time when education was just beginning to recognize itself as an "open" system, Merle Sumption and Yvonne Engstrom used business imagery to suggest that the "educational enterprise" must acknowledge the fact of shared ownership. The school must regard "each individual in the school community as a part owner of an educational venture" (Sumption and Engstrom, 1966, p. 2). As "shareowners" in the school, argued Sumption and Engstrom, members of the community must first have access to clear and effective two-way communication with the school. They must second have opportunities for active participation "in the educational planning, policy making, problem solving, and evaluation of the school" (p. xi). Indeed, the school exists for and is "owned" by its shareholders—who have a right to know when the enterprise is prospering or failing and is well run or poorly run.

As with shareholders in a corporation, the argument proceeds, both school and community have mutual interests—interests that are best realized if the school works actively to bring itself into "close alignment" with its surrounding community. *However*, as with the corporation, the "actual operation of the school is the responsibility of professional schoolworkers" (Sumption and Engstrom, 1966, p. 157). Sumption and Engstrom state unequivocally that

the school must maintain complete independence from the power structure or any other pressure group. It has an obligation to support true democratic government. The public school has the responsibility of serving all the people without fear or favoritism. [P. 33]

The shareholders may unite to appoint or remove the officers of a corporation, but they do not share actively in the day-by-day management of the corporation.

The strategy of walking a fine, and at times tight, line between the interests of the attending community and the norms and pressures of the larger commonweal became a common theme in community-relations textbooks during the 1960s and 1970s. For example, through three revisions (from 1957 through 1984) of *The School and Community Relations*, Leslie Kindred, Don Bagin, and Donald Gallagher offered valuable, down-to-earth suggestions for determining public opinion, encouraging parental involvement, opening channels of communication, "marketing" the schools, servicing complaints, and working with the press. Educators were warned, though, of the dangers of "incursions of power structures into school matters" and cautioned that citizen advisory committees and concerned parents can have a constructive effect only if "properly organized" (Kindred, Bagin, and

Gallagher, 1984, pp. 26–27). The schools must be "open" to the community, however, only in the sense that the corporation is open to its shareholders but also protective of its managers and in control of its own news.

School and Community: Common and Not Separate

Community-relations proponents of the 1960s and 1970s recognized clearly the value of a greater opening of communications between home and school, and the benefits of parental involvement in the schools. Nevertheless, there was still an important sense of separation—a sense that in the interest of its professionalism, the school must guard carefully an independence from the pressures and politics of the clientele.

However, as Richard Andrews (1987, p. 152) has observed, the professionalism of the educator came to be interpreted in many settings as merely "a code word for keeping parents at arm's length, for resisting the development of any meaningful face-to-face contact between school and parent and between teacher and community." Educators in recent decades have been criticized in many quarters for lacking sufficient sensitivity to the concerns of parents and for being party to what has appeared to be a "a widening gap between the schools and the communities they serve" (Andrew, 1987, p. 153). In 1988, while doing dissertation research, Patricia Hulsebosch discovered that teachers who most fully identified themselves as "professionals" were *less likely* to maintain close contacts and communications with parents than were colleagues who did not as closely identify with the professionalism of teaching.

Recognizably, a disappearance of the close linkages between home, school, and neighborhood that reputedly characterized rural nineteenth-century education can hardly be fully blamed on the strains between profession and laity. Other major forces toward a separation of school and community include the very size and complexity of educational organizations, the great diversity and mobility of our modern society, changes in the American family (e.g., far fewer nuclear families and the near disappearance of the extended family), and the many forces that draw today's children away from the influences of both school *and* family (e.g., the television set, the peer group, the automobile, the job in a fast-food restaurant) (Gordon, 1976; Goodlad, 1981).

Indeed, it is at least in part because of these societal forces, particularly the transformation of the family, that advocates of a new approach to community relations are proposing a reintegration of school and community. James Coleman (1987), for example, has argued that there are indications of a serious crisis in the exercise of parental responsibility in America. Simultaneously, there is evidence that the public schools are more effective for children from strong family backgrounds than for children from weak backgrounds. In short, the schools are at their best when they operate from strength, and there is now less and less family-background strength to draw on. Families matter, importantly so, and programs of school-based support for families are becoming increasingly vital (see Booth and Dunn, 1996; Weiss, 1995).

This combination of family breakdown, alongside a complementary relationship between family strength and school quality, suggests to many persons that the schools should now become *community-creating* institutions. As Coleman (1987) has worded it, the public school must now consider its job to be an investment in the "social capital" of its immediate environment, just as educators for years have recognized their roles as creators of "human capital." "What I mean by social capital," defined Coleman (1987, p. 36), "is the norms, the social networks, and the relationships between adults and children that are of value for the child's growing up." While visions of nineteenth-century schools saw the schools responding to strong families and strong communities, a modern-day notion of school and community (faced often with withered communities and fragile families) suggests a turning around of the relationship. The recognition is that the interests and purposes of the school are served well if the schools themselves attempt to create a "sense of community" (Goodlad, 1981), and if the schools work hard to develop solid linkages with and among families (Coleman, 1985).

By no means is the concept of the school as a community-creating rather than community-reflecting institution all that new. Just after the turn of the century, Willard Wirt (Superintendent of Schools in Gary, Indiana) inaugurated a "Gary Plan" of schooling, which innovatively for its time provided gymnasia, playgrounds, auditoriums, adult evening classes, workshops, and extended school access on Saturdays—all designed to provide for the needs of city children and to use Gary's facilities more efficiently (Pulliam, 1987). In addition, with continuing support from the Mott Foundation, the public schools of Flint, Michigan, became nationally known, from the 1930s on, as the center of the "community school" concept. Complete with the special role of community school director, each Flint elementary school sought to broker added resources to its neighborhood (e.g., health, recreation, library services) as well as provide the neighborhood with a range of "community education" opportunities (e.g., adult education, senior citizens' classes, preschool programs) (Seay, 1953; Minzey, 1981). Indeed, the community-creating role of the school in the face of social change was at the heart of John Dewey's pedagogical philosophy as early as 1899 (see Spring, 1986, pp. 172–173).

While not new, the community-creating vision of the school acquired an "its-time-has-come" aura by the late 1980s. A notion of school-site management had become popular, wherein centralized school district organizations were to be decentralized to the individual school building. Each school, with added autonomy, was to be released from bureaucratic constraints toward diversifying its own personnel, setting, and clientele. An accompanying idea was a new "bottom-up" sense of school governance, with classroom teachers and (depending on the locale) parents playing a much larger role in decision structures. Two added developments were (a) a new emphasis on the impact of school "culture" on effectiveness, of which community is a central component, and (b) a rediscovery of the value of integrative, participatory styles of school administration. This latter development was not unrelated to a belated recognition of, and appreciation for, the successes of women in educational administration. As Charol Shakeshaft has observed (1987, p. 197), "Building community is an essential part of a woman administrator's style."

However, despite its fit with the reform temper of our time, the community-generating vision of school and community remains inadequately supplied with a thorough-going definition, a widely understood set of administrative guidelines, or even a shared understanding of what works and what does not. Important inquiry has proceeded toward the clarification of the concept of a communal school organization (see Driscoll, 1989). Intensive, ethnographic-style research in schools has considerably brightened our appreciation of the communitylike characteristics of successful schools (see, for example, Lightfoot, 1984; Metz, 1986; Grant, 1988). And, community-creating projects and experiments in such areas as parent-assisted teaching, parent-teacher-administrator collaboration in school governance, the provision of comprehensive support services to disadvantaged neighborhoods, and parent-training programs have received national attention (see Cavazos, 1989). Nevertheless, community relations from a community-creating perspective remains in its infancy as a tool of effective schooling. Communities differ from organizations, notes Thomas Sergiovanni (1996), in a key effort to address for administrators the task of understanding and building community. A moral voice is important, a sense of "we" must replace "I," and values and ideas override structures. The implications of such notions, their promises and pitfalls, techniques and outcomes are all very much under development (Sergiovanni, 1996).

SUMMARY

With a touch of nostalgia, many modern educators consider the schoolhouse of the nineteenth century a "model" of community relations. The closeness of school *and* community—wherein the schoolhouse joined church, family, government, neighborhood lifestyle, and employment in a mutuality of shared purpose and shared values—represents a time lost but now a time much to be remembered to those who would reform the schools (see Fantini, 1986).

A twentieth-century centralization of educational administration, it is argued, has led to effectively walling the schools off from their parents, neighborhoods, and local citizenry. The schools were no longer very responsive to their communities, and not surprisingly began to discover that their communities began to be much less responsive to them. By the 1950s and 1960s, in an appreciation of their status as "open" systems, despite centralization, the schools began to seek a closer tie with their environments. Although there were some turn-of-the century ancestors in such innovations as the "Gary Plan," a widespread interest in improving community relations is a relatively recent occurrence. Much of the attendant development of community-relations strategies has assumed a public-relations flavor, with educators walking a tightrope, balancing parental involvement, home-school communication, and the preservation of professional discretion and autonomy.

Of late, a reform movement has been pressing toward a decentralization of education, a more participative role for parents, and a sharing of educational responsibility (in an almost nineteenth-century sense). As a result, the definition of community relations in education has been undergoing revision. A new closeness of school *and* community (and an accompanying greater sense of community *within* the school) is the goal—with a major difference between today's route toward closeness and yesterday's approaches. The difference is that with our modern-day complexities and pathologies (e.g., families in disarray), the *community-creating* capacities of the public schools are under consideration. Inadequately explored at this time, however, are questions of "how to," with what effect, and under what safeguards (e.g., of professional discretion, against damaging conflict).

Exercise
CREATING COMMUNITY CAPITAL

Some critics have argued that the schools have traditionally had a "human-capital" bias. That is, they typically focus on preparing individuals for jobs, or for higher education, or for adulthood. What would it take to introduce, as an alternative, a "community-capital" perspective in schooling? How might schools be reorganized toward a community-creating pedagogy in place of their current stress on individual competition and individual performance? What might be some major disadvantages of community-capital-oriented schooling?

Suggested Activities

1. Interview one or more teachers on the topic of their notions of professionalism. What strains do you detect, if any, between professionalism and politics in education? Can the teachers give examples of any past threats to their professionalism?
2. Visit any client-servicing public bureaucracy other than a school (e.g., the post office, a driver's license examination station, city hall, a welfare office). Observe (for a time) some interactions between the public (clients) and employees of the organization. How would you describe the responsiveness of the organization to its clients? Were all clients treated alike? Were all employees alike in their attitudes toward the clientele?
3. Robert Bellah and colleagues (1985) use the term "communities of memory" to describe a potent community-creating force in our lives. Begin a shared-reminiscences conversation with a group of your age-mates—recalling growing up, world events, recreational, educational, and other experiences you hold in common. Reflect on the conversation later. Was there an obvious sense of "togetherness," of experiences and perspectives drawn from a communal past? Try the same conversation with a group from a generation older or younger than yours. Did the same sense of "community" develop? If so, what were the ties? If not, what seemed to block a togetherness?
4. Create a list of what would appear to you to be the separate and possibly conflicting interests of school employees (e.g., principals, teachers) and parents. List as well any interests that school professionals and parents might have in common. Can you think of any strategies in school administration that might create additional common interests out of those that have tended to remain firmly in the "separate" category?

SUGGESTED READINGS

Coleman, James S. (1985, April). "Schools and the Communities They Serve," *Phi Delta Kappan* 66(8): 527–532.

Davies, Don (ed.) (1981). *Communities and Their Schools.* New York: McGraw-Hill Book Co.

Fuller, Wayne E. (1982). *The Old Country School: The Story of Rural Education in the Middle West.* Chicago: University of Chicago Press.

Grant, Gerald (1988). *The World We Created at Hamilton High.* Cambridge, Mass.: Harvard University Press.

Peshkin, Alan A. (1978) *Growing Up American: Schooling and the Survival of Community.* Chicago: University of Chicago Press.

Valdés, Guadalupe (1996). *Con Respeto: Bridging the Distances Between Culturally Diverse Families and Schools.* New York: Teachers College Press.

Chapter Three

SCHOOL-COMMUNITY RELATIONS AND A CHANGING PROFESSION

> The school is a closed system of social interaction. Without pedantry, we may point out that this fact is of importance, for if we are to study the school as a social entity, we must be able to distinguish clearly between school and not-school. The school is in fact clearly differentiated from its social milieu.
> —Willard Waller, *The Sociology of Teaching*, 1932, p. 6

Willard Waller was among the first to argue that the school has a "culture" of its own. While the school is certainly attached to its community environment and mightily influenced by those surroundings, the school also has a special, unique, and separate culture of its own—it is a workplace for teachers, a place for peer socialization, a "sorting machine" (Spring, 1976), a preparer for and "producer" of adult roles.

Imagine yourself a visitor from Mars, suggests Seymour Sarason (1971). You would be struck by the strange behaviors of a school's inhabitants. Why do all those laughing, running, and shouting young people suddenly line up in two disciplined rows and then enter a building, much subdued? Why do they immediately separate, apparently by size and age, into rectangular rooms where they sit in rows, all facing a single adult? Why, after hours of listening to the adult, and occasionally raising an arm in order to be recognized by the adult, do they suddenly emerge from the building once again, laughing, running, and shouting? Why do the adults emerge somewhat later, climb into a number of vehicles, and move off rapidly—leaving the children behind? Why does this activity last for five "suns" in succession, then stop for two?

Indeed, as Waller observed, there is school and there is not-school. This is a fact of importance for three closely related reasons,

39

each of which speaks critically to the concept of "professionalism" in schooling. First, school and not-school can have differing educational goals. W. Norton Grubb and Marvin Lazerson (1982) note that schools typically represent an array of both public and private ends. On the public side, the school seeks to equalize opportunities, communicate common values, develop human potential, and prepare a literate citizenry. On the private side, parents seek to use schooling to ensure the success of their own children, physically protect their children, reinforce their own values, and shield their children from "contaminating" influences. Conclude Grubb and Lazerson: "The mixture of public and private goals has meant that the public schools have always had peculiar and ambiguous relationships to families" (p. 130). While the school may push energetically in one direction, the home can just as energetically establish a counterforce in another. A teacher and a parent are not easily partners or even sharers of a common "wave-length" in communication. Interestingly, teachers complain that the most difficult parents to deal with are parents whose profession is teaching.

Second, while both school and home are engaged in childrearing, one legitimate function of the school is to help wean children away from their parents—to prepare children to leave their families for the larger social and occupational world (Grubb and Lazerson, 1982, pp. 144–145). From communicating work habits, to widening horizons, to teaching language and computation skills, to encouraging an enhanced self-confidence and heightened aspirations, the school is exercising a preparing-children-for-adulthood role that is often distinct from and sometimes at odds with the expectations of parents. As much today as in the nineteenth century, parents may (often subtly) pull their children "back home to the farm," failing to encourage aspirations and "sky-high" goals. Thus, teachers expect children to be increasingly self-reliant as learners and to look to the schools and their teachers for affirmations of their self-worth. They are asked by teachers to compete successfully with their age-mates, but simultaneously to form close attachments to their peers and a shared school spirit. While run by adults and serving as adults' workplace, the school is also fundamentally a children's environment—and it is in part an environment that alienates children from parents.

Third, the very existence of the special societal institution we call school carries the implication, in the words of Gutman (1987, p. 254), that "the good of parents can be separated to a significant extent from the good of their children." In this day of stressed families and often-problematic parenting, many schools and teachers may view themselves as necessary to children's lives in lieu of parental resources. From compulsory-attendance laws, to teacher-certification standards, to "least-restrictive-environment" rules, the notion is that targeted interventions by government are necessary to the welfare and the future productivity of all children, but especially the most needy children. Beyond the nurturing and guiding supplied by parents, this notion of the separate good of the child has led the state to demand that the child attend school, encounter trained teachers, and receive an education appropriate to his or her needs.

Interestingly, an exception that establishes the rule was the landmark U.S. Supreme Court case of *Wisconsin v. Yoder* (1972), in which this very clash of "goods" was represented. In this decision, the "good" of an old Amish community (in refusing to send its children to school beyond age fourteen) won over the "good" as defined by Wisconsin's compulsory-attendance law—but only because the Court determined that Amish religious beliefs had been genuinely and conscientiously maintained for centuries, and took precedence over the right of the state to require schooling to age sixteen. Although a victory for parents, *Yoder* clarifies the tensions between our two definitions of "the good" (Grubb and Lazerson, 1982). It is only under extremely unusual circumstances that a family's definition of what is best for its children takes precedence over a state requirement that the children "be educated."

Thus, school can be distinguished from not-school in its public regardedness, its socialization (even weaning) role, and its extrafamilial sense of what's good for children. Long before the term "professional" became popular in descriptions of educators, it was well recognized that school and not-school must occasionally be a bit at odds. Consider, for example, the "balancing act" that David Malcolm (1927) suggests in some recollections from an early-in-the-century career in rural education:

When a big girl is needed at home to help a sick or overworked mother, there is very little that a teacher can do about it. Here again the teacher should be human and should not add to the poor mother's burden with threats from the county superintendent's office. She should give the child extra help when she returns and encourage her to make up her losses. But on the other hand, if a mother keeps a daughter home in order that she herself may gad about the neighborhood, the teacher must be firm and do her duty. [P. 133]

Or, consider this warning from Willard Waller, in 1932:

The daughter of an influential man in the community does not expect to be treated in the same way as an ordinary child, and yet it is dangerous for a teacher to make exceptions. [P. 36]

Or, finally, consider the all-too-common frustration of the modern-day teacher described in Tracy Kidder's (1989) *Among Schoolchildren*:

Horace said he'd forgotten his book; Manny and Henrietta admitted they hadn't done the homework; Robert just shrugged when she asked where his was; and Alan, of all people, a school teacher's son, had a note from his mother saying that he'd lost the assignment." [P. 41]

In each example, we find evidence of what Grubb and Lazerson (1982) label a central dilemma of the public-service professional— that professionals and parents are both partners and antagonists. At least in part, the current surge in home-schooling is a response by parents to a sense of these antagonisms. The counterurge among professionals has been to ask parents to support their professionalism. David Malcolm was willing to overlook and even help out in a bit of necessary absence, but not for frivolity. Willard Waller warns that some parents may be "more equal" than others. Tracy Kidder shows a teacher's exasperation when even another teacher covers up for her child. All three cases require judgment calls by the professional and all three cases are full of opportunities for antagonism.

Interestingly, a major ingredient in the nation's school-reform movement has been an effort to enhance professionalism in education, especially toward improvements in the autonomy and authority of classroom teachers. But, is professionalism at odds with partnering? What is the likely outcome of a reform movement that simultaneously seeks to enhance the professional discretion of classroom teachers *and* to promote the responsiveness of schools to parents? Will partnership prevail or will school/not-school antagonisms grow? Is it possible to be *both* professional and highly responsive?

THE PROFESSIONAL IMPERATIVE

A central argument of the reform movement is that a necessary further development in the culture of schooling must be toward greater workplace professionalism. This is necessary if teaching is to compete successfully for the best and brightest of the nation's college graduates. The move is also necessary if teaching is to reach a status and prestige consonant with the burden society places on its schools for instructional "effectiveness." And, it is argued that professionalization is necessary if we are to engender commitment, relieve stress, and properly reward accomplishment in one of the most difficult of our nation's public-service careers (Lieberman, 1988; Little, 1993).

Among the suggested changes in the culture of schooling is, first, a transition from an oft-noted isolation among classroom teachers toward an atmosphere of collegiality and collaboration. Despite past experiments in team teaching and open classrooms, most schools are "segmented, egg-crate institutions in which teachers are isolated; objectives are framed in individual, not institutional terms; and problems are hidden rather than examined" (McLaughlin and Yee, 1988, p. 40). Under such conditions, norms of self-reliance and teacher uncertainty develop. "Self-reliance," Susan Rosenholtz (1989, p. 69) argues, "inhibits teachers' knowledge that others suffer common instructional problems, and teachers become turf-minded, unable and unwilling to impinge territorially on the domain of others' classroom practice." Furthermore, "teacher uncertainty constructs the unwitting perception that if others suffer few instructional problems, there is personal shame in admitting one's own." Hopefully, a newly professionalized collegium can reduce teacher uncertainty through a sharing of problems, through mutual assistance, and through social cohesiveness (Maeroff, 1988). Just as curricula and lesson plans are now filled with strategies in "cooperative learning," the reformed school must combat teachers' isolation and uncertainty with a newly professional sense of shared engagement, teamwork, and mutual-mindedness.

A second suggested change in school culture must be toward empowering teachers rather than merely employing them. School management has often been conceptualized in "business" terms, with administrators hierarchically supervising teachers and other ancillary staff (e.g., custodians, librarians, aides, cafeteria workers) in the daily delivery of a complex array of "production-level" services to children. Such a conceptualization tends to leave teachers far removed from important policy-level decisionmaking over matters critical to their own effectiveness as teachers, including curricula, staff development, resource allocation, activity scheduling, pupil placement, and the assessment of student achievement. Empowering teachers, says Thomas

Sergiovanni (1996), can bring side effects that go well beyond collegiality. Empowerment can help to transform schools into valuable "centers of inquiry."

Without control over their own worklives, teachers often find that "their school's policies and practices interfere with their best teaching" (Johnson, 1989, p. 105). Thus, through empowerment, and an accompanying involvement of classroom teachers in school governance, the hope is that pedagogical values rather than managerial values will increasingly define the policymaking culture of the school. Rather than a traditional hierarchy of management and labor, the school can be a collegium of cooperating decisionmakers, planners, and problem solvers. Even the introduction of an added of measure "informed dissent" into the school, argues Judith Warren Little (1993), provides a mark of much-valued professional development.

Third, a professionalization of schooling should alter the nature of the career of classroom teacher. An oft-repeated remark inside education is that fifteen years experience as a teacher tends all too often to be one year fifteen times. For many teachers, their career involves one year of eleven-year-olds after another—held in the same classroom, with little alteration of instructional materials or classroom displays, using much the same teach-and-test schedule, and with a predictable flow and rhythm to the school year. A major "change" in career may be teaching a new grade level or even moving to a new classroom. As the years go by, many teachers find comfort in the lack of change and may resist the odd "innovation" promulgated by colleagues or administrators. Indeed, a teacher might resist an enhancing of career if its cost is to be more time spent in professional collaboration, added training, and less isolation in the "safety" of his or her own classroom.

Among the earliest proposals for changing the teaching career of the 1980s were efforts, often backed by state legislation, to establish "career ladders" for teachers, involving such measures as merit pay, minigrants, and differentiated staffing (see Schlechty and Ingverson, 1987). Opposition to merit pay (who decides and by what criteria) slowed the continued development of many pay-for-performance plans (Johnson and Nelson, 1987); however, the attempt to provide opportunities for professional advancement (through routes other than a traditional shift into administration) continued unabated. By the late 1980s, many local school districts were experimenting with one form or another of a "peer leadership" approach, which typically reduced the teaching loads of first-rate teachers to give them time (with added salary) for mentoring, coaching, staff development, and curricular improvement roles (Smylie and Denny, 1989). Such efforts usually seek to conform to Susan Moore Johnson's admonition that "to professionalize teaching is not to make it something other than teaching." "The purpose," she continues, "should not be to liberate teachers from their work, but liberate them so that they can do their work well" (1989, p. 110).

THE PROFESSIONAL'S DILEMMA: SCHOOL VERSUS NOT-SCHOOL

An essential argument for professionalization is that control over the quality of a process as difficult and as variable as teaching requires appropriate decisionmaking to be lodged at the point of service delivery (Wise, 1988). Although they are typically gathered in classroom lots, education's "clients" are engaged in a largely private transaction with their instructor. These clients are far from standardized. Even when age-graded, they are learners of widely differing needs, prior preparation, motivation, learning styles, and levels of development. Teachers are awash in making daily "judgment calls." What's blocking Jennifer's understanding of long division? Is there a story particularly likely to stir Raymond's interest in reading? How can we get David to complete his homework? What's the best strategy to convince Katey to be a bit less "social" and more attentive in class?

Interestingly, teachers have not always been trusted to make such judgments on their own, effectively. From a 1950s flirtation with "teacher-proof" curricula, to administrator-monitored lesson plans, to state-mandated tests and now "standards," the conventional wisdom has been, more often than not, that teachers may fail to serve their students' needs and interests adequately if uninspected and unsupervised. In the same vein, Linda Darling-Hammond (1988, p. 65) noted that while, to be sure, an empowering and "freeing" of teachers will correctly recognize their professional judgment, such reform "does not adequately answer the obvious question, 'What if more authoritative and autonomous teachers do *not* do what is best for students?' Having weakened other alternative sources of authority, how will we ensure that students' needs are given voice and their interests are served?"

This, then, is the central dilemma of professionalization. If teachers are to be "liberated" and "empowered" to do their work exceptionally well, does the school run the danger of becoming even more solidly closed to not-school concerns and interests? Darling-Hammond (1988, p. 65) put the problem succinctly: "It is precisely *because* practitioners operate autonomously that safeguards to protect the public interest are necessary."

What are these safeguards? We will examine three in depth. The first suggests an important values-shaping (and protecting) role for the school administrator. The second notes that the definition of "professional" in education must increasingly include a respect for, and even the activation of, not-school resources and interests. The third suggests that professionalism in education can safeguard the public if school *and* not-school professionals begin to join forces toward school effectiveness.

The Professional and the Administrator

A rich literature has developed on the topic of public-sector employees' interaction with their clients (Hasenfeld, 1992). Schoolteachers, police officers, health personnel, social security employees, housing administrators, and postal workers have been given a common label by Michael Lipsky (1976, 1980)—"street-level bureaucrats." These client-servicing individuals face common problems in their usually complex and uncertain work environments. Amid complexity and uncertainty, they typically encounter (a) a lack of adequate resources (both organizational and personal), (b) ambiguous and contradictory role expectations, and (c) physical as well as psychological challenges to their authority.

Classroom teaching, for example, is renowned for its limitations of large class size and little available on-task time. Less widely recognized but discussed often by teachers are confusions of role—whether to lose a bit of teaching time in order to prepare an administrative report, how energetically to join in school committee work, whether to "teach to" a much-disliked standardized test, whether to stick to an expected curriculum when one's own students seem to have deeper needs. Not widely recognized as well are the struggles of teachers for authority. Typically, the building principal classroom teachers least admire is one who fails to back the teacher up in difficult (usually disciplinary) circumstances (Morris et al., 1984). Principals who do not back their teachers up may discover diminishing teacher volunteerism in schoolwide discipline, meeting district deadlines, participation in staff development, or help with rules violations (e.g., a willingness to take on extra pupils above the union's class-size agreement).

In response to their problems of resource, role, and authority, street-level bureaucrats develop "simplifications and routines" (Lipsky, 1976, 1980) that help to limit, define, and ease job performance. Police officers, for example, may develop routines for labeling and identifying possibly dangerous people. Teaching is similarly famous for labeling, categorizing, and grouping clients (e.g., underachiever, gifted, at-risk). Similarly, law officers and teachers share a need to protect their authority by communicating to others an expectation of respect for themselves and their position. Public-service personnel, including educators, have furthermore been found to shield themselves from responsibility for events they are unable to control by "blaming the victim" when (as is all too often the case) failure exceeds evidence of success.

It is argued that in no small measure the protectionism exhibited by street-level bureaucrats flows out of an organizational/administrative structure that separates roles and areas of responsibility (see McPherson, Crowson, and Pitner, 1986; also Wehlage et al., 1989). Teachers teach, work developmentally with individual pupils, engage in their own discipline, handle classroom-related paperwork, guide, counsel, and evaluate. The pressures on them (within a profession holding inadequate knowledge about how best to do any of this) are sizable. School administrators manage resources, maintain order, implement policy, supervise, schedule, and handle problems. To be sure, on many occasions one role requires some help from the other (e.g., a discipline case the teacher can't handle, an upper-echelon administrative request requiring the teachers' cooperation). Joseph Blase (1989) has discovered that the separation of roles, combined with their need for mutual support, produces a negotiative relationship between building principals and teachers (e.g., extra work in exchange for extra resources). In line with our protectionism argument, Blase concludes: "Teachers seemed to operate quite individually (almost anarchistically) in their political relations with principals: There was little evidence of collective consciousness or collective action" (p. 403).

Figure 3.1

A Matrix of Administrative Control Types and Forms

Administrative Control Forms

		Commitment	Loyalty	Delegation
	Centralized	Individual to the organization	Blind	Routines
Administrative Control Types	Balanced	Negotiated	Conditional	Authority/ responsibility
	Decentralized	Organization to the individual	Earned	Values formation

Source: Adapted, with permission, from R. Bruce McPherson (1988, Summer), "Superintendents and the Problem of Delegation." *Peabody Journal of Education* 65(4), p. 127.

The evidence is that in their relations with parents and the community, building administrators can display a similar protectionism and maintenance of separation. Morris and colleagues (1984) found principals socializing the clients of their schools into behaviors and expectations acceptable to the organization, guiding parental involvement into nonthreatening activities, and having a few parents be school representatives to the community. Mitigating parental demands, establishing limits to school responsiveness, and buffering teachers from parental intrusions are among the "street-level" behaviors of administrators under traditional structures of schooling.

Arthur Wise (1988) argues that if professionalization and local control are to take hold, school administrators will have to move away from what he terms "the middle ground." From a negotiative and protectionist stance, from a reactor to and manipulator of, and from a politics-minded mediation of competing interests, administrators, says Wise, must now become "champions of educational values," not merely implementors of policy or supervisors of behaviors and outcomes. Administrators will have to work proactively "to exercise the kind of instructional leadership that will allow teachers to meet the needs and interests of the students in their classes. They will have to stand firm in the face of bureaucratic interference" (Wise, 1988, p. 332). Moreover, they must ensure that the schools are "accountable to the public." Similarly, a "Community Theory" in schooling, says Thomas Sergiovanni (1996, p. 58), means becoming a "moral voice" for one's organization and profession—with leadership that serves as a "head follower" of a community's ideas, values, and commitments.

A thought-provoking conceptualization of such "reformed" administration has been offered by R. Bruce McPherson (1988). Figure 3.1, drawn from McPherson, suggests that the administrative control of schools can range from heavily centralized to decentralized, with a balanced type in between. McPherson then suggests that three vital forms of administrative control in modern-day schools are represented in efforts to engender commitment and loyalty and to encourage a meaningful delegation of the work of the school.

Under a centralized system of control, the commitment of teachers, pupils, and even parents is expected to flow from the individual to the organization. The individual is to fit the norms, ideals, and objectives of the school or school system. Similarly, loyalties (important in tying people to an organizational mission) tend to be blind, in that centralized systems just expect such loyalty from their employees, and even from their clientele, as a matter of course. Finally, when the centralized system delegates work (if it does so at all), such delegation tends to be only the routine, for individuals are seldom trusted with anything more. Classroom teaching is famous for its administrative paperwork (e.g., attendance records, tardy slips, fee collections, achievement records, and lesson plans). This paperwork tends to be highly routinized, with little thought given to the loyalty-building or loyalty-damaging dimensions of such standard operating procedures.

Many (indeed perhaps most) control systems in schools and school districts, however, are neither overly centralized nor fully decentralized. They tend to be "balanced," with much top-down authority but simultaneously a sizable leavening of bottom-up decisionmaking. Under such an arrangement, the commitments of individuals tend to be negotiated in ways not unlike the descriptions by Blase (1989) and others mentioned here previously of the workings of "street-level bureaucracies." Similarly, loyalty will be conditional, depending commonly, as McPherson (1988, p. 122) puts it, on whether "the quid finds a quo." To the extent that well-negotiated relationships successfully balance the key forces of commitment and loyalty, then a delegation of authority and responsibility are likely. Nevertheless, warns McPherson (1988, p. 127), "Conditional loyalty yields conditional delegation. There are strings, and they will be pulled if the tentative negotiation . . . begins to come apart." This is the case with the famous "back-the-teacher-up" dictum of the principalship. Teachers' loyalties can be conditional to the backing received from the principal, but the principal's lack of backing can be a response to his or her perceived lack of loyalty among teachers.

Decentralized control turns the direction of commitment around by giving evidence of a solid organizational commitment *to* its individual members and clients in a nurturing relationship rather than in a fit-us-or-leave atmosphere. Similarly, loyalties are earned, through a respect for and service to individuals, unconditionally. As McPherson (1988, p. 123) words it, "If loyalty is a valuable commodity, then advanced payment is required of the manager and not the managed." With nurtured commitment and earned loyalty, the delegation of work can include an opportunity for individuals to participate meaningfully in the formation of the *values* that shape the organization. In other words,

People are invited to share not merely in work, but in determining the worth of that work and the virtue of the organization itself. What is right and what is wrong is not a policy or an edict, but a grounded consideration, a reasonably consensual understanding. Morality is created within the organization in the form of values that carry the hopes of most, if not all. [McPherson, 1988, p. 129]

From routines to policies (e.g., who "backs" whom), the school nurtures the kind of professionalism that defines the very nature and culture of the organization itself.

In sum, the school administrator—long considered a barrier to rather than facilitator of involvement—can help safeguard the public interest *and* serve professionalization. But this is not likely if administrators continue to maintain the middle ground (even though logic would suggest it). Administrators who balance interests, even serving a bit as ombudsmen, leave the schools with conditional and negotiated loyalties and commitments. As parents seek control and teachers seek empowerment, the stakes (the "conditions") can increase mightily. Battle lines are drawn—and harden. If safeguards are to flourish, the administration of a school and a school district must open up; it must delegate to both teachers *and* parents the opportunity to find and serve sets of common values.

The Professional and Outreach to the Parent

Parental involvement in schooling has been found to vary with social class: "There are much tighter linkages between upper-middle-class parents and the school because upper-middle-class parents closely supervise and frequently intervene in their children's schooling" (Lareau, 1989, p. 9). Among the upper middle class, relations with the school display an *interconnectedness*; while among the working class, there tends to be *separation* between family and school (Lareau, 1989).

This perspective has its advantages and disadvantages. Upper-middle-class parents are often actively involved with their children's schooling. They volunteer, they read to their children, they seek information, they reinforce the curriculum, and they value education. They can also be extremely critical of the school, intrusive, and complaining. They do not readily defer to a teacher's expertise and they are quick to make special demands on the school to meet their familial interpretation of what is best for their own children (e.g., a specific teacher, daily progress reports to be sent home, some after-hours tutorial help). Their children, under parental *and* educator pressure, can often be under considerable stress, with school experiences affecting family tensions, and vice versa. Nevertheless, the upper middle class are not about to leave their children's educational success to the schools. They take steps "to ensure that success" (Lareau, 1989, p. 169).

By way of contrast, working-class families tend to leave education to their children's teachers, deferring to the expertise of the educator and intruding little into the life of the classroom. While they may read to their children and support the school, working-class parents are less likely to see school and home as a continuum of shared responsibility. They rarely complain to the school, but they are also less fully involved in the education and academic success of their children. They trust the school to do its separate job of educating their children (Lareau, 1989, p. 169). Indeed, the working-class parents may have a greater faith and acceptance of professionalism than do upper-class parents, many of whom are professionals themselves.

Annette Lareau (1989) develops two important conclusions. First, parents will bring differing, and unequal, resources to their interactions with schools. If school professionals and parents are at odds, it is the upper-middle-class family that is more likely to take the offensive successfully with complaints, expressions of concern, and targeted pressures. Indeed, professionals in education with thin skins or less well-honed defensive skills can be severely tested, for as Lareau notes, "Teachers . . . who lacked good communication skills with adults, were more likely to suffer at the hands of parents" (p. 162).

Conversely, if school professionals and parents are to function as partners rather than antagonists, the upper middle class again holds superior resources (e.g., a ready grasp of the vocabulary teachers use) for establishing good home-school connections. In short, while upper-middle-class parents are better equipped to be adversaries of school professionals, they tend also to be much better equipped to. serve as co-equals in promoting effective education.

The importance of this first conclusion is reflected in Lareau's second observation: The school, in recognizing the resource disparities among the different classes, can do much to activate the cultural resources of the home. As an illustration, Lareau notes that working-class parents place heavy emphasis on the hard evidence of good grades in school. Happy face stickers, good news telephone calls, verbal praise of Johnny's improved understanding, helpful comments on homework assignments, and praise of Johnny's improved cooperation in school may all be far less meaningful communications to working-class parents than would a simple A, B, or C. Hence, says Lareau, teachers of working-class pupils might be better advised to "connect their comments to parents directly to the goal of improving children's grades, rather than, for example, to the broader curricular goal of improving reading comprehension" (p. 181). Well-meaning educators, trying to alleviate the tyranny of grades and grade-level comparisons (e.g., Judy is reading at only the second-grade level), may damage more than promote working-class parents' understanding when they use language full of criterion-referenced comparisons.

It is important to note that while Lareau finds differences between economic classes in the interconnectedness of schools and families, she by no means claims that the working classes are without vital resources. To the contrary, she argues that the schools often fail to tap and to activate working-class families' cultural resources that are ready and waiting but seem currently at odds with the expectations and procedures of the public schools.

In a similar vein, Gary Wehlage and colleagues (1989) suggest four "teacher beliefs" that should be part of what professionalism in education is all about. These are (a) a belief that the educator is personally *accountable* for the success of each student; (b) a belief in an *extended role* of teaching, a role that can include the notion of activating the resources of the home; (c) a belief in the value of *persistence* with less-than-ideal students; and (d) a *sense of optimism* about each student's potential for learning (Wehlage et al., 1989, pp. 135–138).

Myra Cooper (1988, p. 48) sends this challenge firmly by noting that the lore on school professionalism largely ignores the client: "The notion of service, the personal nature of the relationship to youngsters and families, the caring and bonding context of the event, are embarrassingly absent." In our haste toward such attractions as empowerment, she continues, we may overlook the most essential job of the professional—to be a caregiver, a helper, a servant, an "activator." Moreover, adds Guadalupe Valdés (1996), today's professionals must be fully cognizant of the diverse ethnic cultures among a school's clientele—and of the profound differences in values that can surround any "activating" efforts. In his ethnographic study of ten Mexican immigrant families, Valdés (1996) found little professional understanding of either the internal dynamics of the ten families or their deeply traditional values and beliefs.

Thus, safeguarding the public interest can be accomplished by reconstructing professionalism toward an activation of, rather than a protection from, the not-school in public education. By no means is this easy, for public goals and private interests will yet be in conflict, the school will still find itself engaged in weaning children away from their parents, and the needs or "the good" of children will still tend to be interpreted differently by teachers and by parents. A test of professionalism in education will be its success in overcoming these cultural barriers.

The Professional Team

One of the implications to be drawn from a new appreciation of how family background can contribute to school achievement is that the effective professional educator can no longer work independently. Despite a historical drive toward professional autonomy, and the isolation that is built into our one-teacher-per-classroom structure of schooling, today's educator is just one of many professionals (both school and not-school) who have a legitimate voice in each child's development. This notion of shared professionalism, indeed of an integrated-service-delivery professionalism, is developed more fully in Chapter 11.

Few children, even in our most affluent neighborhoods, are untouched by the resources and services supplied by health professionals, law enforcement specialists, parks and recreation experts, and family service professionals (e.g., ministers, counselors). For children in poverty, the additional assistance offered by government, by social service workers, and by charitable institutions can make a significant difference in the likelihood of success in school. Indeed, the argument is that our complex, modern society has forced an unprecedented interdependency among families, schools, and a mixture of community services. Teachers can no longer stand alone, even in the most advantaged of schools. And, even the best of schools with the best of teachers cannot, on their own, overcome the effects of child abuse, drugs, gangs, family breakup, and poor health and housing (McDonnell, 1989; Boyd, 1989b; Kagan, 1993).

Increasingly, attention is being given to the notion of a professional "team" approach to ensuring school success. One much-discussed model, developed by James Comer, has been piloted in two low-income schools in New Haven, and is now being implemented in other schools around the country (Comer, 1980, 1987, 1988b; Comer et al., 1996). Comer argues forcefully that a child's home and school experiences are inseparable in shaping the child's psychosocial development, which in turn influences academic achievement.

As in other interventions, parents in Comer's model are encouraged to participate actively in the life of the school, efforts to "bond" school and community are vital, and the many programs of the school are open to staff and parents in cooperation. An important added ingredient, however, is the concerted work of a professional team (including parental involvement) of classroom teachers, social workers, mental health specialists, special educators, and the school administration, who work together to provide "cohesiveness and direction to the school's management and teaching" and concertedly toward the psychosocial preparation of children for academic achievement (Comer, 1988b, p. 46).

Far from autonomous and isolated, and far from escaping the scrutiny of "the public," professionals in Comer's model are thrust into a collegial relationship with other professionals. This can be a difficult relationship, for experience with PL 94-142 has shown that special educators, classroom teachers, school psychologists, parents, and administrators can all bring differing (even conflicting) interests and perspectives to the meeting place.

Comer extends the concept of a one-child-at-a-time staffing to school-as-a-whole teamwork in governance, program development, and instruction. If not guided and structured well, conflicts can grow and cleavages between professional perspectives can widen under such conditions. Nevertheless, the "team approach" to school management and governance can effectively safeguard the interests of both professionals and parents, bring school and community into closer contact, and augment the impact of each separate professional role on the development and achievement of the clientele.

This, the newest of notions about professionalism in education, assumes that public safeguards accompany professional teamwork, asks for a bonding between school and community, and assumes a sensitivity to and cooperation with parents. The team idea can be, and has been, extended to involve business leaders, university personnel, community organizers, retirees, skilled tradespeople, and others in a new opening of the public school to the community. The test for each school will be whether teamwork replaces antagonism, and whether the combined effectiveness of professionalism as a whole exceeds the contributions of the separate parts.

SUMMARY

The public schools are experiencing both a reform-minded drive toward teacher empowerment and enhanced community responsiveness. Some persons would comment that these two goals are fundamentally at odds. For good reason, the school has long tended to be a closed system of teacher-pupil interaction. The good reason is that teachers serve the professional role of broadening the horizons of children beyond the narrow perspectives of their parents, of treating group and societal needs beyond the special interests of individual parents, and of preparing children for an adulthood that may require some breaking away from the parental environment.

With a further professionalization of teaching, complete with an accompanying goal of teacher empowerment, is there a danger of

becoming less responsive to parents, of solidifying what has traditionally been a barrier between school and not-school? What safeguards
can serve the goal of professionalization but also protect the public
interest and promote community representation?

This chapter suggests three safeguards. First, the school administrator can provide a key safeguard (serving the public interest *and*
professionalization) by leaving the middle ground of a balancing and
compromising role and becoming an active promoter of common values,
uniting both teachers and parents in the school. Second, the concept of
"professional" in education carries its own safeguard if the concept shall
henceforth include the oft-ignored idea that outreach to families and to
the community is part of what being a professional is all about. The
realization here, at long last, is that an activation of the not-school (e.g.,
the resources and attributes of the home) is vital to the success of teaching
in its more familiar within-school environment. Similarly, third, safeguards accompany an emerging realization that many professionals,
both inside and outside schools, affect the lives of today's children.'
Seldom can the educator working alone hope for much success
without the contributions provided by many other highly trained
individuals. The separation of school from not-school no longer
makes sense, as professionals of all types in both the school and
the community learn to cooperate in seeking solutions to shared
problems.

Exercises
PROFESSIONALS AND PROFESSIONALS

1. Interview (or directly observe, if you can) a number of people-serving professionals outside public education (e.g., nurses, social workers, optometrists, dentists, librarians, ministers).
2. Ask your interviewees to talk generally about their professional worklives—the "highs" and "lows" of working with people, their opinions about the profession and its values, their problems and opportunities.
3. What do these professionals have in common? Where do the perspectives of each profession seem to differ? What would it take for a group of people from varied professions to be able to work together on common problems?

Suggested Activities

1. List as many labels as you can think of that are used by education professionals to classify and categorize pupils (e.g., learning disabled, gifted, underachiever). What are the positive effects of labeling in education; what are the negatives?

2. What labels are used by other professionals (e.g., nurses, physicians, lawyers, social workers) to categorize their clients?

3. Walk through an elementary school, observing carefully any wall displays, the condition of the school, the movements and demeanors of people in the school, the interactions between and behaviors of people around the school. What evidence can be found that gives you a sense of the norms and values of that school? Are there observable indicators of the climate or the culture of the school?

4. Write an essay that argues *against* (indeed argues the direct opposite of) McPherson's statement: "If loyalty is a valuable commodity, then advanced payment is required of the manager and not the managed."

5. Interview some parents of school-age children, trying to select parents who represent a diversity of family circumstances. Ask the parents how often and for what reasons they engage in interactions with their child's school. Ask them to describe their personal feelings about these interactive experiences. Did they feel uncomfortable, put on the spot, put down, not welcome? Or, alternatively, did they feel respected, accepted, valued, and responded to?

6. Observe, at a bit of a distance, the relationships of parents with their young (pre school-age) children at a park or playground, at the zoo, in a museum, in a shopping mall, or at the beach. Keep an observational record of the behaviors of both parents and children, and their conversations. Later, analyze your data to determine what resources of an educational value the parents might be supplying to their children.

SUGGESTED READINGS

Comer, James P.; Haynes, Norris M.; Joyner, Edward T., and Ben-Avie, Michael (1996). *Rallying the Whole Village: The Comer Process for Reforming Education.* New York: Teachers College Press.

Grubb, W. Norton, and Lazerson, Marvin (1982). *Broken Promises: How Americans Fail Their Children.* New York: Basic Books.

Lareau, Annette (1989). *Home Advantage: Social Class and Parental Intervention in Elementary Education.* London: Falmer.

Lieberman, Ann (ed.) (1988). *Building a Professional Culture in Schools.* New York: Teachers College Press.

Louis, Karen Seashore, and Kruse, Sharon D. (1995). *Professionalism and Community: Perspectives on Reforming Urban Schools.* Thousand Oaks, Calif.: Corwin Press.

Rosenholtz, Susan J. (1989). *Teachers' Workplace: The Social Organization of Schools.* New York: Longman.

Chapter Four

COMMUNITY GROUPS AND THE SCHOOLS

> Americans of all ages, all stations in life, and all types of dispositions are forever forming associations. There are not only commercial and industrial associations in which all take part, but others of a thousand different types—religious, moral, serious, futile, very general and very limited, immensely large and very minute.
> —Alexis de Tocqueville, *Democracy in America*, 1848

Americans are forever forming associations. It seems that nearly every topic or issue in education has an accompanying association, and that every association has decided to try its hand at changing or monitoring the public schools. One long-established and widely recognized association is the National Congress of Parents and Teachers (the PTA). Somewhat less well known among the general public are other nationally organized associations, such as the National Urban Alliance for Effective Schools, The National Committee for Citizens in Education, the National Community Education Association, and the Coalition of Essential Schools.

As one would expect, many of the associations are formed by professional educators themselves. Among the most prominent are the American Association of School Administrators (AASA), the National Associations of Elementary Principals and of Secondary School Principals (NAEP and NASSP), the Association for Supervision and Curriculum Development (ASCD), the National Education Association (NEA), and the American Federation of Teachers (AFT). Again, there are many, many others of somewhat less public prominence, such as the National Council of Teachers of English, the Council for Learning Disabilities, the National Rural and Small Schools Consortium, and the National Science Teachers Association. Somewhat further distanced from (but simultaneously closely allied with) the professional

61

education community are state and national school boards associations, a flowering of foundation-supported associations, and many university-dominated associations, such as the American Association of Colleges of Teacher Education (AACTE) and the American Educational Research Association (AERA).

However, it is at the local or community level of education that the time-honored propensity of Americans toward associating takes on its most important role in school governance. To be sure, size and complexity will be reflected in a community's directory of associations. A major urban school district is likely to be filled with citizens' councils, school-improvement coalitions, neighborhood organizations, committees of businesspeople, and "task forces." But even the smallest and least urban of school districts is likely to find that the group interests of farmers, homeowners, retirees, business owners, religious communities, and socio-economic strata, whether formally "associated" or informally represented, are each important. Associations are often quiescent, supportive, tolerant, and nonintrusive in local education; but they can also be political juggernaughts, sources of heated conflict, and reflections of something seriously amiss in school-community relations. School administrators pay attention to associations.

The impact of community associations is so widely recognized in American public service that most administrators consider pressure-group interventions a matter of course in their worklives. The schools, like other public agencies, are respondents in a pressure- or interest-group politics of education. Groups of people in association—with interests in reducing taxes, or in alleviating school overcrowding, or in removing some controversial textbooks—make demands on their schools. A complex game develops that involves power, legitimation, some conflict, and a bit of adapting and compromising. The schools eventually respond to these pressures with decisions (sometimes nondecisions) and actions, which then feed back into the political arena (see Easton, 1965).

From this perspective, community relations in local education can be succinctly described as "interest-group politics." Moreover, because interests tend to be in conflict, this style of politics may be further described as "adversarial" (Mansbridge, 1983).

Of late, however, some conceptualizations of community-group relations in education have moved away from an interest- or pressure-group orientation. Much of this has been in recognition of changed interactions between many community associations and the schools. Community volunteerism in education is increasing; school/business or school/university partnerships have been under widespread experimentation; neighborhood residents are increasingly being employed by the local schools; community members are becoming more actively involved in the direct governance of individual schools (e.g., through principal-selection committees and advisory councils); charter schools often combine community and professional leadership; and such traditional interest groups as the PTA are becoming widely varied in their forms of interaction with the schools. In short, the political boundaries between outside interests and inside-the-school interests are breaking down.

In this second case, claims Jane Mansbridge (1983), the politics of public education may possibly be moving "beyond adversarial democracy" toward new forms of associational relationships. This chapter will examine both of these patterns of school-community relations and their administrative consequences—as well as the special interests and potential problems attached to each form.

INTEREST-GROUP POLITICS

The Functions of Interest Groups

Roald Campbell and colleagues (1990) observe that interest groups perform three functions in government. First, they give individuals a chance to join other individuals in collective purpose. What a single individual may be unable to affect, a group of like-minded individuals may powerfully influence. A single taxpayer angry with the budgetary direction of the schools is a lone voice; an angry taxpayers' association is a very serious concern. Second, interest groups can delineate and clarify issues. They tend to stake out positions, often communicating their policy preferences clearly and sometimes forcefully to policymakers. The information that interest groups provide, although often biased in the interest group's favor, can be an important source of policy to political leaders. School policy often begins from the position that one group of consequence has been advocating.

Third, interest groups, by often acting in support of or in opposition to one another, help to facilitate the important policymaking process of compromise and consensus—a process central to our democratic society (Campbell et al., 1990, pp. 378–379). When educational "stakeholders" differ, the savvy leader tries to find common ground.

Varieties of Local Interests

At the local (community) level of schooling, interests are not always "grouped" so much as they are voiced. Homeowners may begin to speak out (at board meetings or in letters to newspapers) against a proposed increase in school property taxes. Sometimes a hold-the-line-on-taxes coalition does form, but more often the group interest is not formally organized so much as it is simply given expression by increasing numbers of individuals who may recognize their own partnership in a groundswell of public opinion. Similarly, interests may coalesce formally or informally around school closings, school district restructuring, curriculum alterations, administrator-board conflicts, or teacher strikes.

Additionally, one finds that at the local (community) level of education, special interests may not even be voiced, but they are still "listened to" by school policymakers. These are the interests described in some of the oldest (and still classic) studies of school-community relations: Havighurst (*Growing Up in River City*, 1962); Hollingshead (*Elmtown's Youth*, 1949); Dollard (*Class and Caste in a Southern Town*, 1937); and the Lynds (*Middletown*, 1929). The subtle influences of social class; of residency, occupation, and social acceptability; and of religion and race can be powerful (even though usually silent) forces in the distribution of educational services. In *Elmtown's Youth* (1949, p. 180), A.B. Hollingshead writes, "New teachers soon learn from their association with other teachers, townspeople, parents, and adolescents 'who is who' and what one should or should not do to avoid trouble." And a bit later, "The honors in the graduating classes from both the elementary and high schools are deliberately given to children from the prominent families" (p. 184).

The people who run things in this town need to say little, but they are still among the most powerful of the interests in school policymaking. Even in a community of the size and complexity of New York City, there are special "core" groups typically lodged very close to the centers of decision making and many "satellite" groups struggling for their voices to be heard (Sayre and Kaufman, 1965).

Patterns of Community Politics

Thus, interest groups serve the important functions of multiplying the powers of individuals, clarifying issues, and helping to resolve issues. In local education, interests may be more often voiced than formally grouped; while simultaneously, powerful interests in local education may be unvoiced (i.e., virtually silent) but still heavily reflected in school policymaking. It is this latter, less positive function of interest groups that is behind a description by Peter Bachrach and Morton Baratz (1962) of "the other face of power" in community politics. This other face is the capacity of some interests to prevent issues from arising, to dominate policymaking, and to channel voices in a single direction. There is, in other words, a power to accomplish but also a power to block accomplishment.

The recognition of the many-faced nature of local policymaking prompted political scientists to develop conceptualizations and categorizations of communities according to their interest-group relations. One typology for education has been offered by Donald J. McCarty and Charles E. Ramsey (1971). They classify communities into four types of power structures: (1) dominated, (2) factional, (3) pluralistic, and (4) inert.

Moreover, they link type of community power structure to a corresponding style of decisionmaking by the local school board, and to a corresponding role of the local school superintendent. Figure 4.1 summarizes the McCarty and Ramsey model.

In a *dominated* community, a small group of individuals at the top (usually an economic elite) directs the course of events. While opposition may surface, it does not receive much attention or credence from this group of the power elite. The board of education shares the perspectives of the dominant group and reaches decisions acceptable to this group. A school district superintendent similarly identifies with and takes his or her cues from the dominant power structure—and, indeed, usually plays the role of a *functionary* vis-à-vis the dominant interests. That is, the superintendent carries out the wishes of or proposals offered by the elite, rather than developing policy on his or her own.

A *factional* community is best defined by its conflict between two major interests of relatively equal strength (e.g., older residents vs. newcomers, farmers vs. town dwellers, blue-collar vs. white-collar).

Figure 4.1

Types of Community Power

Community Power Structure	School Board	Role of the Superintendent
Dominated	Dominated	Functionary
Factional	Factional	Political strategist
Pluralistic	Status congruent	Professional advisor
Inert	Sanctioning	Decision maker

Reprinted by permission of Greenwood Publishing Group, Inc., Westport, CT, from *The School Managers: Power and Conflict in American Public Education*, by Donald J. McCarty and Charles E. Ramsey. Copyright by Donald McCarty and Charles E. Ramsey and published in 1971 by Greenwood Publishing Corporation, page 22.

Power may shift back and forth between factions, or the community may be experiencing a transition between declining and developing factions. The local school board will tend to reflect factional conflicts, with hotly contested elections and with votes following factional allegiances. The local school district superintendent will likely be a *political strategist*, obeying the wishes of the faction in power but anticipating shifts in power by actively keeping his or her fences mended with the temporarily weaker faction.

A *pluralistic* community contains not one or two political interests, but many. Influence over policy is dispersed among an array of competing perspectives, with no all-powerful faction in full control. While school board members may each reflect particular interests, they are generally equal in status and freely give and take in discussions, with no one dominating. According to McCarty and Ramsey, the school district superintendent will tend to be a *professional advisor* engaged often in the statesmanlike act of suggesting alternative policies to the board, then helping the board weigh the pros and cons of these alternatives. Decisions are reached without a necessary obeisance to the special ideology of a faction in power.

An *inert* community demonstrates no viable or visible power structure. There is little evidence of an active politics of education or of any interest in or attention to the deliberations of the local school board. The board tends to follow the lead of the superintendent, sanctioning his or her decisions. The power structure, to the extent one exists at all, may be the local school district itself.

The McCarty and Ramsey typology is now somewhat dated, plus it tends to oversimplify complex relationships between school board, community, and administration. Few communities today are likely to be dominated by a power elite or, alternatively, are likely to be as politically inert as the model suggests. Similarly, few communities are easily pigeonholed today in terms of their seemingly constant power structures. Communities can change extremely rapidly from rural outposts to suburban sprawl, from moderately taxed to heavily taxed, from relatively autonomous to an "edge city" dependency on a nearby city, from economically viable to distressed, from relatively homogeneous to exceedingly cosmopolitan. Community politics accordingly is often in a state of transition, with school board decisionmaking and superintendents' roles as varied as the confusing, changeable environments surrounding them (see Lutz and Merz, 1992).

Nevertheless, the McCarty and Ramsey typology communicates a still-vibrant generalization about community politics in education: (a) the nature of communities' interest-group politics will differ, along a scale that tends to range from little conflict to high conflict; and (b) the nature of interest-group politics in a community (including the degree of conflict) affects mightily the operations of the local school board and the role of the local superintendent. One of the first scholars to make this point for education was David W. Minar (1966), who found that as the level of conflict in school district policymaking increases, the autonomy and discretion of school administrators is reduced. Similarly, in a line of research that has received considerable support in study after study, Frank Lutz and Lawrence Iannaccone (1978) found that a seemingly placid and superintendent-managed politics of education can episodically become full of conflict. This often happens as dissatisfaction builds in a community—leading eventually to a superintendent's ouster (Lutz and Merz, 1992). In short, even when seemingly quiescent, a community's impact on a superintendent's discretion is not to be minimized.

There is some academic disagreement as to whether local schooling is as conflict filled as is popularly believed (see Zeigler, Kehoe, and Reisman, 1985). Nevertheless, Frederick Wirt and Leslie Christovich (1989) and Wirt and Michael Kirst (1989) provide evidence that interest-group pressures have increased in local education. These interest-group pressures flow liberally out of population changes, societal stresses, and fiscal inadequacies in community after community. Even such a phenomenon as the growing incidence of "home schooling" adds substantially, if indirectly, to the sense of "pressure" among educators (Page, 1996). The pressures combine with growth in state and federal programs, increased legal activity, expansion of collective bargaining, and more aggressive special interests (e.g., bilingual education and special education) to put conflict management at the very top of a public school administrator's list of all-important skills (Wirt and Kirst, 1989, p. 194). Again, the prime importance of community conflict and interest-group pressure is that they heavily impact the school administrator's role. Focusing specifically on school superintendents, Wirt and Kirst write: "In short, superintendents will pursue their values differently given different degrees of community conflict" (p. 201).

In brief summary, the public schools are surrounded by political pressures—by special-interest associations, growing in number and diversity, that are not at all reluctant to try to influence school policy and administration. Communities differ widely in their styles of interest-group politics, but by no means can it be assumed that a quiet community is free of pressures and well-entrenched power structures. Nor can it be assumed that a low-conflict community shall long remain quiescent—for in these changing times, conflict can episodically flare, leading often to rapid, unforeseen adjustments in administrative careers. Indeed, one analyst has been prompted to observe that "conflict is the DNA of the superintendency" (Cuban, 1985, p. 28).

BEYOND INTEREST-GROUP POLITICS

By no means would a practicing school administrator be surprised to learn from the research literature that his or her job can be much affected by interest-group pressure and community conflict. The administrative lore in education has long assumed that outside pressures will surround the schools in abundance, that the professional integrity of the school often requires efforts to keep much of this pressure at a distance, and that becoming embroiled in conflict works heavily to the disadvantage of the schools and certainly to administrative careers. B. Guy Peters (1978, p. 141) writes: "The conflict between the demands of pressure groups and the role of the bureaucracy in decision making is, in most societies, one of the most basic in government."

Accordingly, school administrators tend to be wary of the political fray and even wary of outsiders generally. If no longer able to maintain a sacrosanct "four walls" of the school, safe from all intrusion, modern administrators are advised to become astute "poker players"—playing the game of community politics as adroitly as any of its other participants (see Wiles, Wiles, and Bondi, 1981). Strategies for dealing with the community and for stabilizing the school are the new administrative guides, replacing the previous guideline to "avoid politics."

Interestingly, the metaphor of the poker game proceeds from a rich tradition in political theory. In a most influential essay, for example, Norton Long (1958) suggested that community politics functions as an "ecology of games." Its players (e.g., banks, newspapers, chambers of commerce, churches, school districts) each occupy territorial space and interact with one another within well-established rules and roles. There are banking games and education games and business games—all with their own players, strategies, and tactics. Individuals may play in a number of games, but they will usually focus on just one. The players in one game may use the players in another and, in turn, are made use of by them. As in most games, winning and losing are important, and the game playing can become extremely serious.

From this perspective, school district administrators inhabit a special territory (playground?) of education politics. It is important for the educational administrator to realize that players from outside education will have their own games; and while they may participate in the education game, they will play "like bankers," or "like newspaper reporters," or "like businessmen." Although there may be some traditional pulling and pushing among competing political interests, the game is much contained and ordered by its extant rules and rituals. An agreement and its ensuing cooperation, for example, may be less a compromise of competing positions than a fulfillment, often nonconscious, of social roles and expectations. Bankers are expected to act like bankers (e.g., be fiscally conservative), local businesspeople are expected to act like businesspeople (e.g., be leery of tax increases), and school superintendents are expected to act like educators (e.g., ask for more money "for the children"). If the game is played "correctly," each player can protect his or her own territory yet share aspirations and cooperate toward achieving common goals (Long, 1958). In this way, conflict is considerably muted—as long as each actor stays in character, playing the game in the way the other players have come to expect. It is easy to understand, of course, how such expectations about "playing correctly" can become extremely prob-lematic under the conditions of social change, diversity, and differ-ing patterns of family life that now characterize many of our communities (Henry, 1996; Smrekar, 1996b).

A Politics of Common Interest

Long's ecology perspective suggests that political games are underway, and are certainly winnable and losable. Nevertheless, the established patterns, expectations, and "rules" in community politics reduce overt conflict and grow out of shared rather than divergent interests. Even an occasional conflict (heated discussions, threats, leaks to the press) can be part of the larger game—a bit of "squaring-off" from time to time that has its own rules and never gets out of hand.

Alan Peshkin (1978) describes such a common-interest commu-nity, the midwestern town he labels Mansfield, in *Growing Up American*:

It is a community in sociological as well as geographical terms. That is, within a given area its people share common interests and loyalties, not through singularities of language, race, or religion, but through shared outlook, history, occupations, institutions, and purposes. It is a community with integrity and identity. [P. 194]

Mansfield did not find itself in conflict with its schools. Indeed, Mansfielders believed firmly that their schools belonged to them; and it would certainly appear that they did. Academic achievement was not prized above football accomplishment; and teachers would not be hired who were thought to be "too intelligent for this community" (Peshkin, 1978, p. 200). Community participation in educational policymaking was minimal—for the simple reason that for genera-tions the community found no disjunctions between their public schools and themselves.

While we will discuss the dark side of a Mansfield in more detail in the next chapter, Peshkin's findings illustrate well an emerging perspective on local politics. In *Beyond Adversary Democracy*, Jane Mansbridge (1983) argues that political science has tended to over-emphasize differences in interests and the adversarial side of local democracy, to the neglect of common interests and noncombative forms of policymaking. That there are often interests in conflict is obvious; but communities are also much characterized by shared ideals, by consensus, and by commonality.

By assuming a politics of common rather than conflicting inter-ests, one gains quite a different perspective on the relations between citizens and school administrators. For example, in some early work, Merle Sumption and Yvonne Engstrom (1966) captured the essence of this "new politics" by suggesting an image of "shareowner" in community relations. They observed:

The shareowners in the school are also shareowners in the public library, parks, and museum, and many of them own shares in business corporations located in the community. There is a common interest which, if developed, should bring the school into closer alignment with the rest of the community. [P. 4]

Although this "businesslike" language is somewhat dated, the shareowner analogy aptly pictures an integration of community insti-tutions rather than a pulling and pushing among them. Members of a community or neighborhood "share" their social organizations. What they tend to share, in addition to taxpayer support, is a common sense of (and common norms regarding) accessibility, utility, and accounta-bility vis-à-vis these institutions.

To be sure, the public schools may compete for scarce resources with the parks department and the library board; and as "players" in local affairs, officials may behave "like educators" or "like librarians." And in many communities, *all* forms of tax-supported service struggle against little popular interest and a weaker sense of "sharing" than desired. Nevertheless, in many communities, conflict and "combat" are muted in favor of a politics of representation of, and a responsive-ness to, the citizenry's common values. Thus quite appropriately, David Tyack and Elisabeth Hansot (1982) entitled their history of the local school district superintendency *Managers of Virtue*. We will develop in the next chapter this idea of the politics of managing school-community relations.

In fact, active sharing is rapidly becoming part of school operations. More and more parent and community volunteers can be found
in school work positions. Partnerships between schools and businesses
and between schools and universities are popular. Teacher training
is benefiting from a sharing relationship, using the schools as professional-development laboratories. (This theme is developed further in
Chapter 12.)

Integrative Mechanisms

Interestingly, in addition to Sumption and Engstrom's work,
other early research into school politics gives us a sense of some of the
possible "community integrative mechanisms" behind nonadversarial democracy. Louis Masotti's *Education and Politics in Suburbia*
(1967) suggests that school politics can often reflect forces of integration (rather than disintegration) from three important sources: (1) a
foundation of common values concerning community goals; (2) an
effective communications network that ties multiple loyalties and a
community's cross-purposes to shared ends; and (3) a cosmopolitan
leadership, which can turn situations and events toward shared
interests.

Critics might charge that the first of these mechanisms has been
fast disappearing in American life. In fact, much of the argument for a
community-creating role for the schools (in this book and elsewhere)
is predicated on the need to reemphasize and re-create common
values between school and community. Indeed, one position holds
that an integration of values in American life is being achieved today
only at the cost of a larger separation and segregation. Robert Reich
(1991) argues that Americans have been increasingly withdrawing
into their own just-like-us, wealth-segregated enclaves of neighborhoods, clubs, schools, and communities. The fad of "gated communities, for example, is just one sympton of a much larger social
issue. The cities have been left to the poor—demographically, economically, and spiritually. Where there is "community" today, it is
rigidly divided economically and symbolically (see Halpern, 1995).

Alternatively, others argue that deeply shared values have never
been lost—they are still a vital foundation of our body politic. Americans speak a "second language" of tradition and social commitment,
says Robert Bellah (1985)—a language tied to loyalties and obligations in our lives that can effectively override self-interest and

interest-group conflicts. Although one might decry, with Peshkin (1978), the anti-intellectualism of a Mansfield, one cannot but be impressed by his observation: "It is a community with integrity and identity" (p. 194).

The second and third of Masotti's (1967) mechanisms offer some guidance toward a consideration of administrative actions. Traditional interest-group politics may emphasize administrator skills in conflict management and in the "conversion" of (often competing) demands into acceptable policy (Wirt and Kirst, 1989). The "new politics" of administration suggests another set of skills, including being able to communicate loyalties and traditions, identify and develop shared interests, and provide leadership toward achieving a greater sense of community (Sergiovanni, 1996).

Consider the practical example, for instance, of Michael Moore's (1988) description of a town experiencing rising conflict and dissension while trying to accommodate some economic and social changes. A village administrator succeeded in inaugurating a hugely popular "Old People's Day"—an annual festival filled with current and former residents telling stories about the community and its people (amid sing-alongs, picnicking, and socializing). A new sense of tradition rescued the town—interestingly, not at all unlike Bellah's (1985) suggestion that "communities of memory" are among the most powerful components of shared-interest development.

In brief, there is another side to the conflict perspective on school-community relations. Even the games and strategies characterizing interest-group politicizing are often more heavily bound by common values and shared interests than by conflicting values. The politics of common interests can be limiting and narrow-minded, as in a Mansfield. It is, in many ways, the toughest of all administrative jobs in public education, however. "Bringing the community back in," observes Claire Smrekar (1996), comes at present with no recipe, no agreed-upon agenda, no program of training.

SUMMARY

In a society filled equally with freedom and diversity, the public schools "cannot escape being a battleground" (Peshkin, 1978, p. 205), surrounded by interests. When grouped, and especially when groups become coalitions, these interests are a powerful presence in the worklives of educators. From parent associations to teacher associations to athletic boosters to PL 94-142 defenders, divergent political pressures on the schools can be powerful determinants of the nature and style of a school system's community relations.

To be sure, not all communities will display the same styles of interest-group politics. Some may be dominated by a power structure, while others may be pluralistically full of separate interests, none dominant but all with teeth bared in debates over the schools. As communities across the nation engage in the reform and restructuring of their public schools, even groups that have tended to be somewhat removed from education (e.g., corporations, foundations, the media) are now deeply into the fray. It is no news to the practicing educator to be told that school-community relations are likely to be heavily influenced by an adversarial politics of education—a sometimes hotly contested pulling and pushing among competing values.

School-community relations can go beyond interest-group politics, however. There is also a political world of common interests, of value-creating traditions, and of rules and rituals rooted in shared ideals. Community relations from a nonadversarial perspective may stress community building above conflict management and an integration of interests above accommodations to competing interests. A metaphor that has received much attention portrays the educational administrator as a "poker player," amid conflict. However, there has been little discussion of the beyond-adversarial politics of school administration. Some thoughts on this topic are presented in Chapter 5.

Exercises
FIGHTIN'-N-FEUDIN'

1. Track one local school district's board of education through the media (e.g., a local newspaper) for the past twelve months.
2. What newsworthy issues, conflicts, or controversies has the board faced? What reportedly is the nature of the opposition? What interest groups, if any, are involved?
3. How, according to newspaper accounts, have any of the reportable issues been resolved? Was the coverage adequate? Is it possible to determine any "winners" and "losers"? What appears to be the aftermath of the conflict—continued strife, all parties satisfied, no parties satisfied, some new issues developing?

Suggested Activities

1. Choose three or four nearby local school districts, attempting to categorize the power structure of each according to the McCarty and Ramsey typology (i.e., dominated, factional, pluralistic, or inert). What information would you need to have in order to make such a judgment?
2. Develop a descriptive itemization of all the interest groups found within (and connected to) your local school district (e.g., from teacher associations to realtor associations). Interview the presidents or executive officers of at least three groups. How would you describe the central interests of each vis-à-vis the public schools?
3. Consider Masotti's (1967) "integrative mechanisms." Interview at random a number and a variety of persons residing within your local school district—asking each subject his or her sense of what the community's goals should be for elementary and secondary education. Analyze your results, asking whether there appears to be more goal consensus than disagreement among your respondents.
4. Conduct a class debate, or write essays supporting both sides, on the thesis that political interpretations tend to overemphasize differences in interests and the adversarial side of local democracy—to the neglect of common interests and nonadversarial decisionmaking.
5. Observe directly and record the policy decisions made by a local board of education for a period of three to four months. What decisions, if any, are characterized by conflict? What percentage of decisions, on what topics, appear to be free of conflict? What conclusions can be drawn—for example, about what leads to conflict, about how the board handles conflict, about the superintendent's role under conflict?

SUGGESTED READINGS

Bellah, Robert N., et al. (1985). *Habits of the Heart: Individualism and Commitment in American Life.* Berkeley: University of California Press.

Lutz, Frank W., and Merz, Carol (1992). *The Politics of School/Community Relations.* New York: Teachers College Press.

McCarty, Donald, and Ramsey, Charles (1971). *The School Managers: Power and Conflict in American Public Education.* Westport, Conn.: Greenwood.

Mansbridge, Jane J. (1983). *Beyond Adversary Democracy.* Chicago: University of Chicago Press.

Wirt, Frederick M., and Kirst, Michael W. (1989). *Schools in Conflict,* second edition. Berkeley, Calif.: McCutchan Publishing.

Chapter Five

THE POLITICS OF MANAGING SCHOOL-COMMUNITY RELATIONS

The field of politics sets the tasks for administration, but the field of administration lies outside the proper sphere of politics.
—Paraphrased from Woodrow Wilson, *Congressional Government*, in R.B. Hawkins, Jr., "A Strategy for Revitalizing Public Education," 1985, p. 31

No "truism" has had greater impact on the field of public service than Woodrow Wilson's caution against mixing politics and administration. The most frequent expression of this dictum in education is the still-common complaint by local school district superintendents that their school board is having trouble separating its policymaking from direct intervention in school management. The normative world of the superintendent calls for a policy-enacting board, which then stays well out of the executive officer's separate role of converting policy into administration. Although this separation of politics from administration has been labeled "a myth" (Gove and Wirt, 1976), it remains an extremely active belief in public schooling.

Scholars trace this avoid-politics notion to progressive-era efforts toward scientific management and professionalized efficiency in public-sector administration (Callahan, 1962; Tyack, 1974). The central idea from this turn-of-the-century reform movement was that school administrators were to be considered managerial experts— trained to run educational organizations in businesslike fashion, free from political intrusions. Once policy was established, the professional school administrator was to take over in a way reflecting his or her distinctive training and expertise.

Interestingly, the key assumptions behind this separation of

79

functions may go back much further historically. Lawrence Cremin
(1979) draws attention to Bernard Bailyn's (1960) observation that
historians of the colonial period of American educational history may
have asked the wrong question. They asked: "When did the public
school begin?" But they should have asked: "How did colonial Americans educate their children?" (Cremin, 1979, p. 119). The first question reflects a traditional overconcentration on the school *as a separate
institution*, divorced from families and communities (and of course
their politics). The second question finds that the politics for the
community *is* the politics of the school. From this perspective, a
separation of institutions (including a separation of politics from
administration) makes no conceptual sense.

The concept of "the wrong question" provides an organizing theme
for this chapter. From one perspective (the traditional), policymaking
is separable from administration, politics is an outside constraint on
administrative practice, and the school as an institution has its own
managerial identity—albeit heavily immersed in a political arena.
From a second (alternative) perspective, policymaking and administration are not so separable, administrative practice sets the conditions
for its own political environment, and the school is not an independent
institutional or managerial entity. We will label these differing perspectives as follows: (a) school-community politics and administration and
(b) the administration of school-community relations.

SCHOOL-COMMUNITY POLITICS AND ADMINISTRATION

The word *turbulent* is used frequently by political scientists, including Frederick Wirt and Michael Kirst (1989), to describe the
policy environments of local schooling. It is a word with special
meaning to educational administrators—for, as discussed in Chapter
4, the public schools are surrounded by competing interest groups,
community power structures, changing judicial and legislative mandates, and the vagaries of public opinion. The public schools are
decidedly political systems, in that outside demands and supports (e.g.,
tax dollars) permeate the boundaries of the institution and are converted into educative or administrative actions. Seldom are the demands and the conversion processes simple, straightforward, endur-

ing, and uncontested; the political system is indeed quite turbulent.

Three key questions must be asked in interpreting the impact of the outside political environment on the schools:

- How do educators decode the political messages directed toward the schools?
- How do the political messages become translated (converted) into educational policies and procedures?
- How are the internal organizational structures of the public schools influenced by the external political environment?

Decoding Political Messages

Politics has to do with the "authoritative allocation of values" (Easton, 1965). Quite often the values that best characterize a community are deeply rooted in its history, demography, and shared traditions. Such value-integrated communities as Alan Peshkin's (1978) "Mansfield" (introduced in Chapter 4) will tend to select school administrators who have already been heavily socialized (or clearly "buy") into the lifeways and norms of the community. Decoding the messages of the political community may simply involve that which "comes naturally" to such administrators, for they share fully the community's (sometimes narrow-minded) perspectives on education. When political demands intrude from outside the immediate surroundings (e.g., new state requirements), the school executive's key task can be to interpret the outside demands so that they best fit local values.

A long tradition of research into community power would suggest, however, that the values of some residents can carry greater political weight than those of others. This is the central finding in a series of influential studies on the power structures of communities from the 1920s on. The famous study of "Middletown" (in Muncie, Indiana), by Robert S. and Helen Lynd (1929, 1937), found a baronial business elite in effective control of that community. W. Lloyd Warner and Paul Lunt (1941) also discovered a business elite in thorough control of "Yankee City," but found that the community was in a disturbing transition from a live-in industrial elite to absentee ownership and an absentee elite. Other studies (e.g., Dollard, 1937; Davis et al., 1941; Hollingshead, 1949; Havighurst, 1962) were significant in demonstrating the effects of power concentration on less influential groups in the community.

For the educational administrator, "decoding" (interpreting) the community power structure may seem, on the surface, to be a rather simple job of guiding the schools toward the tastes, interests, and demands of the elite. To be sure, there is much evidence throughout the community-studies literature to show that the public schools will often act heavily in favor of residents from the "right side of the tracks" (see Havighurst, 1962; Rist, 1970; Cicourel and Kitsuse, 1963). Nevertheless, a community divided into influential ("ins") and not-so-influential ("outs") poses some extremely touchy political problems for the local educator. In their study of "Springdale," Arthur Vidich and Joseph Bensman (1968) found a school board and superintendent cooperating to keep decisions and issues secret and any conflicts muted—for fear of generating even a hint of breakdown in power-elite solidarity. Inevitably, furthermore, communities do change; and as Frank Lutz and Lawrence Iannaccone (1978) have discovered, dissatisfaction can arise among new power centers in a community, going unnoticed by school board and superintendent until a possible board incumbent's defeat or a superintendent's ouster. Finally, the existence of a power structure can present special decoding problems to the educator who wishes to be especially considerate of the have-nots. As Michael Nunnery and Ralph Kimbrough (1971) indicate, some "dangerous" political strategies may be necessary, such as organizing "latent" centers of power against the elite or bringing pressure from "outside sources" (e.g., state accrediting agencies) on the schools. In large-city environments, as Lutz and Merz (1992) point out, a decentralization of governance power to the individual school site has been one strategy for "decoding" the increasing diversity of urban communities.

Despite the attention community studies have given to power elites, there is by no means an agreement that communities are generally so effectively in the hands of a controlling few. Indeed, one of the most fascinating debates in the community-studies literature has been between Floyd Hunter's (1953) finding of a monolithic ruling elite in Atlanta and Robert A. Dahl's (1960) claim from research conducted in New Haven that communities are more likely to contain distributed or pluralist power structures. Many influentials rather than few and divided arrangements of power that vary with differing decisions and the kinds of issues are far more common locally, Dahl argues, than are all-powerful elites.

The task of decoding the many political messages embedded within a pluralist political system can be given the simplifying label: "conflict management." By no means do researchers agree on how conflict ridden local schooling is compared with other public services; nor do they agree that educators manage conflict more than they avoid or ignore it (see Crowson, 1987). Nevertheless, Wirt (1990) and Wirt and Leslie Christovich (1989) argue that a "new turbulence" is occurring in local education and that the "decisional context" of modern-day educational administration is challenged by increasing numbers of groups with power entering the political arena. The political "codes" reaching the school executive can be many, varied, and overwhelming. It is not surprising that such labels as "besieged," "stressed," and "threatened" have been applied to today's superintendency (Arnez, 1981; Blumberg, 1985).

In an interesting analysis of some field research, Wirt (1990) as well as Wirt and Kirst (1989) suggest that the conflict-management (message-decoding) behavior of local superintendents will vary with the *intensity* of their values. What is the chief executive most likely to fight hard for? Her own job security? An equalization of educational opportunity throughout the district? The professional empowerment of district personnel? An open and responsive partnership with parents? Wirt (1990) summarizes:

As in all human conflict, how hard one fights depends on how much a value is threatened and by how great the opposition is. Like anyone else, superintendents cannot fight with equal intensity over all threatened values; they will give different priorities to what is sacred, what is standard, and what is unimportant. [P. 24]

The politics-of-it-all aside, adds Joseph Kahne (1996), it is a list of social and ethical priorities (e.g., choice, equity, civic virtue) that is truly at the heart of school policy and administration.

Translating Message into Policy

In brief summary, a decoding of political messages begins and ends with questions of value. When elites are in control or there is a close integration of values within a community, the administrator is likely to consider a narrow range of codes. As the political system adds separate and sometimes conflicting interests, the educator's own values become more and more salient: To whom and to what do I owe first allegiance?

This question of allegiance forms a backdrop to the problem of translation: How do political messages from the outside become translated into school district policies and procedures? In one influential approach to this broad topic, Dale Mann (1976) (introduced earlier, in Chapter 1) inquired into the importance of the *representational role* of the local educator. He identified three forms of representation:

1. *The Delegate.* The delegate directs his or her prime allegiance outward to the political community. In exercising his or her within-school administrative leadership, the educator as delegate seeks to represent as faithfully as possible the wishes and demands of the school's external constituency. One problem with the role of delegate is that the pressures from the political community are as often negative as positive. The messages embedded within a failed referendum, a "ban-the-book" movement, or a clash over pupil-assignment policy all present danger-filled agendas for the educator who is trying to respond faithfully to the wishes of the external community. Similarly, as Wirt and Kirst (1989) note, the messages from the community can differ conflictually along fundamentally value-laden lines— often involving issues of race, social class, liberalism-conservatism, and religion. Finally, cautions Mann (1976, p. 25), the delegate orientation "may lead an educator in directions not endorsed by himself or his profession." By no means are political constituencies free of their own prejudices, misunderstandings, and ill-informed opinions about the teaching-learning process. Far too many "Kanawha County controversies" (a famous textbook censorship case) have occurred for educators to feel comfortable in leaving education entirely "to the people" (see Page and Clelland, 1978).

2. *The Trustee.* The trustee directs his or her prime allegiance inward to the professional community and the employing organization. As trustee, the educator seeks to represent as faithfully as possible the best practice that personal judgment, professional knowledge, and collegial experience provide—holding "in

trust," and proceeding from, the expertise of the trained educator. One obvious problem with the trustee perspective is a tendency to close off the schools to many of the wishes, interests, and concerns of the community. As Mann (1976) notes, the schools can often be fooled by a quiet and apathetic community into the false belief that their procedures are thoroughly accepted and are without opposition among the populace. Furthermore, it is often the trustee-oriented educator who most vociferously complains about the lack of parental participation and the lack of community interest in the schools, failing in these complaints to understand the match of behaviors and perspectives represented in parental noninvolvement. Finally, the trustee orientation often reflects an acute sense of "risk" among loyal organizational actors. Mann gives an example of one school principal who provides his own definition of the needs and interests of the community "rather than risk compromising the quality of the school's program by stimulating authentic parental involvement" (p. 24).

3. *The Politico.* The politico responds to some issues and demands as a delegate and to others as a trustee. Mann (1976) cautions that the politico should not be viewed as an indecisive type, blowing with the changing winds of school-community relations. Rather, the politico seeks to balance effectively the "outside" interests of parents and community with the "inside" interests of educators and the school system. One problem, observes Mann, is that "the inconsistencies and compromises that characterize the politico orientation do not recommend it to very many administrators" (p. 31). A related criticism is that the politico tends to make "an adaptable reaction" to community-relations difficulties, instead of operating from the consistent and coherent system of values that tends to characterize either a delegate or a trustee.

Not surprisingly, Mann discovered that most school administrators can be best defined as trustees; although, notably, more minority (blacks and those with Spanish surnames) administrators were likely to be delegates. Fewest in number are the politicos. Mann explains that the trustee orientation reflects a long history of "closed decision procedures" in public schooling and, moreover, a tendency toward bureaucratic defensiveness in the face of conflict. Interestingly, Mann reports, "There was a distinct drop in the tendency of administrators to be trustees as the public they served moved from apathy toward activity" (p. 58). Moreover, "Administrators tend to define their communities as those people who support them" (p. 57).

In sum, the translation of political message into administrative policy and practice is at least in part influenced by representational roles. These roles are, in turn, an outgrowth of the primary allegiances of executives, plus a history of closedness and defensiveness within the profession. By no means, of course, can translation be fully described as a representational problem. Indeed, Wirt and Kirst (1989) devote four informative chapters to the "conversion process"—with much discussion of administrative styles, value intensities, and degrees of conflict in addition to their discussions relating to role. Nevertheless, the question of allegiance looms large. To whom do I owe my allegiance? To the interests of the profession and the organization? To the interests of parents, the community, and their children? Or, as difficult an assignment as it may be, to the interests of both?

Internal Organizational Effects

All three of the representational roles discussed above can be grouped within a construct found often in political and organizational theorizing: These are *boundary-spanning* roles. Boundary spanners are employees who have direct contact with an organization's environment. They interpret the organization to its clientele; they socialize outsiders into the ways and norms of the institution; they collect, process, and pass on information about what is going on in the external environment; and they provide a first line of organizational defense or point of attack (see McPherson, Crowson, and Pitner, 1986).

Boundary spanners play an important adaptive role for the organization, helping it adjust to the constraints and contingencies of its surroundings (Thompson, 1967). Indeed, this task is so vital, notes Karl Weick (1976), that organizations may even contain boundary-spanning units—units that can be sacrificed or "lopped off" in times of trouble, without danger to the core of the institution.

Local public education has, to be sure, boundary-spanning services performed throughout the institution. The board of education and the district superintendent have well-recognized, and even state-mandated, responsibilities in this arena. Similarly, budget officers, curriculum directors, special education directors, and tests-and-measurement specialists also find that much of their work has "boundary" implications.

Nevertheless, much of the investigation on boundary-spanning roles and their internal effects on public-sector institutions has understandably been directed toward the lowest point in each managerial and professional hierarchy—where institutions are engaged in their most frequent and significant contacts with clients. The individuals in these boundary-spanning roles are commonly referred to as "street-level bureaucrats" (Lipsky, 1976, 1980).

The Street-Level Bureaucracy

As introduced in Chapter 3, political scientist Michael Lipsky has developed a theory of the street-level bureaucracy—defining street-level bureaucrats (e.g., police officers, social workers, school principals) as "those men and women who, in their face-to-face encounters with citizens, 'represent' government to the people" (Lipsky, 1976, p. 196). Of importance to the theory is the understanding that the street-level bureaucrats' organizational position calls for much interaction with clients and much discretion in making decisions, and has a fairly extensive potential impact on clients. Furthermore, the street-level bureaucrat typically performs his or her job within a very complex and politically uncertain work environment.

Robert Crowson and Cynthia Porter-Gehrie (1980) and Van Cleve Morris and colleagues (1984) have studied the boundary-spanning behaviors of building principals, using Lipsky's theory. Among the principals' key "coping mechanisms" these investigators discovered were behaviors to (a) guide parental expectations vis-à-vis the school, (b) socialize the school's clients into school-acceptable behaviors, and (c) use certain parents creatively to "disarm" other critics of the school.

Unchecked parental concerns and requests for special consideration, for example, could inundate classroom teachers. The principal may act to screen some parental demands and to calm down parents in areas such as disciplinary action, homework or grading policy, or teaching style, when organizational norms call for the principal to back up the teacher. Similarly, building principals will occasionally go far out of their way (bend the rules) to meet some parents' special requests and help with unusual problems. With other parents (particularly with those who are not as "cooperative"), the principal may use school-system procedures as a ploy to escape parental demands ("I'm sorry but those are the rules") (Morris et al., 1984).

Of importance is the further understanding that while individuals in street-level roles are coping with clientele tensions in their own worklives, their actions tend to create internal, environment-driven *effects* for the organization. A common outcome is the development and use of special labels to distinguish cooperative clients from the troublesome, and supporters from detractors. The ways in which administrators spend their days—that is, how they allocate managerial time—can reflect in some schools the need to guard against client-relations-damaging disorder while simultaneously protecting the school staff from the parent-relations consequences of any errors in pupil management that do occur. Because schools, like other public-sector institutions, are extremely dependent on both monetary and nonmonetary resources (Pfeffer and Salancik, 1978), their managers sometimes bend attendance and admission rules, class-size restrictions, and curriculum guidelines in the interest of adding to or holding steady pupil enrollments. Most school budgets are enrollment driven; thus job protection for teachers and other staff depends heavily on the successes of street-level bureaucrats as creators of strong "holding power" (maintaining student enrollments) within their schools.

Summary

One perspective on the politics of managing school-community relations sees the school, as an institution, well embedded within an often turbulent outside environment. It behooves the policymakers and administrators of public schools to pay close attention to this environment—to carefully "decode" the political messages in the varying power structures of their communities. To fail to act politically is usually to risk conflict and dissatisfaction, and perhaps an eventual loss of administrative appointment.

Beyond the need to decode, political demands require the school administrator to translate environmental messages into institutional practice. While many questions of leadership style, organizational culture, conflict level, and the like are surely involved in this translation, one element well worth highlighting is the *representational role* of the administrator. To whom or to what does the educator owe first allegiance?—to the school's clientele or to the employing institution and its professionals? Or should administrators attempt to be responsive to both? Beyond translation, the role of the administrator can be additionally reflected in the *effects* of environmental interactions on the schools, which can often be found in the boundary-spanning activities engaged in by persons who serve clients at the street level of the organization.

THE ADMINISTRATION OF SCHOOL-COMMUNITY RELATIONS

Far from adequately investigated to date is just how the sense of "boundary" and the street-level bureaucratic role play out in new environments of much closer school-community relationships. For example, with today's recognition that parental involvement can "make a difference" in school achievement, Hoover-Dempsey and Sandler (1995) observe that the central concern now is less boundary than "fit" between parental and school expectations. Nevertheless, they go on to note that today it is *the child* who can be placed in a key boundary role—becoming "the party primarily responsible on a day-to-day basis for negotiating and moving between the demands and expectations of two usually separate entities" (Hoover-Dempsey and Sandler, 1995, p. 324). The dilemma for the child (or student) as boundary-spanner, adds Smrekar (1996b, p. 17), is that "the boundaries between the private zone of family life and public responsibility of education are unclear and constantly shifting, giving rise to confusion on the part of both parents and teachers regarding the expectations of the other."

Thus a second and alternative viewpoint on the politics of managing school-community relations proceeds from these new considerations of boundary and from a presumed "fault" of the perspective summarized above. While accompanied by a rich and informative literature, the first perspective distinguishes clearly between political environment and institutional recipient. Issues of conflict management, boundary spanning, interest representation, power structure, and demand conversion all become important when the school is conceptualized as one political/institutional system surrounded by another. The result is a "delivery system mentality," criticizes David

Seeley (1982), where providers and clients are separate (and sometimes antagonistic) populations. Worse, argues Morris Janowitz (1967),
the public schools have tended to become institutions of "limited
liability" (*gesellschaft* rather than *gemeinschaft* institutions)—restricted
in purpose, estranged from the political community; wary of social
controls; defensive, bureaucratic, and impersonal. Common thinking
in such institutions might be, "We're doing our jobs; it's the parents,
and the children themselves, who are not pulling their weight."

The second perspective reverses this distinction between environment and educational institution. The notion is more in keeping with
the *gemeinschaft* view of schooling—where both institution *and* environment are members of a single political community, more bound
together by shared beliefs and common sentiments than separated by
competing interests and powers in conflict. As Mary Anne Raywid
(1990) puts it, one major impetus to the restructuring movement has
been the conviction that the public schools are "out of synch" with
their external environments. Conceived as *gemeinschaft* institutions, the
shared interests of schools and their clientele, rather than their
differences and conflicts, become the revised focus of political inquiry.

From this perspective emerges a different although parallel set of
key questions. Beyond the earlier concentration on a decoding of
political messages, a translation of politics into practice, and an
adaptation of organization to environment, alternative questions,
vis-à-vis the politics of managing school-community relations, are:

- How do educators perceive the political influences of the public
  schools on the community?
- How do the policies and practices of the public schools become
  translated into community values?
- How do the internal organizational structures of the public
  schools influence the external political environment?

Sending Political Messages

Political scientists have long realized, of course, that the environmental demands placed on the public schools include a powerful
"feedback loop." That is, political influences are processed by educators, decisions are made, and these decisions flow back into community affairs, leading often to new tensions and altered issues. The

school and its parental environment are engaged daily in a many-sided give-and-take. From vacation schedules, to the choice of after-school playmates, to conflicts over homework and "good grades," life in the home is enormously influenced by the local school and its policies.

In a systems-analysis interpretation of exemplary school-community cases, E. Mark Hanson (1979) states that a typical educator response to environmental tension is initially to buffer the school organization from the community. Among the buffering techniques Hanson (1979, pp. 369–370) uncovered were strategic stalling, denying jurisdiction, "talking it out," and strategic ignoring (e.g., allowing some issues to lie dormant). Similarly, Robert Crain (1969) had discovered previously that a typical board and administrator response to demands for school desegregation in cities across the country was to reject these demands initially, until civil rights activities escalated and eventually forced the schools to take a position.

In short, if they can and as long as they can, school executives will tend to prefer "the cloak of bureaucratic invisibility" (Browne, 1980) to action in the front lines of political change. Indeed, Woodrow Wilson's admonition that administration "lies outside the proper sphere of politics" is still a favorite theme of the administrative practitioner. It is not unusual for the more politically active educator to complain bitterly about the political reluctance and innocence of his or her colleagues. Observed one Illinois superintendent:

I got involved in a state legislative committee a while back and found that most superintendents around the state either can't or won't talk to state legislators. It's a shame. Legislators are hungry to talk to superintendents. You can't imagine how hard it is to get most of the superintendents around the state to do such a simple thing as to send off a telegram to Springfield urging a piece of legislation forward. [McPherson, Crowson, and Pitner, 1986, p. 13]

This Illinois superintendent's complaint is not just a reflection of practitioner-only sentiments. In some concluding remarks following a nationally representative conference of university experts on school policymaking, Arthur Goldberg (1979, p. 271) similarly observed:

Let me now turn to what has troubled me about this conference, and that is the view of politics in relation to educational administration, which I have heard voiced from time to time. Politics seems to be viewed too often as either extrinsic or intrinsic. It seems to be viewed either as relating to some necessary evil—usually one from which monies must be elicited (the board of education, the state, the taxpayer)—or as relating to some unnecessary but inescapable intruder into the "normal" operation of the school.

It is therefore easy to understand why both the research and practitioner literatures have devoted insufficient attention to date to the political influences of public school officials on their communities. Politics is to be avoided or worse is something evil. It is also generally regarded as something that happens to administrators but certainly not an activity they engage in. There are discussions of "reconciling interests" (Sergiovanni et al., 1980) and "balancing acts" (Wiles, Wiles, and Bondi, 1981) in school administration. But these discussions of "practical politics" for administrators are still not part of a mainstream imagery for educators. Indeed, David Wiles, Jon Wiles, and Joseph Bondi (1981) use the metaphor of a "poker player" as their example of the astute educator-politician, a metaphor with a smoke-filled-room connotation to some practitioners.

Accordingly, educators tend to have a weak sense of the political influences of the public schools on their own communities. Interestingly, it is often in only the smallest school districts (long opposed to consolidation) that educators tend to realize fully how meaningful the schoolhouse, the football team and marching band, the commencement exercise, and the class reunion are to the political identity of the entire community.

It is from this perspective that Louis Masotti (1967), in some theorizing yet to be followed up on, called attention to the importance of "community integrative mechanisms" in local administration. Some educational leaders, he noted, can be uniquely labeled "cosmopolites." These are the educators who are unusual because they interpret school district "situations and events in terms of their consequences for the plural community, and who have the power to influence the community, opinion and action" (Masotti, 1967, pp. 149–150).

Translating Practice into Politics

In thoughts paralleling those of Masotti, Morris Janowitz (1967) called for a norm of "extended liability"—in place of the emphasis so many public officials place on limited liability. Among the errors of officialdom, continued Janowitz (p. 202), is the increasing tendency toward "social absenteeism" vis-à-vis the surrounding community. This is a loss of the strong community identification common to previous leadership—toward a more detached professional leadership. But worse, it can also be the loss of a feeling of responsibility for community affairs, replaced by a bystander or outside-observer attitude toward the machinations of local politics.

These twin themes of identification and responsibility bear further comment. In a contemporary expression of the identification side of liability, Alan Peshkin (1990) examines carefully the concept of cultural "fit" between school and community. At one time, this may have been a much simpler issue. Tyack and Hansot (1982) note that when Ellwood Cubberley applied for the superintendency of the San Diego schools in 1896, the single concern of the appointing board was Cubberley's religious orthodoxy. Was he a firm believer and a good, practicing Christian?

Today, observes Peshkin, how the school fits (e.g., its curriculum) with its overall culture is inordinately complex. Moreover, judgments of fit are intensely political; they arise from the differing values and concerns of an array of "agents"—from teacher subcultures to parents and parent organizations to state and national (and indeed world) perspectives to business and industry (and on and on). When educators strive to reorganize the schools, change the curriculum, or alter pupil-personnel practices, they almost inevitably will make decisions that fit the interests of some agents better than others.

In a recent case study of family-school relations in one district in southern California, Rodney Ogawa and Susan Studer (1996) found that buffering techniques are still to be found in educational administration. Buffering is most likely to be in use when there is much environmental uncertainty. Such uncertainty often stems from increasing ethnic diversity in a district, from increases in family transiency, and from teacher perceptions that they are increasingly being "threatened" in some way. Nevertheless, in our modern times, buffering is also very likely to be accompanied by much "bridging" (Ogawa and Studer, 1996). Bridging stems from a recognition that the schools depend upon parents and others to provide children with both real and intangible resources necessary to school success. Bridging seeks to find "fit" despite the many uncertainties that encourage buffering.

In short, the practice of education translates heavily into political values. Decisions such as those regarding purchases of instructional materials, teaching methods, how to allocate instructional time, the choice of curricular topic, and the disciplinary rules of the school can all reflect a special sense of fit and a narrow set of (usually implicit) political identifications. What we do not understand at all well, warns Peshkin (1990), are the varying "cultural stakes" of local educators and the resulting determinants of fit between schools and their many-sided communities. Persons who specialize in the evaluation of social-service programs, including education, have written much in recent years of the importance of a "stakeholder"-oriented approach to evaluation. But here too there is often disagreement as to just who the stakeholders are: A program's clientele? The funders? The larger public? The deliverers of services? (Stake, 1986).

The second key liability question concerns responsibility. Again, Peshkin (1978), in his description of the community of "Mansfield," provides a concise statement of the problem. Secure in its conservative, rural traditions and protective of its own values, Mansfield is comfortable with schooling loaded with American "isms" (e.g., racism, anti-Semitism). Peshkin writes:

Although Mansfield has no black citizens, and the possibility of busing does not exist, the community harbors antiblack sentiment. Thus it socializes children with values that conflict with national ideals, albeit disputed ones. [P. 201]

One interpretation of the responsibility of the public school educator is that the community, as narrow-minded as it wishes to be, should be the prime referent. The schoolchildren of Mansfield should be socialized by the schools into a system of values that fits the community and prepares the children for adulthood within that community. Indeed, in Mansfield and elsewhere, the educational professionals themselves are hired with this sense of fit firmly in mind.

Critics of this position charge, however, that it ignores a deeper responsibility. Michael Manley-Casimir (1989) asks that educational administrators pay close attention to "voices of conscience" in their worklives. Administrators can hear these voices in their professional memberships, in the public trust they bear, in the collective memories and traditions of the nation, in their personal moral integrity, and even in their visions of the future. Beyond socialization, the public school has an "enlightenment function," claims Manley-Casimir.

Enlightenment "concerns the development of the capacity of critical reflection such that students become autonomous moral agents capable of evaluating their lives and their world and acting creatively upon them to change them if desired" (p. 3). The responsible educator, concludes Manley-Casimir, is certainly attentive to community mores but harkens "primarily to the voices of conscience" (p. 21).

Amy Gutman (1987, 1989) takes the argument a step further by stating that "a democratic theory of education" is the most morally responsible purpose of public schooling. In simplest terms, her argument is that the intimacy and primacy of the family is sacrosanct in our society; nevertheless, families and their communities-of-value can "predispose their children to violence, religious intolerance, social bigotry, sexism, and other undemocratic values" (Gutman, 1987, p. 290). While the authority of parents must be respected and the school should not interfere with parents in repressive ways, the educational system should prepare children "to participate intelligently in the politics that shape their society" (Gutman, 1989, p. 156). She concludes: "'Political education'—the cultivation of the virtues, knowledge, and skills necessary for political participation—has moral primacy over other purposes of public education in a democratic society" (Gutman, 1987, p. 287).

In sum, proponents of the extended liability of the public official argue that the notion should replace an earlier sense of distancing, of limited liability, vis-à-vis the political fray. This notion is found in an identification, and a "fit," between educator and community (sometimes in a combination of both bridging and buffering). It is also found in an educator's sense of responsibility and "voice of conscience" for community values. As Gutman (1989, p. 186) put it: "To prevent education from being repressive, we must defend a principled limit on both political and parental authority, a limit that in practice requires parents and governments to cede some educational authority to professional educators."

Organizational Effect on Environment

In addition to the values-oriented question of translation is a matter of impact or effect. While the literature on the politics of school-community relations speaks frequently of the political environment's impact on the schools, there has not been adequate attention to the opposite question: What is the school's effect on its political environment? To be sure, the "representational" roles discussed earlier in this chapter carry an environmental side effect. To be sure, as well, the legendary impenetrability of the public school included a clear political message—as illustrated in William Firestone's (1977, p. 279) quote from one urban schoolteacher:

There were parents and kids who couldn't affect anything in a school. It was ludicrous. There were absurd rules and regulations, and there was very little you could do. Parents would struggle to get the least little word in. . . . I've watched school systems make parents feel they don't have any right to interfere.

However, beyond the political messages inherent in open versus closed organizations, there is relatively little information on how the internal institutional characteristics of schools can influence their external environments. A study by Mitchell Koza and Wayne Levy (1977–78) has been one of the few to ask this question. Their finding was consistent with good logic in noting that differences in the availability of school-related resources to the community (e.g., auditoriums, gymnasiums, assorted rooms) and in occasions for community social participation in the schools (e.g., plays, concerts, sporting events) were matched by differences in community involvement and a sense of social integration with the schools.

Interestingly, a key generalization growing out of the famous, decades-old "Tiebout hypothesis" in economic theory is that the economic and political character of a community to a considerable extent *starts* with its schools. Economist Charles Tiebout (1956) reasoned that people "vote with their feet" when they select the communities where they will live and raise their children. A central concern in such voting is the quality of the schools in a community. Although other influences such as pleasant parks, effective police protection, supervised programs for children, and clean air are important, the Tiebout hypothesis nevertheless suggests that good public schools, in part, "create" their own political and social communities— by attracting residents who value education and who in turn will support the schools' efforts to become even better.

In more recent research, Ellen Goldring (1990) discovered that not just the existence of a good school, but more deeply the clarity of a school's ideology—that is, the specificity and definitiveness of the school's educational mission—can translate into increased parental participation in a community. Disturbingly, she also discovered that efforts guided by school principals to develop meaningful partnerships with parents, but unaccompanied internally by a schoolwide consensus on mission, can be unproductive. "These principals," she noted, "did not receive support from their professional community as they tried to negotiate with parents" (p. 30). In other words, a sense of mission needs clarity both inside and outside the school if the school is to bring about meaningful parental participation.

In short, the internal organizational effect of the school on school-community relations is a question not often asked. Most inquiry has preferred to examine the opposite perspective—the community's political impact on the organization. Nevertheless, there are some important hints that institutional resource allocations, the very attractiveness of the school as a service, and the clarity and consensus of an institutional mission can have inside-to-outside (and vice versa) consequences. Similar investigations of the effects on parental participation of such contemporary phenomena as teacher empowerment, choice, charter-schooling, and differing curricular innovations remain to be investigated.

SUMMARY

The politics of managing school-community relations can be informatively examined from both sides of the same coin. From one perspective, a political environment, often turbulent, surrounds and impacts the schools. At great risk of error, and at risk of exacerbating any existing conflicts or stresses, the educator "decodes" the political environment—preparatory to helping to translate community politics into school policies and procedures. A time-honored norm of school administration has been to tread cautiously and warily in political waters—to "be political" to be sure, but also to buffer the professional integrity of the schools from undue interference. The strain in accomplishing this mission is reflected in the differing "representational" roles that educators fulfill and also in the "boundary-spanning" and "street-level-bureaucracy" activities, which together help the public schools cope with their environmental pressures.

From an alternative perspective, the public school is as much the creator of its own political environment as it is a respondent to that environment. The Wilsonian notion of administrative tasks that lie "outside the proper sphere of politics" makes no sense from this viewpoint, for the school is not separate from its community, and the management of the school has its own political effects on the community. From questions of "boundary" between institution and environment, the focus in this second perspective changes to examine both the fit between school and community and the extended liability of the educator who helps to create community values, in contrast to a previous sense of limited liability among educators whose role was to guard the independence and viability of the school from the political fray.

Of course, neither perspective stands well alone. While the public schools are products of their political environments, they are also creators of these environments—a relationship that Ogawa and Studer (1996) discuss. While the organizational structures of public schooling reflect environmental pressures, they also influence the nature of those environments and those pressures. At the same time the schools defend a boundary between institution and environment, they must pay attention to the quality of their fit with (and their bridges across) that environment.

The tensions between these two perspectives have probably never been greater than at present, with our modern-day interests in "restructuring" the forms and processes of school governance. As Raywid (1990, p. 183) writes, there is a growing popular sense that the schools have become more and more insulated from public control, "with more and more decisions made by those operating the system. . . . Direct parent influence has been effectively blocked and walled out." Indeed, some observers are now arguing that "the public is slipping away from the public schools" (Bradley, 1996b, p. 32). But simultaneously, the restructuring movement has been seeking a new set of alliances between schools and their communities at the same time as there is a professional empowerment of educators (particularly those at the school site) and a new freeing of professional educators (often with parents as partners) to deliver improved instructional services, unhindered by flawed bureaucracies and by unrepresentative power structures. Thus, the struggle between "boundary" and "fit" will continue to loom large, and it remains to be resolved.

Exercises
BOUNDARY SPANNING

1. Identify a number of individuals within a local school district whose duties involve considerable boundary spanning for the organization (e.g., a principal, a school clerk, a district superintendent).
2. Observe directly (ethnographically) the activities of one boundary spanner for two to three working days—recording thoroughly all interactions with the district's clientele plus any other outsiders.
3. Categorize and comment on your recorded incidents of boundary-spanning behavior. To what extent did you observe: Conflict management? Organizational buffering? Client socialization? An exercise of extended versus limited liability? Did the person whom you observed appear to operate from a sense of boundary in his or her interactions with client (e.g., what is an allowable intrusion and what is not)?

Suggested Activities

1. Develop an argument (and perhaps a class debate) in support of both sides of Woodrow Wilson's "truism" that administration lies outside the proper sphere of politics.
2. Develop and administer a brief questionnaire, asking school principals to respond to questions about their representational roles. The questionnaire (about a dozen items) could ask principals to respond (from strongly agree to strongly disagree) to such statements as: (a) The principal should always try to back the teacher up in conflicts with parents; (b) In this school, the principal's estimate of what's best for the children comes first; (c) Parents should be fully represented in all decisionmaking in the school; (d) I find it is often necessary to bend board of education rules in order to help individual parents; (e) Small favors to parents can strengthen a principal's hand in running the school.
3. During the course of a small-group discussion, make a list in two columns. In the left-hand column, list the group's sense of the internal organizational effects of the outside environment on the school. In the right-hand column, list the group's sense of the school's effect on its outside environment.
4. Interview a local school district superintendent on the concept of "fit" between school district and community. How can the administrator tell when the fit is good, not so good, improving, eroding? What are some indicators of fit or non-fit? What are the benefits of a good fit; conversely, what are the disadvantages of a good fit?

SUGGESTED READINGS

Gutman, Amy (1987) *Democratic Education.* Princeton, N.J.: Princeton University Press.

Lipsky, Michael (1980). *Street-Level Bureaucracy: Dilemmas of the Individual in Public Services.* New York: Russell Sage Foundation.

Lutz, Frank W., and Iannaccone, Lawrence (1978). *Public Participation in Local Schools: The Dissatisfaction Theory of American Democracy.* Lexington, Mass.: Lexington Books.

Mann, Dale (1976). *The Politics of Administrative Representation.* Lexington, Mass.: Lexington Books.

Peshkin, Alan (1995). "The Complex World of an Embedded Institution: Schools and Their Constituent Publics." In L. C. Rigsby, M. L. Reynolds, and M. L. Wang (eds.), *School-Community Connections,* pp. 229–258. San Francisco: Jossey-Bass.

Chapter Six

SCHOOL-COMMUNITY RELATIONS AND SCHOOL EFFECTIVENESS

Mary Erina Driscoll

The school must represent life, life as real and vital to the child as that which he carries on in the home, in the neighborhood, or on the playground.
—John Dewey, 1897

Writing nearly a century ago, John Dewey called for a school whose hallmark was close integration with home. The task of the school, he argued, was "to deepen and extend his [the student's] sense of the values bound up in his home life" (Dewey, 1897, p. 78). In fact, the "ideal" setting for formal education had

no mystery about it, no wonderful discovery of pedagogy or educational theory. It is simply a question of doing systematically and in a large, intelligent, and competent way what for various reasons can be done in most households only in a comparatively meager and haphazard manner. [Dewey, 1956, p. 35]

Dewey would have found it difficult to imagine an "effective" school that was not predicated on connections between school and home life. The only true measure of school worth was the child's ability to use what the school provided throughout his life. Thus, an ineffective school was by *definition* an institution that stood separate from that home life, distinct from the round of daily events that were so familiar to the child before he ever encountered formal education (Dewey, 1956, p. 75).

In this chapter, we take a critical look at the research that has

103

tried to link parental involvement in schools with children's school achievements. While Dewey in his time might have found this a strange enterprise, today we tend to think of schools as distinct institutions with their own peculiar educational characteristics. We approach the idea of home and school relations with an implicit deficit in mind, and ask, "Given the separation between the two, how best can we bridge the gap?" Since Dewey's plea early in this century for greater coordination between the two key educational settings in a child's life, home and school, we have seen the gap grow wider still.

Moreover, unlike Dewey, we have more and more restricted our notions of what constitutes "effectiveness" to a narrow range of abilities that are measured on standardized tests. In simple terms, we wonder if increased parental involvement will result in an increased level of student achievement.

This chapter broadly addresses the issue of academic effectiveness and community relations. More specifically, it sets the stage for the current definition of and interest in the question with reference to research, legislation, and reform activity over the past thirty years. We review the kinds of parental involvement that have been linked to school performance, giving attention to the variety of interactions that are possible between home and school, the differential effectiveness of these links, and the ways in which current educational reforms embody assumptions about the importance of these connections. We conclude with some cautionary notes and some observations about the strategies and programs that appear to be most useful over a range of educational settings.

THE SEARCH FOR EFFECTIVENESS IN RESPONSE TO CRISIS: DO PARENTS MAKE A DIFFERENCE?

Conventional wisdom dates the impetus for reform during the past decade from the publication of *A Nation at Risk* in 1983 by the President's National Commission on Excellence in Education. Amid cries that the nation's educational system was so bad it constituted a threat to the national defense (Kirst, 1984), the commission called for a return to basic educational values and an increased national commitment to improved education. At the same time, a slew of reports and studies critical of America's educational system appeared, providing the momentum for a movement toward reform and revitalization of the nation's schools. But how to accomplish this transformation was not clear, and thus many of the reforms took off in different directions.

A Nation at Risk confirmed the nervousness in some quarters that the broadened educational goals of the 1960s and 1970s had resulted in a cadre of American students whose grasp of basic academic subject areas was meager. Contemporaneous with this outcry, James Coleman and his colleagues published the first of two high-profile studies that examined the national data sample "High School and Beyond" (Coleman, Hoffer, and Kilgore, 1982c). Their study remains the subject of substantial methodological discussion.[1] Nevertheless, Coleman, Hoffer, and Kilgore's controversial findings that Catholic schools did a better job of educating disadvantaged students than did public schools engendered a lively and provocative national debate (Alexander and Pallas, 1983; Cain and Goldberger, 1983; Coleman and Hoffer, 1983; Coleman, Hoffer, and Kilgore, 1982a; Coleman, Hoffer and Kilgore, 1982b; Heyns and Hilton, 1982; Kilgore, 1983; McPartland and McDill, 1982; Morgan, 1983; Murnane, 1984; Noell, 1982; Salganik & Karweit, 1982; Taueber & James, 1983). A review of this debate, and its particular focus on the role of home and school relations in student achievement, may help us to understand better how deeply beliefs about the role of families in improving education have been embedded in current strategies for school reform.

HOME AND SCHOOL CONNECTIONS IN PUBLIC AND NONPUBLIC SCHOOLS

Specifically, Coleman and his colleagues claimed to have found a "Catholic school effect" that demonstrated students learned more in these school environments. These results were not attributable, they argued, to religious beliefs, or mere "Catholic status"; in fact, Catholics in Catholic schools outperformed their Catholic counterparts in public

---

1. A second wave of research suggested alternate explanations for Coleman's findings. One wave was methodological: the initial research had controlled inadequately for important factors, such as student selectivity (Noell, 1982). Coleman and colleagues encouraged and indeed answered many of these critiques on both substantive and methodological grounds (Noell, 1982; Cain and Goldberger, 1983; Coleman, Hoffer, and Kilgore, 1982a; Coleman Hoffer, and Kilgore, 1982b; Coleman and Hoffer, 1983; Kilgore, 1983; Salganik and Karweit, 1982).

schools. Moreover, Catholic schools seemed to do a better job educating disadvantaged, poor minority students than did the public schools that were historically designed to serve this population. Coleman and colleagues believed that the 1980s' Catholic school was more nearly the "common school" dreamed of over a century earlier than anything they encountered in the public sector. Their research documented a challenging, often traditional academic environment in Catholic schools that encouraged achievement. Here, students encountered both diversity among students and commonality in curriculum (Coleman et al., 1982c).

Coleman and his colleagues offered several explanations for these results. Most of them were related *not* to student's so-called "ascriptive" characteristics (such as race or social class) but, rather, to items that they claimed were affected by school policy. Among these, for example, were the stricter disciplinary and homework policies of Catholic schools. Coleman and colleagues argued that policies such as these could be instituted in the public sector (Coleman et al., 1982c).

A more complex explanation of these findings that attended to the nature of home-school relations followed a few years later, however, as the result of subsequent analyses (Coleman and Hoffer, 1987). Here, Coleman and Hoffer argued that the community surrounding the school—its degree of cohesion and its interest in the general welfare of students—had much to do with students' success. In a closely knit community (found, they suggested, in the Catholic sector and dependent on parish or religious organizational ties), students enjoyed a "social capital" that enriched the resources of information and oversight available to them. Most public schools, especially those in urban settings, had no such tightly knit communities: students and their parents had little connection to other families outside the school, and there was little overlap in students' home and school worlds. This lack of social capital put public school students at a disadvantage, they argued. Their findings suggested further exploration of the ways in which we think about the communities surrounding schools and asserted that parental knowledge of school programs and policies is critical if students are to achieve to their fullest potential.

Those who disputed Coleman argued that the results were explained by a different, far more complex and somewhat less clearly defined set of factors (Murnane, 1984). The central argument focused on the fact that nonpublic schools, unlike public schools, can choose their clientele. Perhaps more important, they have the option to ask students to leave, based on academic performance or behavior. Public schools do not have the option to remove students permanently (McPartland and McDill, 1982). Another formulation of this idea can be found in the work of Laura Salganik and Nancy Karweit (1983). In the original "High School and Beyond" debate, they contended that voluntarism among the students and parents (i.e., wanting to be a part of the institution of one's own volition) so influenced the school and the students' academic investments that comparisons to non-voluntaristic organizations were fundamentally flawed.

Ironically, then, both Coleman and his critics focused on the special nature of home and school relations as an explanation for higher achievement in Catholic schools. Coleman's work suggested that Catholic schools' closer community ties or increased "social capital" was the critical factor in their success. Many of Coleman's critics asserted that parents' free choice of schools for their children itself affected how well those students did in schools. That choice and attention to education, they argued, made those parents and students special, more likely to achieve in school even if they were matched against public school counterparts who resembled them in race, ethnicity, and economic status. While Coleman pointed to Catholic school policies that fostered achievement (arguing these might be instituted in public schools), both sides of the debate agreed that the communities in and around Catholic schools were different from those in the public sector and were important factors in the success of these institutions.

This debate helps to set the stage for our understanding of the nearly two decades of educational reform that have followed *A Nation at Risk*. Perhaps one of the most resilient themes to emerge from these discussions of school improvement has been the belief that it is essential to improve the connections between schools and families in order to restructure education in ways that make schooling more productive. A special urgency in this debate originates in the growing realization that the social and family context of schooling continues to grow more complicated. Emerging demographic trends require that old understandings of parent-school interactions must be revised to take into account new family structures and the increased participation of women in the labor force.

We turn now to some of the research that examines the ways in which family connections to schools affect student academic performance as well as other salient educational outcomes.

EFFECTIVE SCHOOLS LITERATURE AND THE EFFECTS OF PARENTAL INVOLVEMENT

An influential body of research that heightened interest in the greater involvement of parents in schools is the so-called "effective schools" research. Several reviews of research that focused on characteristics of schools that make them academically effective were published in the mid 1980s (Hallinger and Murphy, 1986; Hawley et al., 1984; Purkey and Smith, 1983). This literature provides some evidence that certain kinds of parental involvement promote student learning. Early assessments of this effect varied widely, however. For example, in an article on the social context of effective schools, Philip Hallinger and Joseph Murphy (1986, p. 333) assert:

The role of home-school relations in promoting student achievement is still unclear. The school effectiveness studies report mixed results concerning the impact of parent involvement on student achievement. As Purkey and Smith (1983) note in their comprehensive review of the school effectiveness literature, few of the school effectiveness studies have found parent involvement to be positively associated with academic achievement. Even the few studies that report positive findings are inconsistent with respect to the type of parent involvement that leads to improved student outcomes.

On the other hand, Herbert Walberg (1984, p. 398) reports that "syntheses of 2,575 empirical studies of academic learning show that parents directly or indirectly influence the eight chief determinants of cognitive, affective and behavioral learning." He argues that "extensive evidence suggests that the efficiency of the home in fostering learning has declined for several decades, but cooperative partnerships between the home and the school can dramatically raise educational productivity" (p. 397).

Why the disparity in assessments? One problem we encounter immediately when discussing the direct effects of parental involvement in children's education is the confusion between correlation and causation found in some research. Much as Coleman's critics argued that parents who select their children's schools may not be equated with parents who exercise no such choice, we find it difficult to assess whether parental encouragement and involvement in successful education is cause or effect. As one analyst of the Plowden Report (Central Advisory Council for Education, 1967), a 1967 survey of Britain's primary school system, aptly put it:

Although the report concluded that there was certainly an association between parental encouragement and educational performance, it felt that it was not then possible to say whether "performance is better where parents encourage more" or whether "parents encourage more where performance is better." Not surprisingly, the committee offered the commonsense suggestion that each factor was related to the other and that homes and schools interact continuously. That it is an *interaction* we are concerned with here, and a complex one at that, has emerged since Plowden as both one of the essential features of any investigation into home-school relations and possibly the most inhibiting factor as far as the undertaking and completion of such research is concerned. [Sharrock, 1980, p. 90]

It seems logical that parents who encourage and support their children will help those children persevere in school and may provide an invaluable form of academic assistance. But, as Sharrock notes, from a purely statistical point of view, it is much harder to show that such involvement is an independent cause of academic achievement, even though it may have a strong positive association with high test scores. In other words, it becomes a chicken-or-egg problem, leading us to accept as plausible both the notion that such involvement is a critical factor in children's success as well as the alternate explanation that parents become more involved and praise more when they see visible signs of children achieving.

It is complicated enough to decipher the statistical relations among measures of parental involvement and student test results. A second confusion with the assessment of parental roles in some of the effective schools research lies in an undifferentiated concept of "parental involvement" or "parental encouragement." As Willis Hawley and colleagues suggest, there are at least three purposes to efforts by schools attempting to involve parents in their children's education, namely "(a) to allow parents to make or participate significantly in policy decisions (this may involve parent councils or advisory groups), (b) to engage parents in fund raising and general support (the PTA is a good example), and (c) to involve parents directly in shaping their children's willingness and ability to learn" (Hawley et al., 1984, p. 118).

Each of these approaches has been found to have different effects. Thus it makes sense to look initially at each kind of parental connection with schooling separately. Borrowing from the classification schemes of this research found in review essays (notably, Leler, 1983; Hawley et al., 1984; Dornbusch and Wood, 1989), we will briefly review and summarize some of the research that examines the effects on student achievement of four kinds of home-school connections: (1) programs that directly involve and monitor parent participation in specific academic tasks; (2) programs that attempt to make parents better able to engage in the kind of parenting that supports academic achievement; (3) programs that increase parental governance roles; and (4) programs that involve parents as part of a multifaceted, frontal attack on a range of developmental issues that have an impact on children's performance in schools. Here we will also review some recent reform efforts that use family involvement as one of the tactics in school restructuring. In so doing, we intend also to present an emerging critique of this research and some reflections on its limitations in addressing gaps in our knowledge about how to improve student learning and how to foster better home-school connections.

MAKING CONNECTIONS BETWEEN PARENTS AND THE ACADEMIC WORK OF THE SCHOOL

Parent Participation in Specific Academic Programs

One body of research that has examined efforts to foster home-school connections focuses on the effects of programs that work to engage parents directly in the academic life of the child, perhaps as monitors to see that assigned academic tasks are completed. In 1983, Helen Leler presented a thorough and interesting review of many of the programs that up to that point had looked at how children and parents can work together on preordained academic tasks. Much of this literature, as she noted, is fugitive, found in small-scale project reports and dissertations of widely differing experimental quality. The most unambiguous results come from studies whose design includes a control group, which eliminates the possibility that nonacademic, parent-child interaction of equal frequency and duration may account for increases in student performance. Such designs are few and far between. Nor, as Leler notes, is the research evenly distributed across all domains. Indeed, as Joyce

Epstein (1987) has indicated, there are more parent participation programs in reading than in some other domains that are intrinsically less attractive to parents or in which parents feel they are less competent.

More recent reviews of scholarly work on directed parent involvement note that the research base for demonstrating any effects is improving yet still wanting. In a 1992 review, for example, Epstein suggests:

Research on the effects of students of family and school connections has improved over the years from suggestive to more focused studies. . . . Synthesizing the studies of many researchers, Henderson (1987) concludes that students at all grade levels are likely to benefit from family involvement. Most of the studies reviewed, however, focus on the well-proven family influence on achievement and not on effects of school practices to involve families who would not otherwise be involved. Most omit measures of direct connections between particular school and family practices and longitudinal measures of achievement to determine whether students improve over time because of the partnerships. Despite some recent attention, the most pressing need is for more rigorous, analytic research on the effects of students of specific practices of partnerships. [Pp. 1141–1142]

Although the research as a whole may be less than compelling, some studies do show credible student effects related to directed parent academic involvement. Epstein and her colleagues at John Hopkins have been engaged in a program of research and activity intended to assist teachers and administrators in finding ways to involve parents in their child's schoolwork. Studying the techniques used most often by teachers, Epstein found:

Teachers reported widespread use of three techniques that stress reading and books: having parents read to the child or listen to the child read; asking parents to take their child to the library; and loaning books and teaching materials to parents for use with children at home. Other practices (discussions, informal learning activities, contracts, and parent observations) were less frequently used by teachers, and were less often rated as effective and satisfying techniques. [Epstein, 1987, p. 126]

Epstein also found that parents were willing to spend more time helping their child with homework if they received some direction on how to help. The parents and teachers who worked together on assisting children rated each other more positively than those who did not. Parent-teacher relations were improved generally, extending to more positive attitudes and academic behaviors on the part of students studied as well. In other studies, Epstein found that when teachers and parents use structured parent-involvement practices, students "report more positive attitudes toward school, regular homework habits, similarity and familiarity between the school and their family, and more homework on weekends," noting that the effect is chiefly on student motivation and school-related behaviors (Epstein, 1992, p. 1142, citing Epstein, 1982). Reflects Epstein:

A story builds from all of the sources in the survey: Principals actively support parent involvement, especially in reading activities; teachers request more parent involvement on reading activities at home; parents conduct more learning activities in reading than in other subjects; and the students' achievement in reading is improved, These results suggest the importance of subject-specific connections. If principals exercise leadership, if teachers request and parents give assistance to students in particular subjects, then students' mastery of those skills should improve. [1987, p. 129]

Directed Parent Involvement in the Context of Partnerships

Another stream of literature on academic involvement and parents emphasizes the importance of situating directed parent involvement in the context of broadly based collaborations among schools, communities, and families. Epstein asserts that strategies intended to develop and direct academic connections between parent and child are only meaningful when embedded in an understanding of how all of the key players in a child's life affect student growth and learning. She writes: "The term 'school, family and community partnerships' is a better, broader term than 'parent involvement' to express the shared interests, responsibilities, investments, and the overlapping influences of family, school and community for the education and development of the children they share across the school years" (Epstein, 1994, p. 39). She argues that naming connections in this fashion appropriately recognizes schools as equals in the partnership. This term also encompasses the influences of all family members and of the many social and geographical communities that provide a context for the student's academic life. Moreover, she contends that this broadened understanding also forces consideration of a wider range of student outcomes:

The model assumes that student learning, development, and success—broadly defined—not just achievement test scores—are the main reasons for school and family partnerships. Further, productive connections of schools, families and communities, and pertinent individual interactions of teachers, parents, and students are conducted in order to help students increase their academic skills, self esteem, positive attitudes toward learning, independence, other achievements, talents, accomplishments, and other desired behaviors that are all characteristics of successful students." [Epstein, 1994, p. 42]

Epstein presents a conceptual framework that captures six major types of partnership activities, each rooted in a notion of shared responsibility for child welfare. These include (1) the basic obligations of families; (2) the basic obligations of schools to effectively communicate with families about school programs and children's progress; (3) the involvement of parents at the school building; (4) family involvement in learning activities at home; (5) decisionmaking, participation, leadership, and school advocacy groups; and (6) collaborations and exchanges with the community (Epstein, 1994, pp. 43–49).

Clearly, this approach hearkens back to a Deweyan notion of school and community and orients family involvement in academics in a much larger schema of joint care for student learning.

Another issue, addressed by Epstein (1992) as well as by others (Lareau, 1989; Lareau, 1994), is the importance of considering the abilities of parents in academic involvement programs that make unfamiliar demands upon them. In order to increase parent capacity for this involvement, some programs have been designed that use outside agents to help parents in their efforts to assist students' academic efforts. An example of one such program is the Family Study Institute, a recent effort of the nonprofit Academic Development Institute (Academic Development Institute, 1990a). Building on Coleman and Hoffer's finding that nurturing school community may be a means to improving student achievement (Coleman and Hoffer, 1987), this organization has designed and implemented a three-session program that aims to provide parents with concrete skills and techniques to assist their child. Schools elect to participate in the program for a modest fee. Parents are trained by other leaders (most often, parents themselves) to lead three sessions of a course involving parents and teachers in a highly structured format. The course focuses on teaching parents appropriate grade-level expectations for homework, the importance of establishing routines for the time and place for studying, and the ways in which parents can facilitate their child's homework and academic work in general. Materials and courses focus on reading at home and on studying at home, and sessions are offered in English and Spanish, culminating in a "graduation' ceremony. Designed to be an intervention strategy for schools of many types, especially in city settings, the Chicago-based Family Study Institute has grown in five years from three pilot schools to 116 schools that sponsor the program. Clearly, such an expansion is further testimony to the fact that many parents actively seek direction in how to best assist their child at home.

Other programs, such as those sponsored by the Home and School Institute (Rich, 1987a and 1987b), provide similar guidance to parents in addressing these needs. In fact, some national commissions, including the W. T. Grant Foundation Commission on Work, Family and Citizenship, recommend such outreach efforts as a means of keeping students in school (Youth and America's Future, 1988).

Other Family Behaviors That Support Student Learning

In an effort to understand better the family's role in promoting academic achievement, Schneider and Coleman (1993) present a set of studies that use a recent large-scale data set assembled by the federal government. These data have made possible new examination of some of the family practices that affect the school life of the child. They show that thinking about support as directed involvement in academic tasks misses some of the behaviors that current research identifies as critical to student achievement and attainment.

The National Educational Longitudinal Study 1988 (often called NELS88) was constructed to answer some of the questions about the effects of parent behavior on student outcomes. NELS88 relies on large-scale survey data collected at multiple time points during a student's school career, beginning in eighth grade, and at regular intervals in their adult lives thereafter. NELS88 includes one of the most comprehensive surveys of the parents of students undertaken to date by the federal government. For the first time, students' achievement results, their school grades, and their self-reports of educational attitudes, practices, and values can be linked to school-level data, to information from their teachers, and to reports from their own families about the educational values and practices that characterize their behavior at home and in the community.

Early reports of these data that have zeroed in on the home-school connection (Schneider and Coleman, 1993) illustrate several critical points. Perhaps most striking is the way in which these data show once again that the "typical" family structure continues to depart from a nuclear, two-parent family with one parent as the breadwinner and one parent engaged in full-time child care. For example, in 1988 only two thirds of the eighth-grade students surveyed reported that they lived with their natural mother and father. About 19 percent of the eighth-grade students lived in one-parent families, with most of the remaining students living in families that consist of one biological parent and a step-parent. As we might expect, less than 23 percent of these students live in homes where the mother is a full-time homemaker. The "typical" household is one in which the mother is part of the labor force: 20 percent of the students had mothers who worked at least part time, and well over half of the students had mothers who worked full time (Schneider, 1993). These data clearly show that any assumptions about involving parents must take into account new family configurations and time constraints.

Using the same data, Muller (1993) explores the direct effects of a variety of context variables on student test scores and grades. One of the most important practices in which parents can engage, these data show, is simply discussing school with their children. For eighth-graders, the degree to which parents talked with their children about current school experiences and about their future high school program were significantly related to an increase in the student's grades. These behaviors are also linked to other beneficial practices that indicate the involvement of parents in their child's education, including the degree to which they restrict television viewing, their investment in other educational activities for their child such as music lessons, and the amount of after-school supervision children received (Muller, 1993).

To sum up, a variety of academically focused parent involvement strategies seem promising, even though unambiguous research documenting their effects is hard to find. It is important to remember that parents who elect to seek academic direction and who follow through with the suggestions may exhibit an interest in academics that by itself gives their child a head start. Epstein (1992) rightly points out that the focus of many programs has not been on engaging parents who resist connections with the school or who have work schedules that make traditional linkages difficult to achieve.

But even in the absence of a large body of research documenting achievement gains for the children of parents in these programs, some programs make sense. Linking parent-child practice on academic tasks to subsequent performance on subject-matter assessments has an intuitive logic, especially if the desired outcome is measured using student achievement. Providing opportunities to encourage teacher direction of parent involvement and providing concrete forums in which parents can learn useful strategies seem efforts well worth the price. Finally, encouraging behaviors that demonstrate the importance and value of the child's academic activity also seems crucial to academic success.

Family Processes, Parent Empowerment, and Student Achievement

Parents lay the groundwork for students' success in school by building their child's self-confidence, self-concept, and self-reliance. If these aspects of home training are not completed by the time the child starts school, they become the mutual concern and shared responsibility of the family and the school. [Epstein, 1987, p. 121]

As Leler (1983) and others (e.g., Dornbusch and Wood, 1989) have noted, one strand of research and program intervention has focused on helping children do better in school through strategies that aim to improve the parenting skills of their primary caretakers. These "family-process" strategies work to empower parents and improve the parent-child interaction overall. They may take a variety of forms, including providing job and skill training to parents directly, in the belief that stable employment will improve family circumstances; providing primary health care, nutritional guidance, and information about child development, which are critical precursors to a child's successful performance in school situations; or providing guidance to parents on parenting strategies aimed to improve their disciplinary interactions and their social and emotional relationship with their child.

Such programs reach far beyond the traditional expectations for what schools may do to improve academics. While they may be offered in conjunction with academic institutions or with educational programs, their goals are much broader and even if successful are unlikely to result in improved academic achievement only.

Some of the earliest and most notable of these parent-intervention programs grew out of the Great Society social legislation of the 1960s. As one group of researchers notes (Haynes, Comer, and Hamilton-Lee, 1988, p. 12), the intensive preschool experiences provided through Head Start began a chain of remedial programs whose next logical step was the Follow Through experiment (in 1967), which extended this assistance to elementary school children. The 1965 ESEA Chapter I programs also sought to continue the momentum provided by Head Start and targeted additional resources to aid disadvantaged children in the elementary school years.

From their inception, Head Start programs featured a component designed to improve the community as a whole (as well as the level of education) through the involvement of parents as aides and of teachers in training. An expansion of a pilot preschool program developed in New Haven by a group of early childhood specialists, Head Start continues to function, albeit at a somewhat underfunded level, in the 1990s. Many Head Start children end up in elementary school Title I (originally Chapter I) programs, authorized by the 1965 Elementary and Secondary Educational Act, which provide remedial services, more instruction in reading and mathematics, and greater individual attention for economically disadvantaged children. The Sustaining Effects Study, one of the largest educational evaluation studies ever undertaken, has documented the success of this program, showing that Title I aid enables needy students to more nearly approximate the academic gains of their more advantaged student counterparts (Carter, 1984).

Follow Through was another Great Society program designed to maximize the gains made by preschoolers in Head Start. The Follow Through program was characterized by "planned variation," a design that was intended to allow sponsors to develop their own theoretical models and site-level variations. The framers believed that the evaluation (which became an unwieldy task) would ascertain which program formats worked best. Each Follow Though program had the following components in common: (1) an instructional program, (2) parental and community involvement, (3) comprehensive services, and (4) staff development (Olmsted and Rubin, 1983). Parental involvement was envisioned as a critical component of the Follow Through efforts, and took the form of participation in a Policy Advisory Committee; participation in the classroom as volunteers, observers, or paid employees; home visits by project staff; and participation in educational or community activities developed through the project. Thus the broad educational goals of this compensatory education program were advanced in league with programs designed to increase and strengthen the home-school connection. Reviewing almost a decade's worth of evaluations of Follow Through, Patricia Olmsted and Roberta Rubin remark on the generally positive findings with respect to school-home communication, student attendance, and overall levels of involvement in school by low-income parents who might otherwise not be involved. They note that this trend occurred at most sites, and that the "positive results from the parent involvement data have been reported across the spectrum of sponsors as well as on the national level of the FT program. Evidence of success has been accumulated from a variety of data collection procedures including descriptive, ethnographic, and inferential" (Olmsted and Rubin, 1983, p. 135). Thus compensatory educational efforts may owe part of their success to the parental involvement that became or was designed as an adjunct to the educational program.

Departing from the rubric of social-service-based programs designed to address community issues are the efforts that attempt to affect parenting skills directly. Leler (1983, p. 157) classifies these efforts into three categories. In the first class she groups all approaches based on the personality theories of Alfred Adler (1957) and Dreikurs and Soltz (1964), which stress democratic childrearing methods and parental encouragement. Systematic Training for Effective Parenting (STEP) is a packaged program consistent with this philosophy.

The second group of approaches to improve parent skills is linked conceptually to the works of Carl Rogers (1951), who emphasizes "nondirective interpersonal relationships." P.E.T.: Parent Effectiveness Training, by Thomas Gordon (1970), embodies these strategies—which stress "parental understanding and acceptance of children's behaviors and feelings"—and uses "active listening" as a technique.

Citing works by Becker (1971) and Patterson and Guillon (1971), Leler identifies behavioral management and modification approaches as a third set of techniques used in assisting parents.

These models, contends Leler, are important "because of their effects upon parent attitudes and practices, and child outcomes, such as classroom behavior, self-concept, and achievement" (1983, p. 157). In summary, she notes that the many small studies that review the effects of an individual program implementation "show generally favorable results," with few negative results appearing at all. But the measures of effectiveness tend to correspond to the broadly gauged goals of the parenting program and are not necessarily reflected in an overall measure of achievement or enhanced test performance. More often, improved self-esteem, self-concept, communication, and satisfaction are the results of these programs.

Programs designed to improve parenting skills continue to be popular forms of social service intervention, especially in light of increasing numbers of teen pregnancies that result in exceptionally young mothers and fathers. This interest is by no means restricted to those who provide services through educational agencies. In a recent national survey of the directors of collaborative children's services programs, most of which focused on the provision of based health and support services rather than academic interventions, over 80 percent of the directors listed parenting education as one of the key activities they provided (Driscoll, Boyd, and Crowson, 1996).

We see, then, that a variety of available strategies aims to empower parents and increase parenting skills. Their results, while generally positive, are not always extended to the child's academic performance. Evaluations of these efforts are often so diffuse as to be less than conclusive (as in Follow Through) or reflective of a small-scale experiment that may not generalize to all populations (as in the parenting programs). But using a narrow gauge for assessing effectiveness hardly seems appropriate when linking these efforts to improving schools. These efforts target a critical source of student support: the parent. Since their goals reach beyond the schoolroom, it is not surprising that their effectiveness may be best measured in non-academic arenas.

Parental Governance and School Performance

In a review of many different parent programs in metropolitan locations, Oliver Moles (1980) and his colleagues argue that while independent claims for the effects of the programs are hard to verify, a certain and visible effect of most efforts to reach out to parents is increased communication and parental knowledge about what takes place in the school. This is particularly true of efforts made to include parents in the day-to-day operations of schools (for example, as library aides, lunchroom volunteers, or helpers in various PTA-school projects.) Such a benefit is not incidental, and may be linked to greater parental awareness of the schools' potential advantages and disadvantages for their child. We are reminded of Richard Murnane's argument (1984) that parental choice helps match a child's capabilities with the attributes and goals of a given educational program. He suggests that increased parental investment in education (here achieved through greater participation in school if not school choice itself) may have its own attendant benefits for student performance.

Once again, however, we encounter a different kind of chicken-or-egg problem. Parents who are able to participate in children's school programs must have available time, energy, and knowledge to do so—what some organizational theorists call "resource slack." These parents are more advantaged than their counterparts who live near or at the survival level and must use most of their income for basic necessities. Less advantaged parents usually must work full time, which often conflicts with opportunities for greater involvement, and are thus unable to engage in such increased participation. The children of parents who participate in such programs (and who, theoretically, do better in school because of this) are already more "advantaged," then, than the children of parents who are unable to participate due to increased family and employment pressures. Few studies attempt to disentangle these effects by controlling for the fact that comparisons between children of parent volunteers and those of nonvolunteers may be inherently biased.

Despite potential limits on participation, especially among low-income parents, the past two decades have witnessed a tremendous growth in the programs that substantially increase the level of parental input above this operational assistance level. Instead of using parents as occasional volunteers or as low-level administrative assistance, such programs—most often called "site-based management" or "site based decisionmaking"—include parents in the governance of the schools. Parent members of school councils may have either decisionmaking or advisory power on a range of items that can include such critical issues as hiring principals and some budgetary allocation. Indeed, many plans that began with parent councils as advisors and resources have been extended to include site councils that have real control over the discretionary budget at the site, especially categorical funds targeted at schoolwide improvement.

But, as reviews of the literature on site-based governance assert, the measurable effects of these programs are mixed (Malen and Ogawa, 1988; Malen, Ogawa and Kranze, 1990). In part, this is because there are many variants on "site-based management". In some cases, parents have advisory power only, even when they believe themselves to have decisionmaking authority. In others, mandates for school councils in general and parents in particular are not clear and have impeded efficient functioning of these councils. And third, even when parents possess real power and legislative responsibilities are clear, norms of civility may dictate that parents defer to the "professional" members of school councils (i.e., teachers and principal) and incorporate (at least initially) few new views in school governance.

Amidst all this confusion, there exists little apparent evidence that such councils directly affect school performance. Indeed, Hess (1995) notes that recent research on the Chicago schools shows that organizational change has far outpaced any demonstrable gains in academic achievement (Bryk et al., 1994). Sebring and colleagues also note that governance alone cannot combat some of the structural and social factors affecting the lowest achieving schools, even where levels of parent involvement are relatively high (Sebring et al., 1996).

Does a paucity of solid research on the effects of parental governance mean that these programs are misguided? Not necessarily. While such programs may fall far short of rectifying or even beginning to address all the schools' serious problems, their failure to emerge as a direct cause of increased student achievement is not surprising. There are several possible reasons for this weak relationship.

For one thing, governance, communication, empowerment, and participation—hallmarks of most school-site management councils—are amorphous concepts. Increasing parents' voice may indeed promote school conflict as well as promote school cooperation, depending on the culture of an individual school. And many who argue for increasing parents' role in school governance envision democratic participation and the public discourse it requires as powerful ends in their own right.

Second, even if there is a scholastic effect for children of par-

ent participants involved in governance, this will not be reflected
in school-level achievement scores unless there are universally high
levels of parental involvement. The broader, school-level effects directly attributable to council actions might not appear at all until
the council is itself well-established and stable. Many programs are
still far too new to meet these criteria.

But in a more fundamental sense, the governance arrangements
of schools seem far away in the causal chain of factors that are
known to affect individual test scores—much weaker, we would suspect, than the nature and amount of topical knowledge found in a
child's curriculum, and not nearly as strong a predictor as whether
or not the child took the test on a full night's sleep, in an anxious
state, or on an empty stomach. Indeed, the design of many governance reforms has limited parents' participation in the kinds of decisions that may be most closely related to the technical core of
schooling. In the Chicago plan, for example, the site council is
responsible for developing a School Improvement Plan, but has little authority to hire the teaching personnel of the school who are
in part responsible for the implementation of that plan. In many
sites, the design of the academic and pedagogical program of the
school is greatly constrained by existing state and district standards
and procedures regarding curriculum, textbook selection, and the
kinds of student assessments required. As Astuto and Clark (1992)
have remarked, if the decisions site governance councils are permitted to make are trivial, such "decentralization" is not likely to
produce much in the way of new ideas or procedures.

THE NEXT STEP: RESTRUCTURING SCHOOLS
AROUND PARENT INVOLVEMENT

Many of the recent reforms that have aimed to "restructure"
education include some element of parent involvement as part of
the whole picture. These reform plans vary in the degree to which
substantial parent involvement is included, but all share one trait
in common: involving parents in school governance and planning
is not an isolated feature of restructuring but rather is an important piece of a schoolwide effort to affect the teaching and learning
processes throughout the school. Three recent visions of reform

are Success for All, the Accelerated Schools Movement, and James Comer's School Development Plan.

Success for All

Success for All is a program based on research conducted by Robert Slavin and his colleagues that demonstrates the importance of early diagnosis and intervention in remediating the academic problems of children who fail to read properly. Dubbed by its authors "a relentless approach to prevention and early intervention in elementary schools" (Slavin et al., 1992), its primary focus is a set of pedagogical strategies that are targeted at eliminating key academic problems that occur among early-grade readers. Implemented in over four hundred schools in twenty-six states by 1996, Success for All's central philosophical tenet is that there is no excuse for nonachievement among children in high poverty, who are often deemed "at risk." Moreover, Slavin and colleagues contend that an emphasis on prevention and early intervention will succeed where other remediation has failed.

Success for All employs specific pedagogical and curricular strategies, including individualized tutoring. In addition, every Success for All school has a Family Support Team. The Family Support Team consists of the Title I parent liaison, the vice-principal (if any), the counselor (if any), a facilitator, and any other appropriate staff present in the school or added to the school staff.

Slavin and colleagues suggest:

Parents are an essential part of the formula for success in Success for All. A Family Support Team works in each school, serving to make families feel comfortable in the school and become active supporters of their child's education as well as providing specific services. [Slavin et al., 1996, p. 89]

The Family Support Team works toward improving relations with parents and increasing their involvement across the school. They may initiate "welcoming" activities for new families, plan programs on parenting skills, or implement an academic skills program such as "Raising Readers" that focuses on the ways in which parents can work at home to improve their child's reading skills. A second critical function of the team is intervening when problems are observed. For example, the team will contact parents of children who are frequently absent and determine "what resources can be provided to assist the family in getting their child to school" (Slavin et al., 1996, p. 90).

Family Support Team members also work with parents on issues of student behavior and "provide assistance when students seem to be working at less than their full potential because of problems at home." This assistance may take the form of connecting the family with other social service agencies or seeing that medical conditions affecting school success (such as not having necessary eyeglasses) are resolved. As the program's designers write, "The Family Support Team is strongly integrated into the academic program of the schools. It receives referrals from teachers and tutors regarding children who are not making adequate academic progress, and thereby constitutes an additional stage of intervention for students in need above and beyond that provided by the classroom teacher or tutor" (Slavin et al., 1996, pp. 89–90).

In addition to encouraging volunteers in the school, selected parents take part in a school governance structure that meets four to six times a year, part of an effort to create a school that parents perceive as "an institution that does things *for and with* you" (Slavin et al., 1992, p. 32). In sum, "It is the job of the school to recognize the family as an integral part of the school system and to work with families in devising ways to increase parent participation and encourage community support of schools" (Slavin et al., 1992, p. 32).

Because Success for All is defined and implemented as an intervention program of proven strategies and activities, the involvement of parents, although critical, is limited. Although the Family Support Team works extensively with parents, it is largely made up of administrative and teaching personnel who are charged with linking to parent constituencies. Planning for the school as a whole is not the responsibility of a parent governance system, although parents' involvement in their children's education is underscored as an important part of the overall effort. Operating within a positive climate of school-home relations, the school becomes a responsive provider of services that support academic performance, diagnosing and responding to needs perceived by site personnel. The program is conceived in design and implementation as an "intervention" with an "at-risk" population. It is not possible—nor, Slavin might argue, even desirable—to evaluate the degree to which this component affects student performance independent of any of the other aspects of Success for All, such as individualized tutoring. And it is critical to note that the results of this program are most often measured in standard academic terms such as reading scores, preserving the tight "academic" focus of this intervention-based model. Research sponsored by the program's designers demonstrates that in schools where the program has been successfully implemented students across all grade levels may increase their reading scores significantly (Slavin et al., 1996).

Accelerated Schools

The Accelerated Schools Project is another recent reform, based on the work of Henry Levin (Hopfenberg et al., 1993). Here too the focus is on students traditionally termed "at risk" of poor academic performance or dropping out of school.

Three central principles characterize Accelerated Schools. The first is unity of purpose, or "a striving among parents, teachers, students and administrators toward a common set of goals for a school that will be the focal point of everyone's efforts." The second is school-site empowerment coupled with responsibility, meaning the ability of key participants of a school community in the school and the home to "(1) make important educational decisions, (2) take responsibility for implementing those decisions, and (3) take responsibility for the outcomes of the decisions." Third, accelerated schools use an instructional approach that builds on the strengths of students, teachers, administrators, other staff, and parents "utilizing all the learning resources that students, parents, school staff, and communities bring to the educational endeavor" (National Center for the Accelerated Schools Project, 1991a). The culture of an accelerated school is based on beliefs about equity, participation, communication and community, reflection, experimentation, trust, and risk taking among school staff, students, and parents. According to the literature developed by the National Center for the Accelerated Schools Project,

The organization of the Accelerated School builds upon broad participation in decision-making by administrators, teachers, and parents. Indeed, parent involvement is a central focus of the Accelerated School. Parents are expected to affirm an agreement that clarifies the goals of the Accelerated School and outlines the obligations of parents, students, and school staff. Parents may help make school decisions by joining various task forces and the steering committee. Parents are also given educational and training opportunities on how to help their children educationally. [National Center for the Accelerated Schools Project, 1991a]

Governance structures that reflect this emphasis on participation include cadres (small units of self-selected individuals operative in the priority-setting stage who engage in an inquiry process), a steering committee (a group composed of all constituencies that guide cadres and the process of change) and the "School as a Whole" (all school personnel who together with parent and student representatives must approve all major decisions on curriculum, instruction, and resources allocation (National Center for the Accelerated Schools Project, 1991b).

Because Accelerated Schools is both process oriented and substantively driven, participating schools are likely to derive individualized goals for their population. In this respect, the Accelerated Schools Project represents a sharp contrast to the "proven intervention" focus of Success for All. Such variation in planning and programs also makes large-scale research on the project difficult, although a concerted research effort on the "effects" of this reform is currently underway. But clearly, the themes of democratic activity and collaborative work among families and schools undergird virtually every activity, as does the notion that only a shared commitment to the change process can effect success.

Comer's School Development Program

Conceptually linked to the efforts to improve parenting and foster children's development but moving well beyond them are the programs piloted in the New Haven schools by James Comer and associates over the past three decades and now being realized on a national level. The first incarnation of the School Development Program (SDP) in New Haven is documented in *School Power* (Comer, 1980). More recent literature documents the long-term effects of these efforts (Comer, 1988b; Haynes, Comer, and Hamilton-Lee, 1988a, 1988b) and indicates that by 1995 the Comer School Development Model had expanded to include over 550 schools (Comer et al., 1996).

In essence, the School Development Program restructures the school in ways that fundamentally alter our notion of school as merely an academic agency. As Comer (1988) notes, the model was developed from the observations of research staff immersed in the New Haven schools. The theory of the program is derived from the field of child development and rests on a few key premises: a child's behavior is determined by his or her interactions with the physical, social, and psychological environments; children need positive interactions with adults in order to develop adequately; child-centered planning and collaboration among adults facilitate positive interactions; and all planning for child development should be a collaborative effort between professionals and community members (Emmons, Comer, and Haynes, 1996, p. 29).

These premises, when applied to the School Development Program, result in three guiding principles that are infused throughout the school: consensus, collaboration, and no-fault. These principles are realized in three mechanisms in the school: a school planning and management team, a student and staff support team, and a parent team. Three operations form the agenda for these mechanisms: developing and implementing a comprehensive school plan; engaging in assessment and modification; and staff development (Emmons, Comer, and Haynes, 1996; Comer, Haynes, and Joyner, 1996).

It is important to note that the management team represents all adults in the school community, Typically, it includes the principal, two teachers, three parents, and a mental health team member. The group meets weekly to establish policies for the school in curriculum, staff development, and school climate; to plan and carry out resources allocation and needs assessment; to coordinate the activities of all groups in the schools; and to work with a parent group planning a social activity calendar (Haynes, Comer, and Hamilton-Lee, 1988b).

The parent–participation program is a component of the SDP that is closely linked to the activities of the governance and management team and crucial to the success of the program. As Haynes and colleagues note:

It consists of three sequential levels of parent participation. The first level is concerned with structuring broad-based activities for large numbers of par-

ents. At the second level, approximately one parent per professional staff member
works in the school as a classroom assistant, tutor or aide. At the third level,
a few highly involved parents participate in school governance. The project
provides consultation and material resources to make parent participation
operational at all three levels. [1988, pp. 13–14]

Describing the results from the pilot programs in New Haven,
Comer notes,

The intervention program in New Haven produced significant academic gains.
The students had once ranked lowest in achievement among the 33 elementary schools in the city, but by 1979, without any change in the socioeconomic makeup of the schools, students in the fourth grade had caught up to
their grade level. By 1984 pupils in the fourth grade in the two schools ranked
third- and fourth-highest on the Iowa Test of Basic Skills. By the early 1980's
attendance rates at King were either first or second in the city. There have
been no serious behavior problems at either school in more than a decade.
[Comer, 1988, p. 48]

Evaluations of these sites showed students in SDP schools experience gains in reading and mathematics, have fewer suspension
days, and have better attendance. Recent research continues to
document long-term benefits for students in SDP schools, measured using academic as well as mental health measures (Comer et
al., 1996). It is particularly important to note that the SDP's guiding principles of consensus, collaboration, and no-fault must be
operative in designing and implementing any evaluation of the
program. Part of the ongoing contribution of the program, then, is
finding ways in which "traditional" evaluation may be modified and
re-created to embody these values and to reflect the wishes and
needs of all members of the school and the community.

Like the Accelerated Schools Project, the School Development
program integrates parent involvement into a radical restructuring
of the school that empowers teachers, parents, and students. The
program has a coherent and all-encompassing philosophy devoted
to the improvement of mental health and the provision of resources
essential for teaching and learning. The involvement of parents in
their child's school can vary by degree, but the concept of such
involvement is a central element in the program's success. Comer's
School Development Program demonstrates the benefits that can
occur when a fundamental realignment of the traditional school,

complete with the extra monies needed to address pressing needs, is accomplished. The school takes on far more than an academic mission and addresses key issues of power and collaboration in the process. The cost in personnel and in dollars is not slight, but neither are the results.

THE DARK SIDE OF PARENT INVOLVEMENT

Given the evidence presented above about the positive effects of parental involvement, it is important to sound as well the cautionary note voiced by those who have examined the relationships between parents and schools from another perspective. Annette Lareau, whose qualitative studies of parents in schools have contributed to our understanding of some of the benefits of parental involvement in education, notes as well that there can be disturbingly negative aspects to this interaction (Lareau, 1994).

Too often, she suggests, teachers want parents to engage the school and them on teachers' professional terms only. In these cases, parents are brought into a "partnership" as less-than-equals who are expected to conform to existing power relations if they are to be perceived as "good" or "helpful." Worse, teachers may come to depend on parental assistance (in completing homework problems, for example) but may fail to communicate their expectations in a useful manner to all parents, especially those with limited educational experience or different cultural experiences. This sets up a cycle where an "at-risk" child continues to fail because the parents have not been sufficiently informed or instructed in the tasks that must be accomplished. She argues that this is particularly pernicious when parents of different cultures or low socioeconomic status approach the school. Such encounters have real "costs" as well as benefits, she argues. To be successful, teachers must spend real time and effort ensuring that communication between home and school is clear and interactive. When bringing the worlds of school and home together, she notes, it is likely that problems in either arena will be reflected in both; even a "simple" strategy such as directing parent involvement around homework completion can easily result in interactions between parent and child that are contentious or in patterns of behavior that make completion of homework more stressful. When schools make demands on parents they cannot meet, the costs may be in terms of the parents' own self-esteem and belief in their educational potential (Lareau, 1989; Lareau, 1994).

Other research documents that parents with non-middle class, non-white experiences and cultures may engage the school in very different ways (Delagado-Gaitan, 1994; Kerbow and Bernhardt, 1993; Muller and Kerbow, 1993; Scott-Jones, 1994). The reasons for varying levels of involvement across different economic and ethnic groups may be quite complicated, resulting from an incompatibility between the school's schedule and the worklives of parents as well as a host of cultural differences that affect the comfort with which parents contact or challenge educational professionals. As Lareau (1994) remarks, it is particularly likely that adults who were labeled "at-risk" and underserved as students will bring their own negative childhood school experiences to their encounters with their own children's school parents.

It is important to note that there is evidence that some schools (even those not participating in a major reform program) can mitigate the conditions that work against parent involvement through flexible and sensitive planning. In her study of parents in three schools, Smrekar (1996) found that even in low-income populations, parents could meet school expectations for investment of time when a "contract" was signed between parent and school at the beginning of the year, spelling out the types of support activities that would meet the obligation for parent involvement. Many of these activities (such as baking for a school sale or stuffing envelopes) could be undertaken off-site or on the parent's own schedule. She also found that inflexible work lives and excessive demands on time were not restricted to low-income parents only. Across all social classes, these represented the major constraints on the amount of time parents could give to their child and the school.

Perhaps no issue is more critical to improving the connection between home and school than understanding how established patterns between schools and families underscore the ways in which parents involve themselves in their child's education. Schools must become places that transmit clear expectations, communicate with all parents in ways that they understand, and accommodate the realities of family composition and employment. Most important, all schools must be places where both parents and teachers find respect.

CONCLUSIONS: WHAT CAN WE LEARN FROM THIS RESEARCH?

In a recent book Eric Hanushek (1994) uses economic theory to guide a plan for school reform. He argues that the road to school renewal must be paved with "incentives" for parents and students; absent these, he argues, we will continue to ignore a major force for change and a considerable resource for improvement. The research discussed in this chapter illustrates that it is possible in all schools—not merely in the private sector—to create meaningful interaction between parents and schools. No more powerful incentive could be found than the benefits accruing to students and their families as a result of this involvement.

We should note once again that most of the research reviewed finds few direct links between parent involvement and student achievement scores. Expecting parent involvement to change the school in the absence of curricular reform, remedial services, or adequate resources is unrealistic at best and dangerous at worst.

We should not be disheartened, however, by the relatively small amount of "hard" evidence regarding gains in student achievement. Our lens for examining "effectiveness" has been too narrow for too long. Improved communication, better attendance, more positive teacher-parent rapport—these, it may be urged, should be ends in themselves, and, at the very least, can be seen as harbingers of a climate in which students can learn effectively. In short, as Epstein (1994) intimates in her defense of the partnership metaphor, we need to use a more Dewey-like lens in evaluating our schools, focusing far more on the educational process and the total development of the child than merely on one test score, however important.

There is ample evidence that promising strategies that promote both parent involvement and student gains abound for those schools who desire to implement them. Some are relatively low cost, such as Epstein's (1987) admonition that parents actively seek subject-specific directions from teachers. More and more, however, we see such practices infused into Comer-type strategies that restructure schools, using parent involvement as a key component. The most successful approaches involve a range of professionals and activities that impinge on every aspect of the school organization, its curriculum, and its resources. The payoff for such an extraordinary effort may be extraordinary gains. The implications of such a program are far-reaching, however, and include a redesigned teacher education curriculum, a completely new principal-training model, and a broad array of resources to remedy the deficits children bring to school.

As we move toward the twenty-first century, we have come to realize that schools may be the most stable institutions many children know. Hand in hand with that realization comes the impetus to redesign these organizations and allocate their resources in ways commensurate with that challenge. Many schools are taking on this role by default, unwillingly and with little hope of achieving success. But by facing this challenge squarely and embracing parents in the process, some schools have the added hope that whatever resources are present in the community will not remain isolated. Instead they envision a world in which school, family, and community work together in partnership on behalf of the child.

Finally, it is critical that we learn to think about how all parties interested in the welfare of children can care for the least advantaged students. Models that depend on individual parent input and thus result in individual student gains do not always provide for those students who come from increasingly disorganized family situations. Strengthening the school by creating a parent community may extend benefits to those children who will not benefit under an individual model, enriching the "social capital" that Coleman so extols. At the same time, schools must learn to respect the cultures and experiences students bring with them and find new ways to engage the families that support them. Such nurturing of community is heartening indeed, and brings us full circle to our opening thoughts from Dewey. The most effective schools, he would agree, involve parents in a way that builds such community, including *all* students, and providing the most for those who have the least.

Exercises

1. Thinking about ways to improve student's school experience by connecting home and school in formal ways may involve being acutely sensitive to the needs evident and resources available in the community in which the school resides. On the other hand, you might argue that social context should not dictate the entire program and that some common principles are present in all good home-school programs.

    a. You are the principal of a small, suburban elementary school in an affluent community. Given your reading of this chapter, how would you design a parent program to help improve the reading skills of your students?

    b. Now imagine yourself as the principal in a large elementary school in an inner-city community. How would you design a parent program that attempted to address student reading skills?

    c. Look at your two plans. In what ways are they different? What elements are common to both? Why?

2. At a faculty meeting, teachers agree that parents are underused in the learning process and must be given the chance to get more involved. Each teacher is asked to develop for his or her class parents a set of tasks designed to help them help their children with homework. The fifth-grade math teacher and the seventh-grade history teacher each come to you after school in your capacity as assistant principal for curriculum, asking for examples of such specific directions to parents. What do you say?

Suggested Activity

Investigate in your own community and try to discover any focused academic training programs (similar to FSI and Home School Programs) that help parents to work together with their children on study skills. What organizations are active in this field? Where are the services available, and to whom are they accessible? What changes or additions would you suggest?

SUGGESTED READINGS

Craft, M.; Raynor, J., and Cohen, L. (eds.) (1980). *Linking Home and School: A New Review*, third edition. London: Harper & Row.

Davies, D. (1987). "Parent Involvement in the Public Schools: Opportunities for Administrators," *Education and Urban Society* 19(2): 137–145.

Dinkmeyer, D., and McKay, G.D. (1976). *Systematic Training for Effective Parenting*. Circle Pines, Minn.: American Guidance Service.

Fantini, M.D., and Sinclair, R. (eds.) (1985). *Education in School and Nonschool Settings*. Eighty-fourth Yearbook of the National Society for the Study of Education. Chicago: National Society for the Study of Education.

Ginott, H. (1965). *Between Parent and Child*. New York: Macmillan.

Goodlad, J. (1985). "Rethinking What Schools Can Do Best." In M. Fantini and R. Sinclair (eds.), *Education in School and Nonschool Settings*. Eighty-fourth Yearbook of the National Society for the Study of Education. Chicago: National Society for the Study of Education.

Haertel, E.; James, T.; and Levin, H. (eds.) (1987). *Comparing Public and Private Schools*. Volume II: *School Achievement*. New York: Falmer.

McDonnell, L.M. (1989). *Restructuring American Schools: The Promise and the Pitfalls*. New York: Teacher's College Institute on Education and the Economy.

Macleod, F. (ed.) (1989). *Parents and Schools: The Contemporary Challenge*. London: Falmer.

Maddaus, J. (1990). "Parental Choice of School: What Parents Think and Do," *Review of Research in Education* 16: 267–296.

Moles, O. (1987). "Who Wants Parent Involvement? Interest, Skills and Opportunities Among Parents and Educators," *Education and Urban Society* 19(2): 137–145.

Mortimore, P.; Sammons, P.; Stoll, L.; Lewis, D.; and Ecob, R. (1988). *School Matters*. Berkeley: University of California Press.

Stevenson, D., and Baker, D. (1987). "The Family-School Relation and the Child's School Performance," *Child Development* 58: 1348–1357.

Talbert, J.E. (1988). "Conditions of Public and Private School Organization and Notions of Effective Schools." In T. James and H. Levin (eds.), *Comparing Public and Private schools*. Volume I: *Institutions and Organizations*. New York: Falmer.

Wang, M.; Haertel, G.; and Walberg, H. (1990). "What Influences Learning? A Content Analysis of Review Literature," *Journal of Educational Research* 84(1): 30–43.

Chapter Seven

THE LEGAL CONTEXT OF SCHOOL-COMMUNITY RELATIONS: CONTINUING TENSION BETWEEN STATE AUTHORITY AND INDIVIDUAL RIGHTS

Julius Menacker

> No single tradition in public education is more deeply rooted than local control over the operation of schools; local autonomy has long been thought essential both to the maintenance of community concern and support for public schools and to the quality of the educational process . . . . [L]ocal control over the educational process affords citizens an opportunity to participate in decisionmaking, permits the structuring of school programs to fit local needs, and encourages experimentation, innovation, and a healthy competition for educational excellence.
> —U.S. Supreme Court opinion in *Milliken v. Bradley*, 418 U.S. 717, 1973.

This chapter reviews the role and influence of the law on school-community relations. As new organizational and governance approaches to public schooling are developed, they are often challenged in the courts. The resultant court decisions become the best source for obtaining information and understanding about the legal aspects of school-community relations.

As noted in Chapter 1, the newest interpretation of school-community relations supports the formal representation of parents and other community members in the governance of local schools. Just as dominant conceptions of school-community relations change

135

with cycles of liberalism and conservatism, so do the legislation that affects it and the consequent court interpretations of the law. Most often, the litigated issues involve tensions between government and individual rights. In resolving the disputes arising from these tensions, judges are supposed to concentrate on legal principles rather than on changing political and social attitudes and pressures—a main reason why the U.S. Constitution grants lifetime appointment to federal judges. However, a study of school law reveals that judges, whether elected to state courts or appointed to federal courts, are not entirely free of personal policy preferences or attitudes about how schools should be run. Therefore, they do not always act as strict, legal arbiters of disputes, and sometimes reveal their own liberal or conservative leanings in their decisions (Halpern and Lamb, 1982; Menacker, 1987, 1989).

Even so, the courts represent a relatively stable and independent source of influence over school-community relations, where the focus is not as much on the politics of reform or dominant attitudes about proper school administration as it is on the legality of school board, legislative, or executive policy and decisions. The relative independence of the judicial branch is designed to allow for this focus on the law, rather than on current politics or public attitudes.

Court decisions have a powerful influence on public policy, as judges can invalidate statutes and administrative decisions, thus frustrating the intent of state and federal legislatures and executive departments as well as local boards of education. Since judges focus more on the law and judicial precedent than on current attitudes or politics, court decisions most often act as a conservative force. However, there have been periods of time when the courts have served precisely the opposite function, and have dragged local government and school officials kicking and screaming into significant educational reforms. The assault of the Warren Court upon racially segregated public schools is the prime example of the latter situation.

This chapter will first provide an overview of the legal framework of American education. This framework involves a complex legal relationship that includes tensions among state, local, and national governments as well as conflicts between individual rights and government responsibilities and powers. This overview will be followed by an examination of those legal issues that have had the greatest impact upon school-community relations.

LEGAL FRAMEWORK

State-Local District Roles and Relationships

The U.S. Constitution does not deal with matters of school policy. Indeed, the words "education" or "school" do not even appear in that document. Therefore, legal control of education resides with the individual states by virtue of the Tenth Amendment to the Constitution, which provides, "The powers not delegated to the United States by the Constitution, nor prohibited by it to the States, are reserved to the States. . . ."

In 1789, Massachusetts set the dominant pattern for state public school systems by creating the local school district as a state governmental subdivision managed and supervised by town school committees to which it delegated state authority for day-to-day school management. This arrangement provided the model for the national development of public school systems.

At first, town governments treated schools in much the same way they treated other municipal affairs (e.g., police, fire, streets, sanitation). The idea was that schools were neither more complex nor more deserving of special attention than any other matter of local government. However, for a variety of reasons, public education was separated from general government and achieved special governmental status that included a separate body (the local district board of education) to represent the municipality and the state in the governmental function of education. The school district achieved the status of a quasi corporation, with the local board of education representing the people in directing public school affairs. Then, as now, education government was among the best and purest examples of keeping faith with the Jeffersonian principle that government should be kept as close to the people as possible. Even so, the state always has retained ultimate authority over public education, even while delegating control of daily affairs and decisions to local districts. This must be so, as the state cannot delegate to local subdivisions responsibility that its constitution has assigned to the legislature.

Several principles are important to understanding the legal status of this arrangement. First, states retain plenary power over education; local school districts are creatures of the state. The state legislature can create new districts, alter old ones, and indeed, legislate the entire system of local school districts out of existence and replace it with a centrally controlled state educational government. Many state court decisions illustrate this fundamental power of the state over the nature and function of local school districts. No more explicit statement of the relationship appears than that made by a Michigan court (*MacQueen v. City of Port Huron*, 1916) in the early years of the twentieth century:

Fundamentally, provision for and control of our public school system is a state matter, delegated and lodged in the state legislature by the Constitution in a separate article entirely distinct from that related to local government. The general policy of the state has been to retain control of its school system, to be administered throughout the state by local state agencies organized with plenary powers independent of the local government with which, by location and geographical boundaries, they are necessarily closely associated and to a greater or lesser extent authorized to cooperate. Education belongs to the state.

In 1909 (*City of Louisville v. Commonwealth*), the Kentucky Court of Appeals decided a dispute between the Louisville school district and the state on the issue of the state's requiring the district to levy a minimum tax rate in support of public schools. The court decided that the state had that right, in that public education was a state rather than a local function and concern. A most succinct and direct statement of this general principle was provided by a Michigan court (*Child Welfare Society of Flint v. Kennedy District*, 1922): "The legislature has entire control over the schools of the state. . . . The division . . . into districts, the conduct of the school, the qualifications of teachers, the subjects to be taught therein, are all within its control. . . ." It is important to note that there is no legal requirement that public education be managed by local school districts. For example, Hawaii has no local school districts and manages its educational system centrally.

Another important principle is that once a state legislature has delegated certain authority to local districts, these powers cannot be arbitrarily withdrawn or countermanded by state officials. The state's authority over local districts is limited by state statutes, the state constitution, or the federal Constitution and laws. State officials have no extralegal control over local districts and their schools. The legal authority and independence of school districts come from both express and implied powers. *Express powers* are those explicitly granted to local districts by state constitutions and state statutes. *Implied powers* are those considered reasonably necessary to carry out the responsibilities and mandates assigned to local districts by constitutional or statutory provisions.

An Illinois case (*Aurora East District v. Cronin*, 1982), which adjudicated a dispute between state and local education authorities, is illustrative of the limitations of state agencies over local districts, and of the interpretation of express and implied powers. An Illinois law required local districts to revise attendance patterns in order to prevent segregation. The state board of education then set a policy that each district school must contain no more than 15 percent of the district's minority population. The state board of education required annual reports on this matter, under penalty of potential funding loss. The East Aurora district was threatened by the state board with loss of funding for violating this policy. The district sued, claiming that the board was acting *ultra vires* (beyond the scope of its authority). The state board contended that it had the implied power to take such action under statutory authority "to make rules necessary to carry into efficient and uniform effect all laws for establishing and maintaining free schools in the state" and constitutional authority to "establish goals, determine policies . . . and recommend financing." The Illinois Supreme Court rejected these arguments and found in favor of the local district, holding that the desegregation law vested authority in the local boards, not the state board, to develop rules to facilitate desegregation. The state board's proper course was to appeal to the state attorney general for action, not to assume remedial power in itself.

A New York Court of Appeals decision (*Older v. Board of Union Free District No. 1*, 1971), concerning a state-local dispute over authority governing assignment of pupils to schools, is more explicit about express and implied powers. In finding for the local district board of education, it stated:

There can be no question that the Board of Education, by statute, has the power and responsibility to manage and administer the affairs of the school district, including the assignment of students to schools therein. The Education Law . . . specifically grants district school boards power to have . . . control of the educational affairs of the district and . . . all the powers reasonably necessary to exercise powers granted expressly or by implication. . . ."

The court saw the authority to assign pupils to schools to be among those implied powers related to "control of educational affairs."

Legal Role of the National Government

The national government has exercised influence over education policy from its beginnings. While its authority to do so is indirect, it is nonetheless powerful. The principal constitutional provisions relied upon are the general welfare clause of the Constitution ("The Congress shall have Power to . . . provide for the . . . General Welfare of the United States") and the commerce clause, which gives Congress authority to "regulate Commerce . . . among the several States." Courts have recognized the broad federal authority contained in these provisions for national laws that affect education but do not exercise direct control over public schools.

The national government has used authority granted by these provisions to enact laws that offer money for education programs to school districts that have federal guidelines. Once federal funds are accepted, local districts and state educational agencies become subject to the standards and regulations that attend receipt of federal funds. This constitutes a powerful source of national control over local education policy. Three federal programs clearly illustrate the immense federal influence over local education policy. The National Defense Education Act of 1958 expanded science, mathematics, and foreign language programs and made counseling and guidance services an integral part of public school systems. Then, the Elementary and Secondary Education Act of 1965 and its many amendments through the years introduced programs for disadvantaged students that characterize almost all U.S. school districts. Finally, the Education for All Handicapped Children Act of 1975 has created nationwide programs and policies affecting handicapped students that are relatively similar throughout the nation. These three national laws alone have had considerable impact in moving the nation toward uniform educational policies and programs.

National education policy control equal to that exercised through school funding legislation finds its source in federal civil rights laws and constitutional civil rights provisions. It falls to the courts to determine the scope and intensity with which these legal provisions affect public schools. The most influential law is the Civil Rights Act of 1964, which contains two provisions that have had a powerful impact upon local school policy. Title VI bars discrimination based on "race, color or national origin" in any program receiving federal funds. Title VII similarly bars discrimination based on race, color, religion, sex, or national origin in hiring policies. Title VI was the basis for a Supreme Court decision (*Lau v. Nichols*, 1974) that required public schools to provide instruction that compensated for the learning problems of non-English speakers. Title VII has been invoked in teachers' suits against school boards for various forms of discrimination in employment. Many but not all of them have been successful. For example, in *U.S.A. v. South Carolina* (1978), the U.S. Supreme Court rejected a claim of racial discrimination because more blacks than whites failed a racially neutral teacher certification examination required by the state of South Carolina.

Another important law is the Civil Rights Restoration Act of 1988, which bars gender discrimination in educational programs. Congress passed this act in reaction to Supreme Court limitations placed on the scope of gender discrimination protections found in Title IX of the Elementary and Secondary Education Act Amendments of 1972.

The broadest avenue for federal imposition of policy control over local school districts is found in court adjudication of issues related to constitutional civil rights amendments: First Amendment protections of free expression and religious freedom, Fourth Amendment protections against illegal searches, and Fourteenth Amendment guarantees of equal protection and due process. Persons who believe their rights under these provisions have been violated can apply to federal and state courts for redress. The decisions courts make in response to these plaintiffs override the will of local school boards, state education agencies, and the local communities served by public schools. In a very real sense, state and local judges, the Congress, and executive agencies charged with implementing federal laws have become important actors in school-community relations. Gone are days when a local town meeting or a local board of education could decide school policy. Today, the federal government is as much a part of local school affairs as are the board of education and district superintendent.

It should, however, be recognized that there are limits to federal authority over education. These limits are defined by the Constitution, as interpreted by the federal courts. An example of a limitation placed on congressional authority over education is found in the U.S. Supreme Court decision in *U.S. v. Lopez*, 1995. Congress was concerned about the rising tide of school violence that often involved guns. Its response was to pass the Gun-Free Zones Act of 1990, which forbade "any individual knowingly to possess a firearm in a place that [he] knows . . . is a school zone." Lopez, a student in a Texas school, was convicted of violating the Act. His conviction was appealed to the U.S. Supreme Court, which found the Act to be invalid because Congress had no constitutional authority to pass it. Congress claimed such authority under the Commerce Clause of the Constitution. However, a majority of the Supreme Court held that the Commerce Clause was tied to regulation of interstate commerce, and regulating possession of weapons in local schools was not related to interstate commerce. Cases such as this illustrate that there are limits to federal authority over public education.

Individual Rights and State Interests

The United States is a democracy, based on the underlying cardinal principle that ultimate sovereignty resides in the people. Yet, government must decide policy in the best interests of *all* the people, and courts become arbiters of the proper balance between state interests and individual rights. For example, in 1874, citizens challenged the authority of a Michigan local school district to establish tax-supported high schools (*Stuart v. Kalamazoo*), which the objectors considered an unnecessary frill that should be paid for by parents wishing a high school education for their children. The Michigan Supreme Court decided the controversy in favor of the local board of education, holding that it had the authority to extend tax-supported education to the high school level, when the majority of voters, through their elected board of education, deemed it proper.

It is important to note that the will of the majority expressed through their elected representatives will not always prevail. Courts often weigh the balance between state interests and individual rights and find in favor of individuals. Such was the case in 1925 (*Pierce v. Society of Sisters*), when the U.S. Supreme Court applied this concept to public education policy by rejecting an Oregon law that required all students to attend only public schools. In doing so, the Court explained the relationship between parents and the state regarding schooling of children in this way:

The Act . . . unreasonably interferes with the liberty of parents and guardians to direct the upbringing and education of children under their control. . . . [R]ights guaranteed by the Constitution may not be abridged by legislation which has no reasonable relation to some purpose within the competency of the state. The fundamental theory of liberty under which all governments in this Union repose excludes any general power of the state to standardize its children by forcing them to accept instruction from public teachers only. *The child is not the mere creature of the state*; those who nurture him and direct his destiny have the right, coupled with the high duty, to recognize and prepare him for additional obligations. [Emphasis added]

The Pierce doctrine did not simply place all educational authority in the hands of parents. Rather, it struck a compromise important to the development of school-community relations in America. The "Pierce Compromise" established a relationship of shared authority between parents and schools in the following way:

No question is raised concerning the power of the state reasonably to regulate all schools; to inspect, supervise, and examine them, their teachers, and pupils; to require that all children of proper age attend some school, that teachers shall be of good moral character and patriotic disposition; that certain studies plainly essential to good citizenship must be taught, and that nothing be taught which is manifestly inimical to the public welfare.

Through succeeding decades, this compromise has been the basis for controversy in school-community relations that as often as not has required court resolution. A case in point is the Supreme Court decision in *Wisconsin v. Yoder* (1972) in which Wisconsin state education authorities sued Amish parents for withholding their children from required post-elementary school attendance up to age sixteen. The Amish did so because they believe that high school education alienates Amish children from their distinctive culture. The Supreme Court ruled in favor of the Amish, noting that the Amish place their children in productive apprenticeships and produce law-abiding, productive citizens. Thus, the state's purpose was served without forcing Amish adolescents to attend high school.

LEGAL ISSUES IN SCHOOL-COMMUNITY RELATIONS

The following issues have been selected not only because they are most representative of litigation affecting school-community relations, but also because they illustrate the liberal versus conservative and government versus individual tensions that have historically characterized school-community relations, and continue to do so.

Equal Protection in Public Education

The Civil War produced the Fourteenth Amendment to the U.S. Constitution, which contained the Equal Protection Clause. This clause requires that no state shall "deny to any person within its jurisdiction the equal protection of the laws." Even so, the Supreme Court decision in *Plessy v. Ferguson* (1896) set the pattern for school-community relations regarding race relations in the first half of the twentieth century by holding that the requirements of the Equal Protection Clause could be met by "separate-but-equal" treatment of the races by government, in support of "public peace and good order." This provided the legal blessing for the establishment of segregated public school systems in the South, which mirrored that Court's view of the preeminence of state authority over individual rights in this instance. The lone dissent of Justice Harlan, asserting that "the Constitution is color-blind," was as a voice crying in the wilderness.

Not until over a half-century later would the *Plessy* decision be reversed, due to a more liberal national mood and Supreme Court, headed by Earl Warren. That momentous decision was made by a unanimous Supreme Court in *Brown v. Board of Education of Topeka, Kansas* (1954). In recognition of the deeply felt attitudes of parents and community regarding such an intimate and important activity as public education, the decision avoided making recriminations or assigning guilt. Rather, it summed up the reasoning behind its decision as follows:

Whatever may have been the extent of psychological knowledge at the time of *Plessy v. Ferguson*, this finding is amply supported by modern authority. . . . We conclude that in the field of public education, the doctrine of "separate but equal" has no place. Separate educational facilities are inherently unequal.

This decision, asserting individual rights over state authority, created the classic American school-community relations controversy. Among the questions posed by this decision were: Would the moral and political authority of the U.S. Supreme Court prove sufficient to force changes in public education that were contrary to deeply felt attitudes of the dominant white power structure of the South? Would the national government intervene in the South with sufficient will and force to implement a morally proper but politically unpopular decision? While the ultimate answers to both questions were yes, it would take many years of additional uncompromising Court decisions and tense confrontations between federal and state and local power to resolve these questions. Among the many decisions that showed the Supreme Court's determination to implement *Brown* were opinions that negated state decisions to close public schools (*Griffin v. County School Board*, 1964), ordered racial integration of faculty (*Bradley v. Richmond*, 1965), ordered forced busing to achieve integration (*Swann v. Charlotte-Mecklenburg Board of Education*, 1971) and prevented localities from withdrawing from school districts in order to avoid integration (*Wright v. Council of Emporia*, 1972). Presidential orders brought federal troops to guarantee these decisions when local resistance warranted such extreme actions. Also, federal legislation such as the Civil Rights Act of 1964 and the Equal Educational Opportunity Act of 1974 added statutory weapons for courts to use, in addition to the Equal Protection Clause.

Success in the gradual integration of the South redirected the focus of civil rights advocates on segregation in the North. Unlike the segregation in the South, where clear laws authorized racial segregation in schools, northern segregation was a complex set of official actions, which were more difficult to attack. The U.S. Supreme Court addressed this problem in its *Keyes v. School District No. 1, Denver, Colorado* (1973) decision, which found that school board actions promoting segregated schools constituted *de jure* (by law) segregation, since these public officials made their decisions with "segregative intent." This was distinguished from *de facto* (in fact) segregation, which results from factors unrelated to official action, thereby insulating it from the reach of the law.

By the mid 1970s, the nation, and its Supreme Court, had moved to a more conservative stance. While the unanimity and intensiveness of the legal attack against segregation subsided, school desegregation had by then become an accepted goal in American education. Yet, at the same time, the options available to citizens demonstrated that local community attitudes and unofficial initiatives could confound Court and legislative intention. Chief among these options were the movement of middle-class whites to virtually all-white suburban school systems and the increased enrollment at private schools. A new Supreme Court composition rejected the argument of civil rights proponents that white suburban school systems should be forcibly integrated with black urban school systems (*Milliken v. Bradley*, 1974).

Even so, the Court's decision in *Milliken v. Bradley II* (1977) held that both the Detroit local district and the State of Michigan were responsible for contributing to school segregation, and must share the costs of remedying that condition. The Court required that the remedy must include improvements in reading, in-service teacher training, testing, and counseling and career guidance.

The Supreme Court refused to reorder a school district to desegregate after it had done so and then population change had caused resegregation (*Pasadena City Board of Education v. Spangler*, 1976). Then, in 1991 (*Board of Education of Oklahoma City v. Dowell*), a divided Supreme Court (five to three) ended thirteen years of court supervision of the Oklahoma City schools when it announced that once it was clear that a school district had made a "good faith" effort to desegregate, court supervision must end, even if some vestiges of segregation remain or some resegregation occurs for which the school district had no responsibility. Speaking for the three dissenters, Justice Marshall criticized the decision because it "suggests that thirteen years of desegregation was enough." Marshall's dissent did not sway the view of the Court's majority, as the next year, the decision in *Freeman v. Pitts* (1992) released the DeKalb County, Georgia, school system from court-ordered desegregation in certain areas, even though not all of the factors involved in desegregation had been achieved.

Yet, all traces of the old *Brown* liberalism were not dead. In 1989, the Supreme Court let stand a lower court decision finding a city council's decisions on the siting of public housing equally culpable with the school board for unconstitutional school segregation (*U.S.A. v. Board of Education; City of Yonkers, et al.*, 1988). This decision put city councils on notice that henceforth courts would inquire into the causes of school segregation that went beyond the decisions of school boards and actions of school superintendents. Then, in 1990, the Supreme Court approved a lower federal court order requiring the Kansas City School District to raise local taxes required to fund a court-approved desegregation plan, even though district citizens had voted against any increase and the amount of the court-ordered increase violated Missouri law (*Missouri v. Jenkins*). However, in a subsequent rehearing (*Missouri v. Jenkins,* 1995), the Supreme Court refused to allow the district court to order further expenditures to increase teacher salaries, as the results did not justify imposing additional financial burdens on the state and city.

While efforts at promoting greater racial integration in schools were uneven during the 1970s, the influence of the equality-of-educational-opportunity concept spread to a variety of other areas of public concern. *Keyes v. Denver* (1973) had already expanded equal protection to include Hispanics as a "suspect class" protected by the Fourteenth Amendment. Then, in *Lau v. Nichols,* 1974, the Supreme Court invoked the Civil Rights Act of 1964 to protect the educational opportunity rights of non-English-speaking students. In 1972 Congress passed Title IX of the Education Amendments to protect the educational opportunity rights of females. The Supreme Court provided a narrow interpretation of Title IX by holding that sanctions for violations were program specific; that is, they applied to only the offending department or office of an institution, not to the institution as a whole (*Grove City College v. Bell,* 1984). Congress responded with the Civil Rights Restoration Act of 1987, negating that conservative decision. The legislative response was to strengthen the relatively weak provisions of the Bilingual Education Act of 1968 by amendments in 1974 and 1978.

More recently, Title IX has been successfully used to protect teachers and students from sexual harassment. The U.S. Supreme Court allowed damages from a school district that did not adequately respond to the need to protect students from sexual harassment from teachers (*Franklin v. Gwinett County Schools,* 1992), and lower courts have found school districts liable for not adequately protecting teachers from sexual harassment, as well as protecting students from sexual harassment from other students. For example, the U.S. Court of Appeals (Seventh Circuit) has found that the Equal Protection Clause protects homosexual students from harassment by other students. In the case of *Nabozny v. Podlesny, et al.* (1996) the failure of school officials to protect a homosexual boy from harassment from other boys, when they were aware of the harassment, was held to violate the equal protection rights of the homosexual boy.

School finance was another area brought into the equal protection litigation arena. The question raised was whether equal protection was violated when local districts within a state had great disparities in per-pupil funding. The California Supreme Court answered this question affirmatively (*Serrano v. Priest*, 1971). The U.S. Supreme Court found otherwise in upholding the Texas system of school finance (*San Antonio v. Rodriguez*, 1973), even though noting that while the traditional school finance system was not technically unconstitutional, it was "chaotic and unjust." Texas won the battle, but would eventually lose the war. That state's high court, and many other state courts, eventually followed the path blazed by California, and found radically unequal local district funding to be illegal.

A significant expansion of equal educational opportunity concerns handicapped children and adults. The legislation expanding special education rights stands as a prime example of the influence of school interest groups, combined with court decisions, to affect significant national changes in educational policy. The Rehabilitation Act of 1972, barring discrimination based on handicap in employment and services for any program receiving federal funding, came first. There followed court decisions such as *Pennsylvania Association for Retarded Children v. Commonwealth of Pennsylvania* (1971). Here, a federal court agreed with special education advocates that traditional public school policies that excluded handicapped children from school violated a variety of federal laws. The same conclusion was reached in *Mills v. Board of District of Columbia* (1972) the following year. In response to the district's complaint that educating handicapped students would create an excessive financial burden, the district court replied:

If sufficient funds are not available to finance all the services and programs, . . . then the available funds must be expended equitably in such a manner that no child is entirely excluded from a publicly supported education consistent with his needs. . . . The inadequacy [of] . . . funding . . . cannot be permitted to bear more heavily on the exceptional or handicapped child than on the normal child.

Such decisions, combined with intense lobbying pressure from special education groups, led to passage of The Education for All Handicapped Children Act of 1975 (replaced by the Individuals with Disabilities Act of 1990), which granted strong rights to handicapped children. This was a clear victory of individual rights over state authority. Among the major provisions of the act are the entitlement of a public education for handicapped children in the least restrictive environment; individual education programs tailored for each student, resulting from careful case study; and strong protections for parental participation and due process rights in overseeing the education of handicapped children. Supreme Court decisions have refereed the various disputes arising between school districts and parents in accordance with the Court's reading of the Handicapped Children Act. For example, in *Henrick Hudson District of Education v. Rowley* (1982), the Court majority agreed with the school district that its obligation was to provide a program and services that allowed a student to make adequate progress, and that it was not required to provide services that maximised the potential of handicapped students. However, in *Irving v. Tatro* (1984), the Court majority agreed with parents that the school district must provide the related service of catheterization to enable a student with spina bifida to be educated in the least restrictive environment, as this was not considered a procedure requiring trained medical personnel.

Other Supreme Court decisions about special education include *Honig v. Doe* (1989) in which the Court found California public schools in violation of the Act for successive suspensions of an emotionally disturbed student, which had the effect of changing his placement prior to completion of due process procedures, in violation of the "stay put" provision of the Act. Further Supreme Court decisions have required school districts to pay parents for unilateral placement in private facilities during the pendancy of due process when such placement has eventually been deemed proper (*Burlington v. Dept. of Education*, 1985; *Florence County Dist. v. Carter*, 1993), and permitting a sign language interpreter to be employed at public expense to assist a deaf student attending a parochial school (*Zobrest v. Catalina Foothills Dist.*, 1993). The Supreme Court, as well as lower federal and state courts, continues to do a brisk business mediating disputes between parents and school districts over the proper balance between individual rights and state interests in special education.

Religious Observance in Public Schools

In the formative years of public education, the prevailing religious preference of the community was often integrated into school activity. As state systems expanded, religious aspects of public education assumed a more nonsectarian Christian stance. The customary practices of school prayer, Bible reading, and related religious observances practiced by many state systems or individual school districts were to come to an abrupt halt with the advent of the liberal Warren Court of the 1950s and 1960s. The attitude of this Court clearly favored individual rights over state authority as a general principle affecting all areas of government-individual interaction, and education was not excepted. The religious-observance restrictions placed on public schools created a storm of community protest that continues today. It has stimulated the growth of Christian fundamentalist schools and religion-based home schooling that have often run into conflict with state educational regulatory agencies. For example, refusal of a Christian academy to conform to state curriculum and teacher certification rules led Nebraska authorities to close the school and jail its adult supporters (*State v. Faith Baptist Church*, 1981). Parents opting for home schooling to preserve the religious aspects they deemed essential to education were successful in meeting state challenges in New Jersey (*State v. Massa*, 1967) because the court found the relevant state statute required only academically equivalent instruction, which was demonstrated by the student's standardized test scores.

These developments were first stimulated by the U.S. Supreme Court's *Engle v. Vitale* (1961) decision. A prayer ("Almighty God, we acknowledge our dependence on Thee, and we beg Thy blessings upon us, our parents, teachers and our Country") composed by the New York Board of Regents and recommended for adoption by public school districts was declared unconstitutional, in violation of the First Amendment. The Court reasoned that the "establishment clause" ("Congress shall make no law affecting the establishment of religion") applied to the states and its subdivisions, such as school districts, by virtue of the Fourteenth Amendment, which makes "fundamental rights" applicable to the relationship between states and its residents. It held that "government . . . is without power to prescribe by law any particular form of prayer. . . . Neither the fact that the prayer may be denominationally neutral, nor the fact that its observance . . . is voluntary, can serve to free it from the limitations of the Establishment Clause." This decision was broadened and reemphasized in the following year by the companion decisions of *School District of Abington Township v. Schempp* and *Murray v. Curlett* (1963), which struck down the Pennsylvania practice of opening the school day by reading at least ten verses of the Holy Bible without comment, and the Maryland practice of reciting the Lord's Prayer as a classroom activity. In striking down these practices, the Court noted that it was the *religious ritual* that was proscribed. Bible reading as part of "the study of history, comparative religion or the advancement of civilization" did not violate the First Amendment, as "the Bible is worthy of study for its historic and literary qualities."

This set off a storm of protest in local communities, and a variety of countermeasures soon sprung from state legislatures, school districts, and private citizen groups. Using the "advancement of civilization" theme, Kentucky passed legislation authorizing private funding for placing in public school classrooms posters listing the Ten Commandments. The legislature noted that the Commandments constituted "the fundamental legal code of Western Civilization and Common Law of the United States." The Supreme Court decided against such practice (*Stone v. Graham*, 1980), noting that, taken as a whole, the Ten Commandments "constituted a sacred text in the Jewish and Christian faith."

Another strategy to bring religion into the public schools was stimulated by the Supreme Court's decision preventing states and school districts from prohibiting the teaching of evolution theory, since such action was considered religiously motivated (*Epperson v. Arkansas*, 1968). This decision led to the development of "scientific creationism" (or "creation science"). Promoters wanted this Biblical theory of creation taught to counterbalance the study of evolution theory, which they considered antithetical to religion. This strategy got no further than the federal district court level (*McLean v. Arkansas State Board of Education*, 1982), which struck down "equal time" for creation science because it is not "science" at all, since science "is guided by natural law, . . . its conclusions are tentative . . . and it is falsifiable." None of these principles were found to characterize "creation science." This issue was put to rest by the U.S. Supreme Court in *Edwards v. Aguillard*, 1987. A Louisiana statute authorized that when either evolution or creationism was taught, "equal time" must be given to the other theory. The Court declared that act violative of the Establishment Clause, as its purpose was to promote religion in public schools.

Still another strategy was to pass state legislation that allowed for a moment of silent meditation or prayer as a classroom procedure. The Supreme Court has held that the "free exercise" clause of the First Amendment prohibits government from "hostility to religion" (*Zorach v. Clausen*, 1952). Some statutes providing the option to either silently pray or meditate have survived court challenges (e.g., the Massachusetts statute in *Gaines v. Anderson*, 1976). But the Supreme Court struck down the Alabama statute because of evidence that it was motivated by a paramount interest to introduce prayer into the public schools (*Wallace v. Jaffree*, 1985) rather than to allow for choice between silent prayer and meditation.

Another prayer controversy was adjudicated by the Supreme Court in *Lee v. Weisman*, 1992, in which the Court held that nondenominational prayers led by clergymen at public school graduation ceremonies violated the Establishment Clause. Schools wishing to have prayer at graduation ceremonies then allowed for student voting to authorize it, since this was seen as removing government decisions from the matter. However, this approach also was seen as violative of the Establishment Clause by a federal appellate court (*American Civil Liberties Union of New Jersey v. Black Horse Pike Regional Board of Education*, 1996).

Another example of judicial limitation of the entanglement of religion and government occurred when the State of New York passed special legislation allowing a community of orthodox Jews to create their own school district so that their disabled students would not have to go outside of the religious community for their education. The U.S. Supreme Court found that this government action violated the Lemon Test, as it violated the Establishment Clause requirement that government be neutral toward religion (*Board of Kiryas Joel Dist. v. Grumet* (1994).

Free Expression Policies for Teachers and Students

Through the first half of the twentieth century, First Amendment free expression rights (speech, press, assembly, petition) did not apply to either students or teachers. However, the "privilege doctrine" did apply to both students and educators. It was a privilege to be afforded a public education, and a privilege to be appointed to the position of teacher. Courts often offered teachers a choice between exercising their civil rights and getting or keeping a job as a teacher—they were not necessarily entitled to both simultaneously. Students had even weaker individual rights. The superintendent and school board had complete control over their educational life. State interests were paramount, and individual rights had little applicability for teachers or students within the public education arena.

An extreme example of this lack of individual rights was the period in the 1950s known as the "McCarthy Era," in which suppression of individual rights was motivated by fears of communist subversion. Teachers were required to sign loyalty oaths attesting to their conformity to the principles of patriotism as defined by their employers and swearing that they had not been nor presently were members of a variety of organizations that state officials had decided were subversive, without any particular evidence to support these decisions. When a New York teacher protested that such practices violated his First Amendment rights to free expression, the U.S. Supreme Court responded that teachers "have no right to work for the . . . school system on their own terms. . . . They may work . . . upon the reasonable terms laid down by . . . New York. If they do not choose to work on such terms, they are at liberty to retain their beliefs and associations and go elsewhere" (*Adler v. Board*, 1952).

But about fifteen years later, this assertion of state interest over individual rights fell along with "McCarthyism" when the Supreme Court began to reverse its support for such loyalty oaths. In reversing its decision in *Adler*, the Court decided that "[t]he vigilant protection of constitutional freedoms is nowhere more vital than in the community of American schools." The decision held that the First Amendment "does not tolerate laws that cast a pall of orthodoxy over the classroom" (*Keyishian v. Board of Regents*, 1967).

Teachers' rights were expanded much further the next year, as the Warren Court began warming to the task of radically altering the balance between state authority and individual rights in public education. In *Pickering v. Board of Lockport* (1968), the Court laid to rest the privilege doctrine as it applied to teachers. A teacher had written a letter to a local newspaper, criticizing the school board's decision on spending new funds gained from a recent voter-approved tax increase. He was promptly dismissed, and he brought suit against the board for violating his free expression rights. The Court found in favor of teacher Pickering, holding that "the interest of the school administration in limiting teachers' opportunities to contribute to public debate is not significantly greater than its interest in limiting a similar contribution by any member of the general public."

The next year, the Court pronounced the death sentence for the privilege doctrine's application to students in its landmark *Tinker v. Des Moines District* (1969) decision. Here, students planning to wear black armbands to school in silent protest against government policy regarding the Vietnam War were warned not to do so. They wore the armbands anyway, and were suspended. They sued, asserting First Amendment expression rights. In this dramatic reversal of unlimited adult authority over schoolchildren, the Court explained:

It can hardly be argued that either students or teachers shed their constitutional rights to freedom of speech or expression at the schoolhouse gate. . . . In order for the State in the person of school officials to justify prohibition of a particular expression of opinion it must be able to show that its action was caused by something more than a mere desire to avoid the discomfort and unpleasantness that always accompany an unpopular viewpoint. . . . In our system, state-operated schools may not be enclaves of totalitarianism. School officials do not possess absolute authority over their students.

In dissent, Justice Black warned:

[I]f the time has come when pupils of state-supported schools . . . can defy and flout orders of school officials to keep their minds on their own schoolwork, it is the beginning of a new revolutionary era of permissiveness in this country fostered by the judiciary. . . . [T]axpayers send children to school on the premise that at their age they need to learn, not teach.

Just as the lone dissent in *Plessy v. Ferguson* would eventually become majority opinion as the national mood and concerns changed, so too would the dissent of Black in *Tinker v. Des Moines* eventually become the majority view. However, while it took over a half century to reverse *Plessy*, it would take less than two decades to see *Tinker* severely limited. By the mid 1980s, conservatism had reasserted a national social and political dominance. In the educational arena, this was manifested by concerns for falling academic achievement levels and standards, along with concerns for deterioration of school order, safety, and discipline. Among the causes ascribed to these problems was the abdication of adult authority in school promoted by educational liberals and given legal sanction by court decisions such as *Tinker*. The Supreme Court responded first with its decision in *Bethel District v. Fraser* (1985). In this case, a high school senior was suspended after he delivered to a student assembly a speech some considered to contain "graphic and explicit sexual metaphor." Distinguishing this situation from *Tinker*, the U.S. Supreme Court upheld the suspension, noting that "the schools, as instruments of the state, may determine that essential lessons of civil, mature conduct cannot be conveyed in a school that tolerates lewd, indecent or offensive speech. . . ." In dissent, Justice Stevens stated: "The fact that he [Fraser] was chosen by the student body to speak . . . demonstrates that he was respected by his peers . . . [and] was in a better position to determine whether . . . his contemporaries would be offended . . . than a group of judges who are at least two generations and 3,000 miles away from the scene of the crime."

Notwithstanding such criticism, the Supreme Court moved two years later (*Hazelwood District v. Kuhlmeier*, 1988) to further erode the *Tinker* doctrine, in order to more closely align student expression policy with the court majority's perception of community standards and attitudes. In *Hazelwood*, a school newspaper was censored because it contained articles about students' views of teenage pregnancy and parental divorce. The Supreme Court majority sided with the school authorities, distinguishing the issue from the *Tinker* doctrine as follows: "[T]he standard articulated in *Tinker* for determining when a school may punish student expression need not also be the standard for determining when a school may refuse to lend its name and resources to the dissemination of student expression." Such decisions illustrate how changing court and national attitudes can influence changes in constitutional interpretations and resultant school policy.

The constitutional guarantee of free expression has, to date, proven to be the most successful strategy used to allow certain expressions of religion into the public schools. This avenue was first taken in the higher education case of *Widmar v. Vincent* (1981) when the Supreme Court held that religious groups had the same rights to meet as an extracurricular activity as secular interest groups, since the university had created an "open forum" requiring that all interest groups be allowed equal access to public facilities. This was followed by congressional passage of the Equal Access Act of 1984, which holds that when secondary schools created an "open forum" for extracurricular groups, prayer groups could not be excluded. This avenue for introducing religious ritual into the public school through the extracurriculum was further strengthened by the U.S. Supreme Court's decision in *Westside Community Schools v. Mergens* (1990), which held that the Equal Access Act did not violate the Establishment Clause of the First Amendment by allowing religious groups to meet on school property as part of the extracurricular program created as an open forum. Legislation such as the Equal Access Act and decisions such as *Widmar v. Vincent* and *Westside v. Mergens* signal the reemergence of national judicial and legislative support for reasserting a religious presence in public schools.

The "open forum" approach has also been used by community religious groups to gain entry into the public schools. A New York law authorized local school boards regulate the use of school buildings for after-school community events, except those that were religious. When an evangelical church was denied use of a school to show a film series emphasizing family values from a Christian viewpoint, the board denied access. The issue was eventually resolved by the U.S. Supreme Court in *Lamb's Chapel v. Center Moriches District* (1994). By unanimous decision, the Court held that the school had created an open forum. Therefore, a film series on family values could not be excluded because it expressed a religious viewpoint on the subject, as this would be viewpoint discrimination, which is forbidden by the First Amendment. This decision was followed by Congressional enactment of the Religious Freedom Restoration Act in 1993, which requires that government must show a compelling interest in restricting free expression of religion before it may do so.

Free Expression and Community Activism Seeking Control of Education

The Chicago case of *Stevens v. Tillman* (1988) illustrates the tensions between central and community authority as large urban districts move toward greater community control. Community activist Tillman led a group of local African-American residents bent on removing the white principal from a school serving African-American students. Principal Stevens was publicly accused of being a racist, running the school like a plantation, working to destroy the minds of the children in the school, and similar wrongs. Boycotts, "eviction notices," and criticisms made of Stevens by Tillman to the Chicago Board of Education eventually resulted in Stevens going on sick leave and then being involuntarily reassigned to another school.

Stevens then sued Tillman for violating her civil rights and for defamation of character. The suit began in 1983, and finally ended with the U.S. Supreme Court refusing to grant *certiorari* to the case in 1989. The district court had limited the statements Tillman had made to just those that could be objectively verifiable as true or false. Charges of being a racist and running the school like a plantation were excluded from consideration. A jury found in favor of Stevens on the civil rights claim, but awarded her only one dollar in damages. Stevens appealed, claiming that the accusation against her of being a racist should have been considered, along with other defamatory statements made by Tillman. The appellate court affirmed the decision of the trial court, holding that "accusations of racism no longer are obviously and naturally harmful. The word has been watered down by overuse, becoming common coin in political discourse."

The appellate judge went on to explain that even though Tillman's accusations contained some falsehoods, Stevens' position as principal did not insulate her from criticism by the community she served. The judge lamented "the limited reach of federal law" in this case, and even suggested that Stevens' cause would have been better served by a suit in state court based on assault, as she had been placed in fear of bodily harm. This case illustrates the broad leeway given to community activists who criticize the schools serving their children.

Discipline and Control of Students and Teachers

No subject directs as much community concern and attention toward the school as that of behavior—of both students and teachers. Before the "privilege doctrine" crumbled under the review of the Warren Court, students' and teachers' behavior were firmly directed, controlled, and punished (if need be) by the school board and the administrators they hired. Teachers could be refused positions or dismissed from their positions for any behavior that the school board or superintendent deemed improper or inimical to the best interests of the school district. Possible improper behavior included personal decisions about dress or grooming, life-style, choices of friends, marriage, and whether or not to have children. Students had even fewer rights than their teachers.

That legal situation conformed to a conservative view of school-community relations favoring state interests over individual rights. Beginning with its *Tinker* decision, the Warren Court reversed the balance, creating an abrupt, severe reversal of power relationships. The liberal trend would continue even after Warren Burger succeeded Earl Warren as Chief Justice of the U.S. Supreme Court. The due process concept, contained in both the Fifth and Fourteenth Amendments to the U.S. Constitution, was the chief legal principle relied upon to free students and teachers from excessive control over their behavior. In simplest terms, due process means fairness. It involves fairness in both the steps (e.g., notice of charges and a hearing on them) required in making a decision affecting one's interests and welfare (procedural due process), as well as the fairness of laws, regulations and actions (e.g., not arbitrary, capricious, overly broad or vague) taken by officials (substantive due process). Justice Frankfurter, in *Joint Anti-Fascist Refugee Committee v. McGrath* (1951), explained the meaning of due process this way:

> "[D]ue process " ... [represents] ... that feeling of just treatment through centuries; ..."due process" cannot be imprisoned within the treacherous limits of any formula. Representing a profound attitude of fairness between ... the individual and government, "due process" is compounded of history, reason, the past course of decisions, and stout confidence in the strength of the democratic faith which we profess. Due process is not a mechanical instrument. It is not a yardstick. It is a process. It is a delicate process of adjustment inescapably involving the exercise of judgment.

It is easy to see how this broad concept can be easily adapted to suit one's views on the proper conduct of teachers and students.

The Supreme Court and lower federal courts of the 1970s set about interpreting due process as favoring individual rights. The courts began by bringing teachers under the protection of the due process umbrella. Decisions supported the tenure rights of teachers as protection against arbitrary dismissal (*Perry v. Sindermann*, 1972); the right of pregnant teachers to continue teaching while it was medically safe to do so (*Cleveland Board of Education v. LaFleur*, 1974); the right of a female teacher to have a male guest (an out-of-town friend of her son) sleep at her home, even though community people objected (*Fischer v. Snyder*, 1973); and the right of a homosexual teacher to retain his job when this did not affect his role as a teacher (*Sarac v. State Board of Education*, 1967). These examples are but a few of the decisions supportive of individual rights.

The major decision supporting the individual rights of students over control by government authority was *Goss v. Lopez* (1975), which stated that public schools could not suspend or expel students without first providing them the protection of procedural due process. In the words of the court: "The authority possessed by the State to prescribe and enforce standards of conduct in its schools . . . must be exercised consistently with constitutional safeguards." These "safeguards" demanded, as a minimum, that students "must be afforded some kind of notice and afforded some kind of hearing." Henceforth, schools would have to justify suspensions and expulsions as reasonable and conforming to constitutional principles of fairness. This decision, and others that would follow, greatly increased student protections against potential dismissal or other disciplinary actions by school authorities. Even after the Supreme Court decided that infliction of corporal punishment by school authorities did not require procedural due process, as was necessary for suspension (*Ingraham v. Wright*, 1977), a student still won a suit against a teacher who used corporal punishment that violated the student's *substantive* due process rights, because the judge considered the teacher's action to be "literally shocking to the conscience" (*Hall v. Tawney*, 1980).

During the 1980s, the courts set about shifting the balance back to support of government interest in matters concerning the control of student behavior. The first U.S. Supreme Court case in that direction was the Fourth Amendment search case of *New Jersey v. T.L.O.* (1985). Prior to this case, the U.S. Supreme Court had not ruled on a public school Fourth Amendment search case. However, the Warren Court, with its emphasis on individual rights, had developed legal protections against unreasonable searches and required that evidence used in criminal charges was legally obtained. However, when the Court heard this case involving student Fourth Amendment rights, the Court supported government interests in education over individual privacy interests. *New Jersey v. T.L.O.* involved a high school student (T.L.O.) who was suspected of smoking in a restricted school area. She was reported by a teacher to the assistant principal, who searched her purse and found cigarettes. However, he did not discontinue his search at that point. Additional search of her purse revealed contraband drugs and drug paraphernalia, as well as evidence of illicit drug trafficking. In this first student search case to reach the Supreme Court, the majority held that the usual standards that govern reasonable suspicion or probable cause did not apply in school situations. While the Fourth Amendment did apply to public school students, there was no need for educators to obtain warrants to search for evidence that might be used in criminal proceedings against students. All that was necessary was that educators act reasonably in searching students and seizing evidence, which would "spare teachers and school administrators the necessity of schooling themselves in the niceties of probable cause and permit them to regulate their conduct according to the dictates of reason and common sense." If the search was justified at its inception and reasonable in its scope, the Fourth Amendment was not offended. The reason given for relaxing traditional restraints on educator searches of students was the problem of school discipline and safety. In the Court's words:

Against the child's interest in privacy must be set the substantial interests of teachers and administrators in maintaining discipline.... Maintaining order in the classroom has never been easy, but in recent years, school disorder has taken particularly ugly forms: drug use and violent crime in the schools have become major social problems.... Accordingly, we have recognized that maintaining security and order in schools requires a certain degree of flexibility in school disciplinary procedures.

This reasoning starkly contrasts with the thinking of the courts that decided *Tinker v. Des Moines* and *Goss v. Lopez*. In *Tinker*, the majority held that neither "teachers [n]or students shed their constitutional rights . . . at the schoolhouse gate," and that "schools may not become enclaves of totalitarianism." Then, in *Goss*, the majority held that "the claimed right of the State to determine unilaterally and without process whether . . . misconduct occurred immediately collides with the requirements of the Constitution.... We have imposed requirements which are, if anything, less than a fair-minded principal would impose upon himself in order to avoid unfair suspensions." In contrast, the *T.L.O.* court majority placed a higher value on allowing "flexibility in school disciplinary procedures" so that school authorities could cope with the "particularly ugly forms" of school disorder.

This view was reinfoced by the Supreme Court's *Vernonia School District v. Acton* (1995) decision in regard to school efforts to control student drug abuse through urinalysis testing. The Vernonia, Oregon, school district imposed a regulation that students participating in interscholastic athletic programs must, as a condition of participation, submit to random urinalysis testing for drug use, as the district found that there was a higher incidence of drug abuse among athletes, who served as role models, than the general student population. Suit was brought claiming that this policy violated the Fourth Amendment privacy rights of students, as it was a blanket search without particularized suspicion. The Supreme Court found in favor of the school district, further strengthening the search authority of school officials.

Encouraged by the greater court deference given to school authority, combined with growing concern regarding school order and safety, many school districts have opted to enact "no tolerance" discipline regulations requiring suspension or expulsion for a variety of student offenses. While such policies have appeal to the general public, they can run afoul of due process concepts, as they tend to be overbroad and vague, as well as arbitrary, as imposition of penalties allows "no tolerance" for individual circumstances. An example is found in the case of *Dothan City Board of Education v. V.M.H.* (1995). The school board adopted a Code of Student Conduct that included the following section: "Possession of any item which may be conceivably used as a weapon on the school grounds" was cause for expulsion or placement in a long-term alternative school. A school official saw an unloaded air rifle in plain view inside a student's locked car, leading to the student's expulsion. The expulsion was overturned by the Alabama trial court, which found the regulation to be arbitrary and unjust. Upon appeal, the appellate court affirmed, adding that the code section was both ambiguous and vague. The enthusiasm of school boards to "come down hard" on student disorder and violence must be tempered by consideration of the due process rights, both procedural and substantive, to which students are entitled.

While the recent spate of conservative decisions has not brought policy on student control back to pre-*Tinker* and *Goss* conditions, they have shifted the balance back from the liberal position on students' rights established by those earlier decisions. It is instructive to note that this shift in the liberal-conservative balance parallels the shift in national attitudes regarding public education. As the public and its representative interest groups become more critical of public schools, in terms of both academic performance and standards of order and safety, courts and legislatures respond with decisions consistent with those attitudes. This is true at local, state, and national levels. In a very real sense, this condition exemplifies the democratic nature of the United States and its systems of public education.

THE LAW AND SCHOOL REFORM STRATEGIES

The current direction of school reform strategies throughout the United States emphasizes transferring authority from central school boards and educational bureaucracies to local schools, communities, and parents. The major strategies developed for this purpose are school-based management programs, voucher programs, and charter school authority for local groups of educators and citizens. These reforms represent significant restructuring of traditional administrative and legal arrangements. As might be expected in this litigious nation, these approaches to school reform have encouraged significant legal challenges.

School-Based Management

Chicago is the scene of one of the most far-reaching exeriments in school-based management. The Chicago School Reform Act of 1988 transferred a large amount of authority over local school management from the central school administration and board of education to newly created local school councils, composed of six parents elected by school parents, two community representatives elected by nonparent community residents, two teachers elected by each school's faculty, and the school principal. Other provisions of the Act stripped principals of their former tenure and placed them on four-year renewable contracts. Local school councils were given authority to offer and terminate these contracts.

As a result, suit was brought in the Illinois courts to invalidate this legislation. In the case of *Fumarolo v. Chicago Board of Education, et al.* (1990), the Illinois Supreme Court found the Act unconstitutional, as the greater voting power given to parents violated the U.S. Supreme Court's standard of one person, one vote. Having done so, the Court went on to respond to the claim that withdrawal of tenure violated the due process right of the formerly tenured principals. The Court held that the principals were entitled to due process, but that they had received sufficient due process because the legislature had carefully considered its tenure withdrawal decision, including holding public hearings on the matter. Further, since the legislature had provided the benefit of tenure to Chicago principals, it could also withdraw it.

The Act was revised to satisfy the demands of the Illinois Supreme Court. However, this did not end litigation related to Chicago school reform. Subsequent cases, among a variety of other cases stemming from the reform Act, dealt with charges of discrimination against local school councils in their decisions on principal retention (*Pilditch v. Board of Education, City of Chicago*, 1993) and principal incompetence (*Board of Education of Chicago v. VanKast*, 1993). Dismissed Chicago principals even tried their due process argument in federal court (*Pittman v. Chicago Board of Education*, 1995), but the result was the same as in the Illinois Supreme Court.

A further Illinois concession to local district autonomy was created by an act that allowed school districts to apply for waivers of state legislative mandates and administrative rules and regulations. This has led to approval of a variety of district requests for relief from state mandates and regulations, most of which are in the areas of required physical education programs and rules governing personnel matters.

Voucher Plans

Another important effort toward stronger community influence over school policy is the voucher movement, which advocates that parents receive state-funded vouchers that they may use at the school of their choice to defray educational costs. The idea is to improve education by subjecting schools to marketplace competition—parents choose the best schools for their children. Voucher plans vary regarding allowing vouchers to be used at public schools only, at both public and secular private schools, and, in some cases, at parochial schools as well.

Many of these state voucher plans have resulted in court challenges. In 1970 the Supreme Court of Massachusetts unanimously advised the state House of Representatives that its plan, which included payments to parochial schools for instruction in secular subjects, would violate the state constitution, which forbids state payments to private schools (*Opinion of the Justices*, 1970). A similar scenario in New Hampshire ended the same way when that state's Supreme Court advised the state Senate that public payments to sectarian schools violated the state's constitutional prohibition of public support of sectarian schools (*Opinion of the Justices*, 1992). In 1973 the Supreme Court of the State of Washington unanimously struck down the state's proposed voucher program for disadvantaged students because most of the funds went to Catholic schools, thereby violating the state constitutional provision requiring schools supported by any portion of public funds to be free from sectarian control or influence (*Weiss v. Bruno*), and later reached the same decision in *Witters v. State Commission*, 1989.

The Wisconsin Supreme Court upheld the Milwaukee Parental Choice Program, which provided state vouchers to low-income parents to defray costs at either public or nonsectarian private schools. Court approval was based on the view that public funds were spent for a public purpose (*Davis v. Grover*, 1992). This decision suggests that a "public purpose" argument for voucher programs has a reasonable chance for success when sectarian schools are excluded from receiving state funds. However, it has been argued (Kemerer, 1995) that if and when federal courts become involved in legal disputes over voucher plans that center on the Establishment Clause, the Religious Freedom Restoration Act of 1993 may prove to be a legal avenue for state vouchers paid to parochial schools.

Charter Schools

Twenty-five states now allow over five hundred publicly funded charter schools that receive freedom from a variety of state education regulations in order to experiment with innovative approaches to teaching and curriculum (Johnston, 1996). The legal arena in this movement is in the state legislatures, as supporters and opponents battle over state or community control of educational regulations and standards, along with a variety of other related policy issues. For example, the South Carolina charter school legislation requires that charter school enrollment must match, within 10 percent, the racial composition of the district in which the school is located.

The 1993 Michigan charter school law was challenged in state court (*Council v. John Engler*) due to its provisions allowing public funds to a charter academy that was a collection of home schools that had religious elements. The court found the law to be in violation of the Michigan Constitution. The reasons given by the court for reaching that conclusion were that (1) the charter schools (academies) were not structured in a way that met the test of a public school according to the Constitution, and hence had no right to receive public funding; and (2) the act usurped the constitutional authority of the state board of education to oversee public education by placing this authority in the hands of others. The act was subsequently revised, but sapped of much of the independence the previous act had conferred on those operating Michigan charter schools. Similar actions in state courts may be expected as the charter school movement continues to grow and as unanticipated issues related to charter schools develop.

SUMMARY

States have plenary power over public education. This statement, while true, hardly begins to explain the legal complexity affecting schools. State authority is mitigated by a multiplicity of federal laws and programs as well as by state policy delegating significant policy authority to local boards of education. The task of sorting out the power relationships and managing disputes among these levels of government has fallen to state and federal courts.

A judiciary independent from politics, particularly at the federal level, was designed to insulate government against the potential danger of tyranny by an extremist majority. In education, the courts have become increasingly active in this role. The most significant policy impact made by the courts upon public education was the 1954 U.S. Supreme Court decision in *Brown v. Board of*

Education, which outlawed racial segregation in public education. Courts have also prevented states from abolishing all forms of nonpublic education, limited the role of religion in public education, clarified and strengthened the civil rights protection afforded teachers and students in public education, and interpreted the meaning and effect of various federal and state education programs and policies.

Analysis of court decisions illustrates that judges are no more immune from the influence of public opinion and pressure groups than are legislatures or local boards of education. As the national mood becomes more liberal or more conservative, courts often follow suit. This view is confirmed by observing the clear retreat of the conservative Rehnquist Court from the school policies carved out by the liberal Warren Court. Even with such tendencies, the judicial system remains the branch of government most insulated from political pressure and the potential dangers of single-issue interest groups capturing control of the public schools and converting them to reflect their narrow, particularized interests.

State legislatures, bent on reforms emphasizing various approaches to reducing the centralized authority of urban school boards and districtwide administrations in favor of local school authorities, have developed various choice plans, such as voucher programs, charter schools, and school-based management designs. These new developments, which are very much at the heart of school-community relations under reform, have already produced court litigation. It can be expected that many more suits will follow, as such issues as the rights of special education students and minority student admissions within charter schools, acceptance of vouchers presented by minorities to particular schools, and competing interests of school-based policymaking boards are presented to the courts for resolution.

Exercise 7.1
ANALYSIS OF EDUCATIONAL CIVIL RIGHTS ISSUES

Select one controversial state or school board policy affecting students and another affecting teachers. Analyze them in terms of whether or not they might be challenged on the basis of constitutional civil rights protections. Identify the policies as either liberal or conservative. Then decide whether these policies would be approved or rejected by the current U.S. Supreme Court. Would the decision be different if the Warren Court were deciding the case?

Exercise 7.2
IDENTIFYING PERSONAL POLICY PREFERENCES AND BIASES

Separate the following cases into two lists; one for decisions with which you agree, and the other for decisions with which you disagree. Review your two lists and determine if your judicial preference reveals a clear liberal or conservative bias. See if your bias (if any) relates to a particular issue (religion, race, etc.) rather than to a general principle.

Abington v. Schempp
Bethel v. Fraser
Brown v. Board of Education
Cleveland v. LaFleur
Davis v. Grover
Fumarolo v. Chicago Board of
   Education
Goss v. Lopez
Hazelwood v. Kuhlmeier
Hudson v. Rowley
Lamb's Chapel v.Central
   Moriches District
Lau v. Nichols

Lee v. Weisman
Missouri v. Jenkins
New Jersey v. T.L.O.
Oklahoma v. Dowell
Pickering v. Lockport
Pierce v. Society of Sisters
San Antonio v. Rodriguez
Swann v. Charlotte-Mecklenburg
Tinker v. Des Moines
U.S. v. Yonkers
Vernonia School District v. Acton
Westside v. Mergens
Wisconsin v. Yoder

Suggested Activities

1. Select a few U.S. Supreme Court decisions or decisions of your state courts affecting policy in your school district. Then ask a random group of teachers whether or not they are familiar with these decisions. Do the same with school administrators. Make a judgment as to whether or not each group has sufficient school law knowledge.

2. Review the rules and regulations of your school district. Can you identify any that could result in a successful court challenge?

3. Interview special education teachers and administrators about the Individuals with Disabilities Education Act. Ask their opinions about the provisions of this legislation and the roles of the federal government, the state government, and the local school district. Ask them what changes they would make if they were members of Congress.

4. Identify an educational interest group active in your community. In what ways do they attempt to influence board policy decisions and state legislation. Do they use the courts as one avenue for promoting their interests?

5. Ask a representative of your teachers' union or association about the group's most recent involvement in court suits. Do the same with a school administrator.

6. Read various sections of your state school code (curriculum, teacher certification, student discipline, etc.) in which you have a particular interest. Can you find provisions that are being ignored by your school? Are there items of permissive legislation that you feel should be adopted by your school, or items adopted by your school that could be discontinued?

7. Reread the material about the case of *Stevens v. Tillman*. Could school-community relations in your school district ever reach the sorry state exemplified by this case? Why or why not? If yes, what could and should be done to prevent such a breakdown in school-community relations?

SUGGESTED READINGS

Kluger, Richard (1975). *Simple Justice.* New York: Alfred A. Knopf.

LaMorte, Michael W. (1996). *School Law: Cases and Concepts,* fifth edition. Boston, Mass.: Allyn & Bacon.

Fischer, Louis; Schimmel, David; and Kelly, Cynthia (1995). *Teachers and the Law,* fourth edition. White Plains, N.Y.: Longman.

Valente, William D. (1994). *Law in the Schools,* third edition. Columbus, Ohio: Merrill.

Part II
Toward Effective School-Community Relations

Chapter Eight

STRATEGIC PLANNING

The plan can contribute toward a centralizing tendency or it can serve the purpose of creating a framework within which participation can be made more viable.
—C. Arnold Anderson, "Potentialities for Popular Participation in Planning," 1974, p. 275

Curiously, there is a rejuvenated interest these days in *planning*. The curiosity is that planning has long been considered a highly rational and usually centralizing (or "top-heavy") activity. Managerial professionals, it is claimed, typically seek to impose planning from above on lower-level employees and on an organization's clientele. Nevertheless, despite an emphasis now on bottom-up decisionmaking (decentralization, empowerment, and democratization), the vitality of planning is being discovered anew—by business and industry, by government, and by an array of social service agencies, including education.

The current label is *strategic planning*—a not-yet-thoroughly-defined term that includes a deep sense of the relationship between organization and environment, a good deal of "futures" visioning, and considerably more bottom-up than top-down managerial implementation (Melcher and Kerzner, 1988; Koteen, 1989). Far from being viewed as a chief executive's prerogative, planning is now considered a vital activity in engendering among workers a sense of participation and belonging in organizational accomplishment, including an opening up of opportunities for people to be involved in the decisionmaking process.

Interestingly, a now decades-old book encouraging the centralization and consolidation of rural schools urged planning as a device to stay in close touch with "the neighborhoods" (see Essert and Howard, 1952). More recently, in 1989, the law in Illinois to decentralize the governance of Chicago schools to the neighborhoods

173

included a planning mandate, for the school site, as a device to bring grassroots control in touch with larger concerns for systemwide accountability (see Walberg, 1989; Hess, Jr., 1989; also Cooper, 1990).

As a testimony to the new importance of planning, the preparation of a three-year "school-improvement plan" was legislatively identified as one of the central priorities for each of Chicago's parent-dominated Local School Councils in the first year of reform. With little time to learn techniques, each Chicago school's staff, parents, and community representatives spent the spring of 1990 preparing strategies for school improvement—including the Illinois General Assembly's priority of improving reading and mathematics skills, pupil attendance, and drop-out and failure rates (*Substance*, 1990). Interestingly, the central office for the Chicago schools was to plan systemwide as well—in a confusion of top-down and bottom-up that has not been easily resolved (Crowson and Boyd, 1996).

In short, Chicago's reform has focused on planning as a major vehicle for educational improvement under that city's drive toward attaining a heavily decentralized, and more participatory form of school governance, while simultaneously maintaining "oversight" from above. Similarly, many other communities less radical than Chicago have been exploring site-based management and other "empowerment" alternatives—with many looking toward strategic planning as a key procedural tool. Unfortunately, despite the renewed interest, little attention has been given to strategic planning (and particularly participatory or shared strategic planning) in the school-community relations literature. In this chapter, we will just scratch the surface of this important topic—providing a bit of background to strategic planning, then considering some strategic planning practices, pitfalls, and possibilities.

BACKGROUND

A curious piece of history regarding public education is that the modern technique of strategic planning has roots in the notion formed years ago of a community needs survey—an idea traceable to the very beginnings of administrator training and professionalization (Callahan, 1962). Such institutions as Columbia's Teachers College led the way, shortly after the turn of the century, in offering formal coursework (and soon one or more graduate-level degrees) as preparation for administrative roles. Central to the ideology of the time was the understanding that public education requires persons who are thoroughly trained to run schools professionally, in businesslike fashion, freed from the vagaries of pressure politics. The irony is that while these early programs taught the necessity of an administrative distancing from the public, they found it necessary to simultaneously instruct professionals in how to ascertain the needs of their publics.

The needs assessment became, over the years, a common tool of local school administration. Indeed, state and federal funding began to require evidence of local need as a key part of the application process within a number of grant-in-aid programs. It has not always been easy to agree on just what an educational need is, who should determine need, or which or whose needs should have priority. Furthermore, there are individual needs, community needs, and school system needs—all of which may or may not be compatible.

Finally, *need* has different meanings if used as a statement either of means or of ends. As a means statement, one could suggest that the Creekside schools need additional reading specialists, another learning disabilities teacher, resources for asbestos removal, and some curriculum revision in elementary science. However, Creekside's needs could also be expressed as a set of desired ends—as an indication of a gap between current educational conditions and some prescribed goals. If a sizable number of fourth-graders are reading below grade level, or teacher absenteeism is on the increase, or standardized test scores in science are below the national norm, Creekside's needs could then be identified as the discrepancy that exists between actual and expected performance in reading, science, or coming to work. It is this latter, outcomes-oriented approach that is commonly favored by experts engaged in educational needs assessment (Witkin, 1984; 1991).

With its roots in a turn-of-the-century interest in "surveying" the surrounding community, a mainstay of needs assessment in education has been the public opinion questionnaire and the personal interview. Over the years, a sophisticated technology has developed with which to sample respondents systematically, fashion questionnaire items clearly, collect opinion data efficiently, and scale and analyze the results with interpretive meaning for program development (see, for example, Conway, Jennings, and Milstein, 1974). One of the most difficult tasks in needs assessments is the establishment of priorities, which involves making value-laden decisions about which needs take precedence over others. Here, too, a sophisticated technology has developed, with survey methods (e.g., forced-choice items) and data-analysis procedures (e.g., rank-order-of-difference scoring) specially developed to facilitate the prioritizing of needs (Witkin, 1984).

As sophistication in needs assessment techniques increased over the years, it became common for many school districts to use the process as part of a larger effort to keep the community informed. After a school district's "needs are reviewed and ranked and resources are determined," urged Susan Otterbourg (1986, p. 26), the results should be "reported to the entire community through a district newsletter or reporting form." This, said Otterbourg, informs the community of needs and resources, provides commitment-generating feedback to persons who had responded to the survey, and encourages the future participation of those who had not responded.

Briefly summarizing, strategic planning has its roots in one of education's oldest administrative techniques for gauging community values—the needs survey. As new administrators were receiving training in how to separate themselves from politics, their trainers were simultaneously recognizing the necessity for understanding community opinion. Over time, needs assessment techniques grew in sophistication. And interestingly, over time, these techniques acquired many of the characteristics of modern-day strategic planning—particularly a goals orientation and procedures for feedback to, and later the participation of, the community.

The vitality and continued viability of the needs survey is attested to by the popularity of the national Gallup Poll in education, whose results are reported annually in *Phi Delta Kappan* and whose questions are often copied by local districts for their own comparisons. For example, Table 8.1 shows responses to a key question in the 1996 Gallup Poll. Nationally, most respondents considered "drug abuse" to be the top-rated problem of public schooling, whereas one year earlier, in the 1995 poll, "drug abuse" came in fourth place behind "lack of discipline," "lack of proper financial support," and "fighting/violence/gangs."

Of interest as well are the findings that "overcrowded schools" jumped to fifth place and "pupils' lack of interest" ranked sixth in the 1996 poll. In 1995, the sense of a "problem" in these two domains was much smaller. Over time and even markedly from year to year, such polls as the Gallup indicate changing national trends

Table 8.1
**Perceptions of Problems in the Public Schools
(1996)**
What do you think are the biggest problems with which the public
schools in this community must deal?

	National Totals		No Children in School		Public School Parents		Nonpublic School Parents	
	'96 %	'95 %	'96 %	'95 %	'96 %	'95 %	'96 %	'95 %
Drug abuse	16	7	17	7	14	7	12	8
Lack of discipline	15	15	16	17	12	11	18	18
Fighting/violence/ gangs	14	9	14	9	15	8	17	17
Lack of proper financial support	13	11	14	10	13	12	7	3
Overcrowded schools	8	3	6	3	11	5	15	3
Pupils' lack of interest/ truancy/poor attitudes	5	2	5	2	6	1	4	2
Lack of family struc- ture/problems in home life	4	3	5	3	1	1	1	5
Crime/vandalism	3	2	3	2	1	2	3	2
Poor curriculum/low curriculum standards	3	2	3	2	3	1	5	1
Difficulty getting good teachers	3	2	3	2	3	3	3	*
Integration/segregation/ racial discrimination	2	2	2	2	3	2	2	*
Lack of respect for self/ others	2	3	2	3	1	4	2	6
No problems	3	3	2	2	7	6	3	2
Miscellaneous	9	4	8	5	10	3	11	3
Don' know	13	11	15	12	9	10	10	6

*Less than one-half of 1 percent.
(Figures add to more than 100 percent because of multiple answers.)

Source: "The 28th Annual Gallup Poll of the Public's Attitudes Toward the Public
Schools," by Stanley Elam, Lowell C. Rose, and Alec M. Galleys, *Phi Delta Kappan*
78(1), p. 49. © 1996, Phi Delta Kappan, Inc. Reprinted with permission.

and provide the basis of valuable local-to-national comparisons, both extremely helpful to the local practitioner.

STRATEGIC PLANNING

The community survey and the needs assessment were small cracks in the traditional armor of the administrator against pressures from the outside. The cracks became sizable as from the 1970s on, administrators in both public and nonpublic sectors came to the realization that the attainment of institutional goals and objectives must *begin* with consideration of the environment. While planning was by no means new to the management community (including educational administrators), the preferred terminology from the mid 1970s on increasingly became "strategic planning" (which, notes Witkin [1984], is also occasionally labeled "open-systems planning").

Strategic planning differs from long-range planning in two major ways. First, observes Witkin (1984, p. 246), strategic planning "stresses *effectiveness* (doing the right thing) rather than *efficiency* (doing things well)." Effectiveness in the private, corporate sector comes from a sense of organizational improvement goals far beyond simple profit and loss, stockholder returns, and let the buyer beware (Melcher and Kerzner, 1988). In the nonprofit sector, effectiveness is demonstrated by a special concern with "the basic character of the organization" (Witkin, 1984, p. 246)—with the organization's values and purposes, its quality of life rather than simple quantity of output, and of course the quality of the organization's relationship with its clientele.

Second, strategic planning (as practiced) includes a participative focus. Strategic planning is not considered the responsibility of "a planner," operating at a chief executive's level of officialdom with a technically trained support staff. Rather, strategic planning is meant to provide participative integration throughout the organization, stimulating decentralization and delegation as planning activities unfold (Koteen, 1989; Melcher and Kerzner, 1988; Carlson and Awkerman, 1991). Consequently, the strategic planning process tends to be qualitative as much as quantitative, more inductive than deductive, and more art than science (Witkin, 1984). It is this participative rather than top-down flavor to strategic planning that has increased its appeal enormously to educators who are striving for teacher empowerment or, as in Chicago's reform, added parent empowerment.

Still, planning is planning. As in all planning, strategic approaches attempt to identify goals, assess courses of action for goal attainment, determine the resources needed to achieve the goals, and eventually monitor the organization's effectiveness in reaching its goals. In a list of activities that incorporates strategic planning's open-systems flavor, as well as its value ladenness and its organizational holism, J.M. Bryson (1988, p. 48) offers the following eight-step process:

1. Initiating and agreeing on a strategic planning process.
2. Identifying organizational mandates.
3. Clarifying organizational mission and values.
4. Assessing the external environment: opportunities and threats.
5. Assessing the internal environment: strengths and weaknesses.
6. Identifying strategic issues facing an organization.
7. Formulating strategies to manage the issues.
8. Establishing an effective organizational vision for the future.

In a shorter list, which differs from Bryson's (1988) in that it begins with consideration of the environment and then returns to that environment, Robert Cope (1978, pp. 10–11) suggests four interrelated activities in strategic planning:

1. Identification of opportunities and problems in the institution's environment and estimation of the degree of opportunity or degree of risk associated with alternative decisions.
2. Assessment of the institution's strengths and weaknesses.
3. Consideration of the personal values, aspirations, and ideals of staff members, donors, and publics.
4. Contemplation of the institution's responsibility to the public.

Some Differing Approaches to Planning

Whatever steps may characterize strategic planning, there is latitude for some major differences in conceptualization and procedure. The planning process can be complex and require much explanation plus lengthy training—thus we do not attempt in this brief chapter to communicate planning methodologies or tools and skills. What may be of some help instead to those exploring school-community relations issues would be an examination of three quite different forms of strategic planning and their community implications: (1) a "systems" approach to planning, (2) a "strategic leadership" approach, and (3) a "deliberative" approach.

The Systems Approach. Systems analysis techniques have been popular in school administration for a number of decades. Indeed, the 1960s saw rather widespread experimentation in education with such "systems" ideas as PPBS, PERT-charting, and measurement by objectives. The central difference in the systems approach between then and now, offers Roger Kaufman (1988), is that the concentration in the 1960s was on the many *parts* of the larger educational system, while the newer approach is much more global and holistic. That is, systems analysis planning now incorporates much of the awareness of the environment and the future of the modern-day strategic initiative.

Otherwise, the systems approach today uses essentially the same terms and philosophy as did the 1960s technology. Figure 8.1 shows one simple yet extremely attractive model developed by Roger Kaufman (1988; 1991), who suggests that the essence of planning is how to get from "what is" to "what should be." In other words, the key challenge is how to overcome whatever gaps lie between an organization's set of objectives and evidence of its success in meeting those objectives.

As Kaufman's (1988) model shows, some improvement-relevant discrepancies between the "is" and "should be" are likely to be found in a number of "organizational elements." These range from inputs to processes; from products to outputs and outcomes. Inputs of consequence include school facilities, personnel, and other budgetary choices; but important inputs can also include assessed community needs, school board policies, and state law. Processes include doing whatever is necessary to convert inputs into outputs—including curricula, instructional materials, teaching strategies, matters of classroom organization, grouping practices, and the like. Then, finally, Kaufman (1988, pp. 34–35) suggests the examination of gaps in products, outputs, and outcomes. Products are direct educational results (e.g., completed curricula, tasks fulfilled, instructional objectives reached). Outputs are the collected products that the educational institution delivers to its environment (e.g., numbers of graduates, numbers of persons performing at an acceptable level of

Figure 8.1

The Systems Approach to Strategic Planning

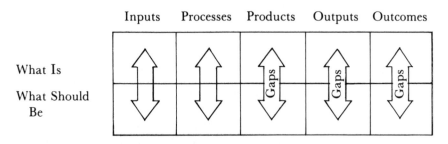

Reproduced with permission from R. Kaufman, *Planning Education Systems*. Lancaster, Penn.: Technomic Publishing, p. 35.

competency). And, outcomes are the more elusive impacts on society of a school system's outputs (e.g., reduced welfare dependency, enhanced employability).

One of the strengths of the systems approach is its attention to detail and its clarity and specificity of means-ends relationships. Kaufman (1988) provides an informative example of this perspective in his treatment of the planner's key task of determining mission (the "what should be" side of the systems analysis equation). "A mission objective," Kaufman states, "is a precise statement expressed in performance terms" (p. 93). Such a statement as "Hire new teachers of exceptional quality" would be unacceptable as a viable mission objective. Rather, the objective should be expressed in measurable, attainment-oriented terminology, such as: "Over the next five years, at least 90 percent of all new faculty hires will have scored at the 95th percentile or above on the National Teachers Examination."

It is only with such a performance-related statement of mission, continues Kaufman, that the next important step in planning can proceed. This is to add function to mission—that is, to determine *what* is to be done if the mission is to be accomplished. A flow charting of tasks, needs assessments, and constraint analyses can then "flesh out" the mission, in what Kaufman terms a "mission profile" (p. 103).

The central strengths of the systems approach are its conceptual clarity and its consistent focus on a linkage of means to ends. Even without the technology of needs assessments and mission profiles, it is enormously beneficial for any school and community to ask, then attempt to answer, the simple strategic questions: "What should be" in schooling for this community, "what is" educationally for this community, and how do we get from the "is" to the "should be"? It is not at all necessary for a school's staff and its parents and community to be highly trained and sophisticated planners—for the exploration of "gaps" between the desirable and the present conditions is an extremely powerful starting point toward improving schools. How can we bring a larger percentage of our pupils up to grade level in achievement? What strategies over the next few years will upgrade the quality of our teaching staff? What activities will maximize the quality of our instruction in science?

The Strategic Leadership Approach. The major strength of the above systems approach can, however, also be a prime weakness. An emphasis on ends (and particularly measurable ends), then an effort to work systematically toward the elimination of gaps in reaching those ends, places the central focus of planning on organizational deficiencies—that is, on the elimination of gaps between the desirable and the actual. The emphasis, accordingly, is not on the strengths of the organization—what it does well—but on its weaknesses in accomplishment—what it yet needs to do in order to reach valued ends.

While neither ignoring nor downplaying the importance of analyzing problems, identifying issues, and assessing needs, John Mauriel's (1989) approach to strategic planning nevertheless emphasizes strengths, productive change, and vision above gaps in accomplishment. Strategic planning here is not quite the measurable and technocratic exercise of the systems method. It tends to be more loosely defined, less formal, and certainly less specific. In a major deviation from the systems perspective, for example, Mauriel (1989) agrees that the strategic planning process should certainly begin with a clarification of mission and organizational purpose—but it *should not* include "the *determination* or *development* of precise wording for either" (p. 135). The process of communicating, clarifying, and testing a not-so-precise mission can become, in itself, the very essence of a participative planning process.

An assessment of a school or school system's resources, strengths, and capabilities is an important early step. To be sure, an awareness of limitations will also emerge. However, this early analysis, says Mauriel (1989, p. 75), should focus on two basic questions: "What is this organization uniquely qualified to do? What can it do especially well?" In answering these questions for schools, one may wish to take a special, focused look at such key "resources" as teacher quality and experience, administrator quality, board-administrator relations, student characteristics, finances, and facilities. But no less important are such often-ignored intangibles as the reputation and image of the school system, any unique features in the development of the school system, the leadership history of the organization, the enthusiasm and motivation quotient of the school system, and the overall support of parents vis-à-vis the schools.

Out of the organization's capabilities and strengths (as well as an awareness of its limitations) emerges the strategic plan. Rather than an end-results plan, or a removal-of-gaps plan, however, the strategic leadership approach emphasizes a *change process*. Strategic planning from this perspective is a matter of implementing a collective vision for a better school (i.e., exercising leadership) rather than reaching highly specific goals.

The key difference between the two approaches to strategic planning can be illustrated by comparing Figure 8.2 with Figure 8.1. While both figures compare an organization's desired future state (what should be) with the current state (what is), Figure 8.2 indicates that the major attention in strategic planning is not so much on input or output as it is on the *transition* between present and future. The vital task of leadership in planning, notes Bunker (1989, p. 264), "should be to spearhead this transition."

Strategic planning for "transition" may require quite a different set of planning and management skills. Far from merely analyzing and manipulating resources and their effects, transition planning requires careful attention to such matters as (a) the politics of organizational change; (b) the psychology of change (e.g., the fears and insecurities of persons who are "in transition"); (c) the work-group relationships, or sociology, of change; (d) the conflict-resolution, or decision and communication, ingredients in change; and, (e) the norms, beliefs, and incentives of the changing organization. More-

Figure 8.2

Strategic Planning as a Transition Process

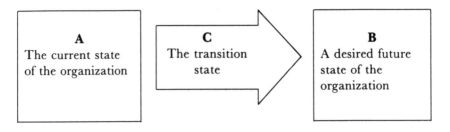

Source: Adapted with Permission from Barbara Benedict Bunker, "Leading School Systems Through Transitions." In J.J. Mauriel (ed.), *Strategic Leadership for Schools* (1989). San Francisco: Jossey-Bass, Inc., p. 265. Adapted by Bunker from R. Beckhard and R. Harris (1977), *Organizational Transitions*. Reading, Mass.: Addison-Wesley.

over, planning for transition must also pay obeisance to such important nonsystems concerns as maintaining momentum, fostering involvement, and articulating some commonly accepted symbols of the changed organization (Mauriel, 1989).

In sum, the central strength of the second ("leadership") approach to strategic planning is that it focuses heavily on the *process* of organizational improvement itself rather than the products. Although it recognizes the importance of trying to move from one organizational state to a more desired state, this second approach emphasizes strategic change above strategized effectiveness and efficiency. Accordingly, planners look for organizational strengths to build on above organizational deficiencies, value the leadership aspects of planning above the mechanical and technical, and worry less about making precise mission statements than generating a collective agreement regarding mission.

It can be extremely important to the success of process, of course, to make sure that each of the key groups of "processors" (of ideas, viewpoints, interests, positions) is well represented. Increasingly, parents and community members are being viewed and valued as process participants. However, what is often not well recognized is that parent-community advocates may often need much time to learn just what the process is all about—to have time and an opportunity to form their own judgments of both strengths and deficiencies in the school organization and to bring their own important assets to bear, as Sarason (1995, p. 46) puts it, "in regard to matters educational."

The Deliberative Approach. Maurice Holt (1987) is highly critical of the more structured routes to planning, which are represented in our first two approaches. They tend to be bureaucratic, technocratic, logistic, and mechanistic. Moreover, there is little evidence, he says, that the systems style of planning can fulfill its close-the-gaps promises—despite all of its "lists of objectives, detailed question-naires, taxonomies of categories and instruments, and performance tests of every kind" (p. 34).

Holt prefers a *deliberative* alternative. The deliberative model has also been labeled a "transactive" style of planning (Friedmann, 1973) and "collaborative planning" (Miller and Buttram, 1991), with the emphasis quite simply on collective judgment (judging with), shared values, commitment building, and empathy—above mission state-ments, needs assessments, and transition strategies.

"Planning," offers Holt (1987, p. 93), simply "means some considered—and, inevitably subjective—judgment of what values might be attached to surroundings and the quality of life they per-mit." Efforts to move from "what is" to "what should be" are fine. And, plans to change an organization from a present to a desired state are certainly welcome. But both of these approaches give insufficient first attention to a careful deliberation and inevitably a judgment of just what values reflect the collective organizational experience.

There are no hard-and-fast rules for how deliberative planning is to occur. To deliberate is to weigh and consider fully, to take time in making up one's mind, to be careful and not hasty in reaching a judgment. Beyond this think-it-through-carefully admonition, advo-cates of the deliberative approach also caution that planning should by no means try to be so "scientific" as to ignore moral considera-tions. Indeed, the careful consideration of alternative values is of such importance to effective deliberation that at least one procedural sine qua non must be to plan with sufficient participation (e.g., from teachers, parents, community representatives, students, administra-tors, support staff) to ensure that the values of every "stakeholder" group are given worthy consideration (Miller and Buttram, 1991).

The importance of this combination of participation *and* deliberation for parents is attested to by Geraldine Markel and Judith
Greenbaum (1979, p. 6), who note that parents are often "at a loss
when faced by the educational system." Anxious, aware they are
uninformed, often awed by but wary of school authorities, they can
feel simultaneously powerless, incompetent, guilty, and angry" (p. 6).
When critical of the schools, they can have teachers in mind, says
Sarason (1995), because they are still ignorant of how power is actually
allocated and protected within the school organization. An effective way to help parents resolve these conflicts, manage anxiety,
become more knowledgeable, and learn to express their own concerns, suggest Markel and Greenbaum, is to incorporate parents
into planning and help them view themselves as *problem solvers* by
allowing them to join actively in conferences and deliberations and
permitting them to "contribute to the educational planning process" (p. 115).

While there is no established procedure to be followed in
deliberative-style planning, Holt (1987, p. 90) draws informatively
from Walker (1975) in suggesting three stages. These are:

- *Platform*—the foundation of initial ideas, perspectives, and values
  shared by a deliberative body. An effort to work toward a sense of
  shared beliefs and working principles.
- *Deliberation*—"a string of episodes during which the group gives
  sustained attention to one topic or problem. The problem is stated,
  a solution proposed and *arguments* offered for or against the *proposal*.
  In the course of these *arguments* another *proposal* is made and
  arguments offered for or against this one" (Holt, 1987, p. 90).
- *Policy*—establishing agreements, plans, statements, procedures, or
  materials.

One interesting example of successful deliberative planning is that
of the development of a "constitution" for the Glenview, Illinois,
Public Schools (Community Consolidated School District #34,
1989–1992). In the 1989–90 school year, Glenview's constitution
replaced the traditional collectively bargained contract, as a set of
guidelines for professional relationships and for a reorganization of
responsibility and authority throughout the district. The constitution offered a structure for "collaborative, consensus decision-making"

in the form of a major redistribution of administrative controls to committee, councils, and faculty-selected "PEER's" (teacher-leadership specialists), who were to fulfill special curriculum and staff-development roles.

The constitution emphasized "building-based decisionmaking," with a Local School Council (LSC) for pairs or "clusters" of the district's schools, which was responsible for broad goals and expectations and for evaluating the success of the cluster's schools. Each LSC was composed of four parents, four teachers, and the principal of each cluster school. At the separate building level, each school contained a "Building Council" whose composition was left to the discretion of the staff and principal in the building and whose open-ended responsibilities were "to develop policies and/or procedures related to the organization, budget and educational program for each respective school."

There were also districtwide committees for personnel, for finance, and for the curriculum/staff-development/evaluation responsibilities included in the teacher-leadership specialist roles. These districtwide committees included three classroom teachers, a principal, a district administrator, the superintendent, and the president of the teachers' association. An additional districtwide committee was the District Coordinating Council, charged with monitoring the constitution and acting on appeals of any lower-level committee or council. The District Coordinating Council included the chairpersons of the other districtwide committees, a principal, the president of the board of education, the president of the teachers' association, and the superintendent.

The constitution's agreement was to abide by a "consensus model of decision-making," and indeed, a charge to the district's superintendent under the constitution was to "develop and implement a training program on decision-making by consensus." Beyond its emphasis and reemphasis on consensus, the explicit provisions of the constitution were remarkably minimal. Essentially it (a) established a from-the-building-up structure of committees, (b) peopled those committees, (c) provided a broad scope of responsibility for each committee (e.g., to oversee and coordinate all districtwide curriculum efforts), and then (d) left the implementation of the constitution to a shared faith in deliberation (the "consensus model").

For Glenview, such a faith was not misguided, because the constitution itself was the product of a year-long deliberative planning process. The process began with lengthy meetings to formulate shared "we believe" statements, then moved to a collective sense of district mission and a set of agreed-on principles, which together formed the preamble of the emergent constitution. Interestingly, as the product of deliberative planning, the constitution itself became hard evidence of Glenview's continuing faith in the worth (and practicality) of collegial and consensual deliberation.

Glenview's constitution set up a somewhat elaborate, perhaps too elaborate, structure to guide its deliberative planning. Interestingly, however, deliberation is not an activity that educators engage in easily. Isolation, autonomy, and minimal professional interaction are more common organizational characteristics than "talking-things-through." As a learning activity, as a set of first steps in becoming deliberative, a bit of "structure" may often be important—particularly if there is to be a concerted effort to structure-in the contributions of parents and the community.

COMMUNITY RELATIONS, SCHOOL ADMINISTRATION, AND PLANNING

Each of the strategic planning approaches has strengths and each has weaknesses. The more highly technical method of systems planning can show a community forcefully and can demonstrate with direct clarity the gap between where it wishes its schools to be and where they are in terms of measurable indicators of school effectiveness. Closing the gap is a matter of planning well to effectively use the means of education to reach valued ends. However, the simplicity of the concept of gap closing and of using resources effectively toward attaining measurable ends belies the hard administrative realities and difficulties of putting plan into practice. Both communities and school administrators can become frustrated and disenchanted as the ends of schooling fail stubbornly to respond to the means that have been conscientiously programmed to lead to the improvement of these ends.

The emphasis of a strategic leadership approach is on the source of much of that frustration—that is, the difficulties in changing the typically loath-to-change organization. Less input-output oriented, the planning process in this second model is more attuned to such "transition" variables as employee motivation, incentives and perceptions, communications, symbol management, shared values, and of course, leadership. A precisely worded goals statement may be far less important than a vision of organizational objectives; and planning from a sense of organizational strengths may be a more effective change strategy than targeting organizational weaknesses or gaps.

Interestingly, a central weakness of the second model is its possible overemphasis on change to the neglect of resources and ends. If organizational participants and their key publics are in disagreement or have conflicting interests vis-à-vis goals, or if agreement is lacking and there is widespread uncertainty about what resources to use toward what ends, the planning process may be doomed (Brown, 1986).

Thus, while not fundamentally at odds with either of the two earlier models, a third approach to planning suggests the importance of careful deliberation (whether it concerns ends, means, or transitions) as a key planning strategy in and of itself. In these democratizing, empowerment, and choice-oriented times, the deliberative model has much intuitive appeal—in that it places a premium on planning for full stakeholder participation in the determination of organizational directions.

This mode of planning has been used by small farmers in rural India, and in reporting on their efforts, L. David Brown (1986, p. 127) notes that "dialogue encouraged participants to take initiatives in analysis, discussions clarified agreements and common concerns among participants, and problem-solving exercises required participants to work collectively so [that] they learned by experience about skills required for joint action." The same set of outcomes as those in rural India would be similarly valued results in most deliberations among teachers, parents, students, administrators, and community representatives on the direction of their local schools.

Deliberation can be dangerous, however. It can bring deep conflicts and divergent interests to the surface. It can lead to politicking and coalition building. It can enormously delay getting any work done, as reaching for consensus goes on and on and on. It can bring to light uncertainties, ignorances, and philosophical differences that professionals might prefer to keep hidden from public view. It can lead to compromises and face-saving agreements that may not be the best choice of policy for the organization's clientele. But these are the chances one takes with the deliberative planning model.

SUMMARY

To many persons, planning has the image of a highly rational, centralizing exercise—something the staff of a chief executive engages in without much concern for public participation. Nevertheless, planning is experiencing a rejuvenated interest in both public and private sectors of our economy. The emphasis now is on strategic planning—in a form that includes an awareness of the environment and of the importance of value differences, and an appreciation of the worth of broadened participation. The current interest in planning has been extended to public education, with a special focus on the usefulness of planning at the local school site amid initiatives to decentralize controls from the central office to parents and teaching professionals. Three forms or models of strategic planning were examined in this chapter. One, a systems approach, would focus on gaps between what is and what should be in the effectiveness of a school. A second, a strategic leadership approach, would emphasize the planning involved in school change. A third, deliberative planning, would emphasize planning for wider participation in the decisionmaking process within schools.

Exercises
EVERYONE'S A PLANNER

Nearly every participant in school engages in some form of planning.
1. Enter into informal, one-on-one discussions with a range of school "actors": teachers, administrators, cafeteria workers, maintenance personnel, guidance counselors, students. Discover what each does as an individual to plan his or her own (a) allocation of time, (b) use of resources, and (c) work products. Do some persons think ahead and plan more actively than others? Are there differences of opinion among your respondents as to the value of planning?

2. Continue your investigation of planning in one school by discovering where and in what form any group planning occurs. Do teachers plan curricula together? Do administrative staff members plan collectively? Is there any "cross-role" planning actively underway (e.g., teachers together with parents, administrators, and support personnel)? What gets planned in group fashion (e.g., class schedules? pupil placement? curriculum development?), and what does not?

Suggested Activities

1. Develop and administer a questionnaire to survey perceptions of educational needs in one school attendance area. Administer the questionnaire to differing groups of respondents— teachers, parents, administrators, and so on. Do the respondents' perceptions of need differ significantly?
2. In discussion with a group of professional colleagues, try to identify a set of at least three gaps between what the group acknowledges as what is in their school and what should be. For each gap, consider a number of alternative strategies (plans) for the removal of the gap. What are the strengths and weaknesses of each strategy?
3. Interview a group of teachers in your school, asking them to identify the strengths of the school. Interview a second group of teachers, asking for an identification of the weaknesses of the school. List the strengths and the weaknesses—then see whether a plan for school improvement might differ significantly depending on whether one starts by looking at strengths or weaknesses.
4. Join a group of colleagues or classmates in imagining yourself a member of a faculty committee determining new standards and procedures for teacher evaluation and teacher compensation by results. Work toward a decision consensus. What problems, difficulties, and compromises accompany this search for consensus?

SUGGESTED READINGS

Bryson, J.M. (1988). *Strategic Planning for Public and Nonprofit Organizations: A Guide to Strengthening and Sustaining Organizational Achievement*. San Francisco: Jossey-Bass.

Carlson, Robert V., and Awkerman, Gary (eds.) (1991). *Educational Planning: Concepts, Strategies, Practices*. New York: Longman.

Holt, Maurice (1987). *Judgment, Planning and Educational Change*. London: Harper & Row.

Kaufman, Roger (1988). *Planning Educational Systems: A Results-Based Approach*. Lancaster, Penn.: Technomic Publishing.

Mauriel, John J. (1989). *Strategic Leadership for Schools*. San Francisco: Jossey-Bass.

Witkin, Belle Ruth (1984). *Assessing Needs in Educational and Social Programs*. San Francisco: Jossey-Bass.

Chapter Nine

PARENTAL INVOLVEMENT

There was a man named Jensen who had a big boy attending the school where you are planning to teach. The boy was in trouble. I had to see Jensen, but since I had been warned that he was a dangerous man and that I mustn't go near his house unarmed, I borrowed a revolver.
—David J. Malcolm, *The Letters of a Country School Superintendent to His Daughter*, 1927, p. 4

Although it did not quite have the tension of a "High Noon," David Malcolm's recollection of his turn-of-the-century meeting with the parents of a wayward pupil was certainly thrill enough for a country schoolteacher. Stopping his horse, old Molly, within sight of the Jensen farmhouse, Malcolm loaded the revolver, then bravely faced an angry father and a torrent of "cuss words." After talking nearly two hours, Malcolm "began to think that perhaps I would not have to kill the man after all" (p. 5). Finally, and with a gift of maple sugar from the family, Malcolm rode away—assured "that they were grateful to me for being honest and straightforward with them" (p. 5).

Weapons aside, the tribulations of educators in meetings with angry parents are "the story" of school-site management no less today than yesterday. Public education has always been firmly, and often fiercely, in contact with its community at the level of the individual school. School board and chamber of commerce dimensions of school-community interaction are far removed from the often emotional encounters between school officials and children and parents. Academic failure and success, the distribution of rewards and opportunities, the realities of ability versus expectation, the burdens of accepting responsibility and experiencing competition—all these are the stressful forces that surround the relations of the school with its parental community, then as now.

If the individual school has always been the focal point of community relations, its importance in the near future is likely to increase manifold because education is now immersed in a reform movement that is steadily transferring autonomy to the local school while empowering the teachers within the school. By no means, however, does either autonomy or empowerment remove the tensions in school-parent relations or calm the stressors behind these tensions. Indeed, these may be increasing—for an "estranged public," says Bradley (1996b, p. 20), is beginning to express new expectations for involvement. It is the central purpose of both this chapter and the next to examine the implications of reform-minded changes in school-site governance, in parental-involvement, and to suggest some practical measures for managing and improving community relations under reform.

THE TRADITION OF PARENTAL INVOLVEMENT

In our vignette of the "Showdown at the Jensen's Farm-house," David Malcolm was communicating a bit of hard-earned knowledge to his daughter who was about to take a job as a one-room school-teacher in the same district Malcolm had served in years earlier. In a later letter, Malcolm (1927, p. 80) passed on some practical advice about planning for a parents' night:

Sandwiches, cake, and coffee (but cocoa for the children) are all that are needed to satisfy everyone. You should take special pains with the sandwiches, however, to see that they are dainty and delicious. Since you must not run the risk of insulting anyone by trying to tell her how to make sandwiches, be careful in selecting the people whom you ask to make them. If it so happens that no one in the district knows the difference between a sandwich and two slabs of bread and a slice of meat, then you had better make them yourself.

Fortunately for educators in most neighborhoods, sandwich, cookie, and brownie makers are to be found in abundance—and it is seldom necessary for the teacher to "make them herself." However, this getting folks together, complete with foodstuffs, covered in David Malcolm's advice is part of a great and valued tradition in local education. The "open house" or parents' night has deep historical roots and is still a fixture of school-community relations. Even today, when both parents in a home often work, many elementary schools continue to ask "room mothers" to coordinate a bit of classroom partying through the year (e.g., for Halloween or Valentine's Day). And school bazaars, game nights, carnivals, and "haunted house" transformations at Halloween are still common throughout public education.

This coffee-and-sandwiches tradition has important nineteenth-century roots in an integration of school and community (Tyack, 1974; Fuller, 1982; Spring, 1986). The nineteenth-century school was a "social institution" (Tyack, 1974, p. 17) as well as a place of concentrated book learning; it was a place where dainty and delicious sandwiches could be just as important as the three Rs in communicating a neighborhood's faith that the public school is *the* path to upward mobility.

What's wrong with this great tradition? Is it not just as important as ever for today's school site to be a community center, a social institution? The tradition is perhaps much more difficult in this age of magnet schools, paired schools, and bused-in enrollments—but for these reasons it is perhaps an even more important function now than before. Schools today tend to be more cosmopolitan and therefore more than ever in need of the ties that "getting together" provides.

There is nothing wrong with the tradition, note critics; and to be sure, the school as a "social" institution is a vital aspect of good school-community relations. Nevertheless, continue the critics, there is something problematic in the "old" tradition of parental involvement in the schools; and the whole notion bears careful reexamination. At least in part, reexamination is needed, observes Susan Swap (1993, p. 13), because parents and teachers now agree on the importance of parent involvement while simultaneously "parent involvement in the schools is surprisingly minimal."

The criticism can often be found in the research conclusions following investigations into parental involvement at the school site. One finding is that parental involvement is frequently *guided*, even manipulated, by local school authorities (Wong, 1990). Van Cleve Morris and colleagues (1984), for example, found building principals busily "socializing" and reeducating parents into behaviors acceptable to the school. Principals were observed to mitigate and screen parental demands in such sensitive areas of professional discretion as disciplinary action, homework or grading policy, teaching style, and curricular emphasis. Similarly, parents were carefully manipulated into reshaping their expectations of school responsiveness into limits permitted by the school. As a reward to certain parents for "acceptable" behavior, principals would often go far out of their way to secure special individual help, extra resources, a bending of school district rules, or some outside community services. For less compliant parents, the response may be "Those are the rules," with no special consideration offered (Morris et al., 1984, pp. 116–121).

A second finding is that parental involvement has often been *constrained* into professionally acceptable roles within the school. Enlisting parents as sponsors of field trips and partners in fundraising via candy sales, bakery goods exchanges, and holiday bazaars has for years marked the limits of parental intrusion into the curriculum of the school. From the late 1960s on, however, it became increasingly common to find parents employed in paraprofessional capacities— often with close-to-instruction duties as teachers' aides. Nevertheless, the teacher and aide relationship has not always been smooth, with common complaints by teachers that the aides often try to "take on" the professionally trained teacher's work (Crowson, 1974). Innovations in recent years have continued to open the local school to tutorial help from retirees, parent-sponsored interventions such as READ, and parent-advisory participation on curriculum committees. Still, the typical school remains warily protective of its professional prerogatives and maintains a careful (often subtle) distancing between parental involvement and teachers' work roles.

A third criticism is that educators traditionally have perceived parental involvement in local schooling as a *representational* rather than a participatory activity. Increasingly, schools and school districts have shown a good-politics-minded willingness to reach out for parental advice, especially as critical and potentially controversial decisions must be made. As a superintendent interviewed by R. Bruce McPherson and colleagues (1986, p. 12) put it in a school-closing case: "With the first, I just went to the board and said 'We should close Wildwood.' Well, Wildwood is still open today. By the time we'd reached our fourth closing, we'd figured it out. We had meetings on the closing nearly every night—wore the opposition down." Although wearing down the opposition is only infrequently the object of obtaining parents' advise, the effort to elicit a cross section of parental viewpoint, through representation, usually is. Schools are famous for using the "Noah's Ark Principle" in forming advisory committees— two from this ethnic group, two from that one; two from the east side of town, two from the west side; two business types, two blue-collar people.

To be sure, meaningful representation is at the heart of American democracy. Better decisions, of wider acceptability, derive from a consideration of well-represented group interests. The difficulty, critics charge, is that a representational way of thinking about parental involvement can be far removed from a participatory attitude toward parents. Furthermore, family demographics have been changing over the last few decades with astonishing rapidity. It is not at all easy, any longer, to determine just what "representation" means (e.g., whose interests in just what combination of family styles and backgrounds?) (Swap, 1993).

An oft-used illustration of the dark side of a representational approach is the typical special education staffing (or pupil-placement meeting) required under the provisions of Public Law 94-142. Surrounded by professionals (teachers, psychologists, social workers, administrators), the parents at a staffing are usually informed of a recommended special education placement for their child, told of the scientific rationale behind this placement, informed of the expected improvements in the child's performance as a result of the placement, and asked for parental approval of the placement. At the staffing, parents are expected to represent adequately their side of the placement equation; they are encouraged to ask questions and are further encouraged to communicate their own perceptions of the child's developmental and educational needs. However, many emotion-filled parents are so thoroughly intimidated by the presence of an array of highly educated professionals, all offering negative-sounding judgments about the parents' offspring, that they tend to be little capable of effectively representing their own familial interests. They tend to sign and leave, having said little (see Illich et al., 1977; Baker, 1989; Espe-Sherwindt and Kerlin, 1990).

Finally, critics of parental involvement strategies charge that parents have typically been the *passive* recipients of information from the schools rather than active members of the teaching-learning community (Cervone and O'Leary, 1982).

The typical high school open house is a good illustration. Parents gather initially in the auditorium or gymnasium for welcoming remarks from the school's administration. Then, in ten-minute intervals, the parents follow their child's class schedule in a shortened version of the school day. After the confusion of finding the right classroom for each subject, the parents listen briefly to the English, or history, or chemistry teacher explain the course of study and the teacher's expectations for student performance. A bell rings and the parents rush to the next classroom on the schedule, after perhaps taking a bit of time for a handshake with the teacher they just met. There is no time for dialogue; and the evening ends informally with coffee and cake in the cafeteria—a get-together most of the faculty avoids.

Beyond such special events as the open house, the school's consideration of parents throughout the year tends to be dominated by an information-reporting or a spectator philosophy. Newsletters, parent-teacher conferences, and "good news notes" all tend to be highly valued communications; and parents excitedly watch their children perform in the annual music festival, dance club recital, or class play. Nevertheless, continue the critics, the emphasis remains on the parent as a passive participant in (and recipient of) one-way, school-directed communications rather than as a member of an active, two-way parent-relations process.

Passiveness can also have the side-effect of a normative separation of the instructional roles of parents from the instructional roles of the schools (e.g., what *should* the school do, what *should* parents do?). Indeed, some educators in earlier years urged parents not to "confuse" their children by becoming too active in the learning process. Consider these reminiscences from a person thinking back, nearly four decades lalter, about some changes in her own family's "involement" in learning:

My mother had been a primary-grades school teacher in a 2-room school when she was 18 to 21 from 1931 to 1933. When her oldest son began school in 1945, she was very involved in providing parental support at home that reinforced the lessons he was given at the school. She listened to him read, went over his spelling words with him until he knew them, made certain that he memorized his math tables and that he understood the applications he was learning, talked with him about his geography lessons, and went over his homework with him after he had completed it.

In the spring before her youngest child started to school in 1952, my mother started back to college to work toward a degree in education. She was told during this time by the "educators" who were her professors that parents should keep hands-off and let the teaching be done solely by the child's teacher to avoid the parents' "confusing" the child. She listened to her professors and did not actively involve herself in her youngest child's learning progress. Her two sons were relatively equal in intelligence and in their ability to relate to their peers. But the older son achieved far beyond the younger one, both in schoolwork and in community activities.

The older son participated in Boy Scouts, played in the band, was a first-stringer on the football, basketball, and track teams, and was a B+ student. The younger son was, from the sixth grade on, a discipline problem for the teachers and for his parents. He was a mischievous, laugh-a-minute, hard-drinking, wild-driving teenager; but he was not mean or a trouble-maker type. He participated in sports in junior high but was too small in size to be on the high school varsity teams and dropped out of sports at the end of his freshman year; his grades were C's, D's, and F's; he did not go through the high school graduation ceremony with his class but had to go to summer school to get his diploma. In comparing the two sons at the time they finished high school, the older son had a much more solid sense of self-worth; more productive self-discipline; a greater sense that he was appreciated and valued—by his parents, his teachers, his coaches, and other adults; and a better understanding of how to build positive relationships with others in the community.

In college, the older son was captain of the track team, a leading member of several clubs, and was selected "most popular" by his classmates. At the same college, the younger son lived off campus and never participated in any of the school's organizations; he did pass all his coursework and graduated in four years. Now that they are middle-aged, the younger brother has caught up with his older sibling and is a successful businessman and a past-president of his local Chamber of Commerce. But he took a lot of flack along the way. Life has been very much harder for him. I have many times thought that if, during the primary grades, he had been given the attention from his mother that his older brother had received, life would have been much smoother for him. It appears to me that it is not only the reinforcement of what he was learning at school that was missing in his life but also the undivided attention of his parent—the special attention that a child gets when being given out his spelling words, when practicing his reading, when saying his math tables. This must be a very valuable factor in the development of a child's self-worth, of a child's perception of where he stands in relationship to the world around him.

You may ask, "But what about yourself?" I was the middle child, the quiet one, the book-reader, the A student. I played in the band and was on the basketball and softball teams from sixth grade through high school. I received the music medal and the scholarship medal at the end of my sophomore year; I was third-best flute player in the state contest during my junior year; my classmates chose me to be editor of the high school paper during our senior year; and I was salutatorian of my class. However, my self-esteem was very low, and I thought much less of myself than my classmates and teachers thought of me (learned from their comments and interactions with me as the years, 36, have gone by). I remember my mother helping me *one* time with my homework—in the third grade when I couldn't understand fractions, and she found me crying over my homework. Although I didn't need her help to understand my schoolwork, did I need those times of special, undivided attention? I'm sure that I did.

For too many years, the education profession has undervalued the role of parents as teachers of their children. They have encouraged parents to discipline their children, to provide them with the time and place suitable for doing homework, to see that the children are fed a balanced diet, reminded to brush their teeth, and sent to bed to get sufficient sleep at night. We have seldom read any literature emphasizing the importance of the time parents spend teaching their children daily living skills—cooking, cleaning, clothing care, house repairs, auto maintenance. And parents were discouraged from being actively involved in the schoolwork of the children for two generations, so that current parents do not even have parental role-models to remember as guidelines for their own involvement in their children's learning. [Personal vignette volunteered, in discussion, by a member of the author's community]

EMERGENT FORMS OF PARENTAL INVOLVEMENT

Table 9.1 summarizes researchers' criticisms of parental-involvement strategies, as these have typically (traditionally) been implemented at the school site.

All too often, claim the critics, parental involvement is *guided* (even shaped) toward modes of interaction, patterns of behavior, and topics of discussion that are acceptable to the school. Additionally, the involvement of parents is typically *constrained* by separate role expectations for professionals and nonprofessionals, including some strains between them. Third, much of the involvement of parents in the local school, even that legally mandated in the special education staffing, tends to be viewed by school authorities as a *representational* rather than fully participatory activity. Finally, parental involvement has tended to mean a *passive* and recipient role for parents rather than an active relationship with the school.

One fear, not without justification, is that the school-reform movement toward teacher empowerment and professionalization could *add* to a distancing of teachers from parents. As the schools change, ambiguities and uncertainties can increase (Glickman, 1990; Malen and Ogawa, 1990; Louis and Kruse, 1995). The short-term response, despite the goal of democratization, could be to try to reduce uncertainty by additionally guiding and constraining parental involvement. For this reason, it is important for emerging forms of school-community relations to be thoroughly understood not only as new perspectives on parent roles in schools but as important elements as well in the larger reform of public education.

Table 9.2 offers four emergent forms of parental involvement, as

Table 9.1

Traditional Forms of Parental Involvement at the School Site

	Traditional	Emergent
Forms of Parental Involvement	Guided	
	Constrained	
	Representational	
	Passive	

Table 9.2

Traditional and Emergent Forms of Parental Involvement at the School Site

	Traditional	Emergent
Forms of Parental Involvement	Guided	Responsive
	Constrained	Open
	Representational	Participative
	Passive	Active

alternatives to the four traditional, often criticized forms discussed in the previous section. These new forms are *responsive, open, participative,* and *active.* Each is described below.

Responsiveness. Janet Atkin and John Bastiani (1988) warn that all of the rhetoric about cooperation and partnership is "cozy and uplifting." However, an improvement of school-community relations might best begin with the basic and seemingly simple task of *listening to parents.*

This can be a surprisingly difficult thing to do. Parents bring to school their complaints and concerns. They also ask often for a bit of special treatment, or extra help, or some favoritism to be shown to their own offspring. They can cover up, offer excuses, and overprotect their children, while placing blame for problems on the children of other parents. They can be "stressed to the max" in their own worklives and "volatile" when they feel "that they or their child's rights have been impinged upon" (Ogawa and Studer, 1996, p. 13). They can also harm collegial relations by complaining to Miss Brown about Mrs. Jones' teaching, and vice versa. Somewhat harshly, Jack Greenstein (1983, p. 31) concludes: "We must recognize that there is often a convenient transference of guilt to the teacher by parents who know that their own efforts and those of their children have been inadequate."

Beyond a goodly amount of patience vis-à-vis these negatives, the act of listening responsively to parents can require considerable understanding of where the parents' concerns come from—or where, through self-understanding, one's own viewpoints originate. Furthermore, schools have not learned how to deal constructively with conflict, nor do they have traditions of finding and spending the time necessary for either handling crises or building relationships (Swap, 1993). Figure 9.1, adapted from Atkin and Bastiani (1988), suggests five important areas of separate understanding (and potential misunderstanding) between parents and teachers.

For example, parents bring to their meetings with teachers a deep sense of their own contributions to their child's development. This usually stems from an intimate knowledge of the child from birth on, from years of past experience as a family of origin, and from years of communication between parent and child. Teachers can often be skeptical of the parent's interpretation of the child's needs and abili-

Figure 9.1

What Teachers and Parents Bring to Their Conversations

Parents Bring		Teachers Bring
1. A view of their own contributions to their children's learning	*Mediated by*	1. A view of their professional status
2. A view of the status of teachers		2. A view of parental status in the learning process
3. A philosophy of education	Class, Culture Race, Gender	3. A philosophy of education
4. Outsider knowledge of a particular school		4. Insider knowledge of a particular school
5. Stage in the family life cycle	The Child	5. Stage in the schooling system

Adapted from J. Atkin and J. Bastiani (1988). *Listening to Parents*, Figure 4.1 (The Making of Home/School Relations), p. 24.

ties, can fail to understand that the child's at-home persona may be quite different from her or his at-school persona, and can denigrate the intimate (one-child) knowledge of the parent from the viewpoint of the broader (many-children) knowledge and training of the professional (Heck and Williams, 1984).

Teachers usually bring a formal philosophy to their work, plus a sense of status or role; but parents are similarly equipped. A parent's philosophy of education may not be easily articulated and may not be a conscious or reflective artifact, but it is often found in the parent's expectation of the educational system and the parent's questions and concerns about his or her children's experiences in school. Annette Lareau (1989) discovered, for example, that when the Colton School (in California) dropped letter grades in favor of growth-in-performance comments, the school's (largely Hispanic) community was angered and perplexed. To the parents, their children's opportunities for and progress toward upward mobility in the United States were clearly and cleanly represented by an A or a B on the report card. Anything else amounted to shortchanging the lives and futures of their children.

Not often credited sufficiently by teachers (who after all are "inside") is the parents' "outside" knowledge of a particular school. Schools and their teachers have reputations in the neighborhood. There are networks of parental acquaintances who pass on suggestions, stories, here's-what-happened-to-Sally warnings, and teacher-by-teacher judgments. Parents draw conclusions from the experiences of an older child in a school, just as teachers can approach every child from the Smith family warily, after their experiences with eldest son Richard. Neither the perceptions of parents nor the perceptions of teachers tend to be fully justified. But they are seldom completely unjustified; and a bit of careful listening can garner useful information (Lightfoot, 1978; Heck and Williams, 1984).

Finally, although it is something that school professionals recognize and do credit as important to success in school, the impact of each child's "family life cycle" is not usually a matter of shared home-school understanding. Educators are well aware that latchkey situations, single-parent families, unemployed-parent households, and frequent-mover families can all display home-to-school learning effects. Yet, although parents will often share with teachers some personal struggles with a divorce, sudden illness, or recent job loss, it is usually uncomfortable for teachers to learn of these problems, and it is not considered professional for teachers to make special provisions for one or two in a classroom of thirty-five children. Consequently, the educator's practical knowledge of the specific family life cycle effects on learning remains rather meager.

A *responsive* school should not be asked to lose its own professional identity and pander to parents, but there are ways in which the typical school can improve its capacity for *listening* to parents. Here, for example, are just a few ideas for the elementary-level teacher that Susan Swap (1987, pp. 26–27) has gleaned from practicing teachers: (a) a breakfast conference with parents before school starts; (b) a parent get-together in the evening, early in the school year; (c) a fathers' (or mothers' or grandparents') workshop wherein dads are invited to share special skills or interests; (d) an open invitation to parents to join the class for lunch; (e) a special day to share family backgrounds for each child, at some time during the year, with parents invited; and (f) a potluck meal, with each family supplying its own special dish. Swap (p. 31) notes that one of the best ways to open up a two-way listening environment is to provide occasions wherein parents as well as teachers can be "just people" with one another (e.g., breakfasts, potluck dinners, Saturday morning activities).

Bradley (1996, p. 1) has described one school district near Seattle that pushed the notion of responsiveness to a new level, with "multilayered" efforts to reach out to parents and the community. There is full involvement at a "policy level" (e.g., setting standards, designing schools, hiring principals) as well as constant involvement at a learning-together level (e.g., math nights, bedtime story nights, focus group meetings). Uniquely, the district has also distributed a "calendar" of the curriculum framework as well as brochures and videos to parents that describe in detail the ingredients in, and provide examples around, the district's standardized testing program.

An Open School. It is one thing to suggest to the school that it needs to listen to parents and be more responsive to their concerns, problems, and needs. It is quite another to suggest that the public school should take positive steps to open *itself*, warts and all, to parental and community scrutiny.

It is no secret to anyone familiar with educational environments that inside the four walls of the school, staff rivalries, hostilities, power politics, pedagogical differences, and long-lasting feuds can abound. Behind any school's veneer of professionalism can be strains between factions, between departments, between faculty and administration, between the "old guard" and some "young Turks." These conflicts tend to be kept hidden from parents. Indeed, a strong norm of teaching is to refrain from any washing of a school's dirty linen in the presence of outsiders. The faculty of the Hawthorne School may agree fully that Mr. Wilson is a burned-out educator who has come to hate his job and now dislikes kids, but it would be wrong professionally to share this consensus with persons who are not faculty or staff colleagues.

For this reason, there are legitimate concerns when proponents of a fully open school-community relationship suggest the benefits of an *equal* partnership. Such a partnership, urges Ryan (1976), implies a full *sharing* of concerns, as well as risks and benefits. Indeed, continues Ryan (p. 17), the sense of "colleagueship" that drives the sharing and keeping of faculty and staff secrets should be extended to parents and the nearby community.

Risky business; and is there much to be gained from such an open partnership? Yes, if done correctly, suggest Gary Wehlage and colleagues (1989) in *Reducing the Risk*. One key is to open the school in a manner that communicates a broad *sense of school membership* to the school's many publics—a sense of collegial sharing that places trust in the positive and productive roles of parents when given insider information, no less than the school trusts its professionals. Some practical suggestions, offers Carl Marburger (1990), are to:

1. Create a school that's open, helpful, and friendly.
2. Communicate clearly and frequently with parents (about school policies and programs or about their children's progress).
3. Treat parents as co-workers in the educational process.
4. Encourage parents, formally and informally, to comment on school policies and to share in some of the decision making.
5. Get every family involved, not simply those most easily reached. Pay special attention to parents who work outside the home, divorced parents without custody, and families of minority race and language.
6. Make sure that the principal and other school administrators actively express and promote the philosophy of partnership with all families.
7. Encourage volunteer participation from parents and other members of the community. [Pp. 87–88]

Participative Parental Interaction. William Firestone (1977, p. 280) quotes a classroom teacher, who observed about her school: "Parents would struggle to get the least little word in. . . . I've watched school systems make parents feel they don't have any right to interfere." Interference, of course, is exactly what educators fear most; and it is primarily for this reason that the schools have historically been ready to offer representational involvement to parents but seldom much participation. Participation, says Don Davies (1981, p. 86), can be defined as citizen and parental influence "in the most significant areas of school affairs: budget, personnel, and programs."

Budget, personnel, and programs are exactly the areas of the most jealously guarded professional control in schooling. What does the professional community stand to gain by broadening participation in these domains of school decisionmaking? Although much additional research is needed, and such fully participatory reforms as Chicago's remain to be fully evaluated, the evidence to date is that broadened participation in decisionmaking improves the local school.

First, it is claimed that a participatory/partnership approach to decisionmaking can yield a common effort toward attaining common goals (Seeley, 1982; Moles, 1982). Interactive, supportive relationships between the home and school are possible, ending a destructive distinction between client and provider—each of whom usually blames the other for failure (Heck and Williams, 1984). Indeed, a productively redefined "social contract" is possible, joining the teacher and parent in the realization that each supplies a vital resource toward reaching shared objectives (Olson, 1990b).

Second, there is evidence that participation can translate into what Alberto Ochoa and Vahac Mardirosian (1990) have termed a "transformational empowerment" of parents. That is, by participating, parents themselves can be "empowered" toward becoming (a) more actively engaged in teaching their own children, and (b) more receptive of "parent leadership training" toward the improvement of their home-based teaching skills (see Ochoa and Mardirosian, 1990; also, reports of the Academic Development Institute, 1990b).

Third, the indications are that a cooperative participation/partnership between school and home can raise school achievement (Henderson, 1981, 1987; Walberg, 1986; Gordon, 1976; Epstein, 1985; Olson, 1990b; Dornbusch and Wood, 1989; Reynolds, 1989). The reasoning is simple and compelling, as illustrated in N. Ray Hiner's (1989) quotation of a remark by James Coleman (1988b):"If there is one thing that recent research has shown, it is that a child's education depends on what goes on in that child's life, not merely on what goes on in that child's school." Herbert Walberg (1984) adds teeth to this observation by noting that twelve years of schooling add up to about 13 percent of a child's waking life in his or her first eighteen years. During this same period, parents nominally control 87 percent of a student's waking time. Walberg (1984, p. 397) concludes with the question: "Can educators and parents cooperate to use this out-of-school time more efficiently for the welfare of students and of the nation?"

The evidence thus far is that through parental involvement and cooperative home-school partnerships, Walberg's question can be answered positively. Lynn Olson (1990b, p. 20) summarizes Anne Henderson's (1987) synthesis of research as follows:

- Students in schools that maintain frequent contact with their communities outperform those in other schools.
- Children whose parents are in touch with the school score higher on standardized tests than do children of similar aptitude and family background whose parents are not involved.

● Students who are failing in school improve dramatically when their parents are called in to help.

One of the central difficulties in moving toward a more participative form of community relations, however, is that parents are often reluctant to join the partnership. The reasons for this can be many. The demands of breadwinning and parenting can leave little time for becoming involved in the school. A residue of distrust and wariness can continue to fuel parental apathy and anger toward the public school long after the school changes from closed to open (Comer, 1986). There has been an "erosion of confidence" in the public schools among parents (Gamble, 1996, p. 13). Parents in some neighborhoods (and particularly from some cultural backgrounds) may feel that it is *the school's* job to educate and that it is not proper for parents to interfere (Ogbu, 1974). Finally, parents may avoid contact with the schools simply because they feel out of place, insecure, and ill-prepared to converse with college-educated professionals.

For these reasons, the effort to secure participation must often rest on schools' doing some hard work in "outreaching" to the community. James Comer (1986, p. 444) warns, furthermore, that unfortunately "even when parents are invited into schools, there is frequently no mechanism for using them effectively to improve the relationships there."

In this regard, Susan Swap (1987) notes that improving school-community relations most commonly begins with the formation of a school advisory council, with about equal representation from parents and teachers. The secret to ensuring advisory council effectiveness, with carryover into the whole tenor of parental involvement, is the degree to which parents are authoritatively involved in decision-making concerning the significant areas of school affairs: budget, personnel, and programs (Swap, 1987, pp. 89–92).

Active Parental Involvement. A good description of the participatory form of involvement might be: "Parents as cooperative educational decision makers"; or in another, complementary vein: "Parents as teachers." The notion turns the parent as a passive recipient and client into a more active and coequal teaching partner.

The reexamination of a long-accepted historical interpretation of the relationship between families and schools provides a background to this fourth form of involvement. Until recently, historians believed that industrialization destroyed the capacity of the (extended) family to act as the primary vehicle for preparing children for adult life and work. The inability of the family to educate its children adequately for an industrializing society spurred a demand for public schooling. The school became *the* central agency for the transition to adulthood (Hiner, 1989).

Modern historians and ethnographers now find that this interpretation erred significantly in its overemphasis on the power of the school and on its undervaluing of the family as a viable source of twentieth-century socialization (Clark, 1983; Hiner, 1989; Mintz, 1989). From family and kinship assistance in the immigrant experience; to the transmission of core cultural knowledge, linguistic skills, and values; to the provision of role models; to the development of a sense of self as well as a sense of mutual responsibility—it is the family that continues to serve as the child's primary educator (see Ogbu, 1974; Clark, 1983; Comer, 1980).

Within the public schools, a casualty of the earlier historial interpretation was a respect for, and an understanding of, the family's role in a child's education, which school and home share (Epstein, 1985). It just was not within the educator's conceptual framework to understand that *both* parents and school authorities are teachers—and that they might be more effective as active partners in instruction than as independent (and often antagonistic) forces.

This historically influenced interpretation is changing among educators, and schools across the country are now reaching out to parents as fellow educators. Extremely influential has been the Parents as Teachers (PAT) program of family support and early intervention started as the Harvard Family Research Project and adopted throughout Missouri's public schools. A much discussed and rapidly spreading brainchild of Stanford's Henry Levin—the Accelerated Schools Program—includes a heavy emphasis on the involvement of parents in their children's education. The attractive and rapidly disseminating ideas of James Comer, in an approach that integrates children's services in inner-city schooling, include a heavy emphasis on active parenting (see Reed and Sautter, 1990). And, a growing organization, the Family Study Institute, has developed an elaborate program of school-by-school parent education, using a unique intervention model that combines assistance to parents in guiding their children's learning with teacher education and building-level assistance to parents in becoming partners in the determination of school goals (see Family Study Institute, 1990).

ORGANIZING THE SCHOOL FOR PARENTAL INVOLVEMENT

The transition to an emergent style of school-community relations and parental involvement is unlikely to be reached through some wishful thinking, right-mindedness, or good intentions. Schools must be carefully *organized* for responsive, open, participative, and active relationships with parents.

As in other goal areas (e.g., school effectiveness), the evidence is that the building principal's role is a key to success (Sergiovanni, 1996). Mitchell Koza and Wayne Levy (1977–78) found that irrespective of the school *district's* emphasis on community relations, the individual building principal's *receptivity to the community* was the single most important determinant of any community-relations differences between one school and another. Indeed, similar research (Goldring, 1986) discovered that even when district superintendents evaluate principals on the degree of parental involvement, the principals in what are perceived as "uncertain" (e.g., overly assertive, hostile, demanding) neighborhoods would still, more than likely, fail to meet the superintendent's expectations of openness.

The principal's role becomes no less difficult in the context of a school-reform movement and teacher empowerment. A deeply held norm of the profession, for example, is that it is the principal's responsibility to "back the teacher up" in showdowns with parents (Becker, 1961; Morris et al., 1984). Indeed, as described earlier, the principal serves teachers professionally by buffering them from an occasionally turbulent environment (Crowson and Porter-Gehrie, 1980; Goldring, 1986). By no means is "turbulence" or are "showdowns" likely to disappear as the school takes steps to become more open, receptive, and participatory. Teacher expectations of administrative backup could even increase as added stress on professionalism occurs. Simultaneously, parental pressures on teachers and the administration could increase as the school delivers new messages of openness and receptiveness.

Ellen Goldring (1990) provides a comparative case study of

community relations in two Israeli schools, which illustrates the problem nicely. In one school, the principal took many reform-minded steps to establish active parent committees and to increase parental participation in the "informal" aspects of schooling (e.g., social events, afternoon enrichment courses). The principal drew a clear line, however, against parental intervention "in areas which should be left to the experts" (p. 20). Unfortunately, serious conflicts developed in this school as parents attempted to "discuss problems" with the principal; and eventually a parent-drafted restatement of school goals was accomplished, without even discussing it with the principal.

In Goldring's second case-study school, interestingly, the principal was far less enamored of parental involvement. Nevertheless, the school had long had an identifiable "ideology" of its own, and a widely shared (between school and family) sense of mission. Moreover, parents had long felt free to express their opinions (and to be heard) regarding "all aspects of the school's functioning" (p. 21). Goldring concludes: "The extent to which parents are an integral part of the school's community in terms of the definition of the school's ideology, mission, and value system (rather than being called upon to support or aid the school in fulfilling its ideology), will be a major factor in determining principal-parent interactions" (p. 2). Sergiovanni (1996) adds that one important aspect of a shared sense of mission may be a collective vision of the school as simultaneously a learning, a caring, and an inquiring community.

John Ogbu (1974) tells a story similar to Ellen Goldring's in his analysis of school-community relations in the low-income community of "Burgherside." School authorities repeatedly stressed the need for parents and community to become more involved in the education of their children, showing more interest in their children's education and learning some techniques to help their children succeed in school. However, by "involvement," notes Ogbu (p. 171), the school district meant that "Burghersiders should participate in the noncurriculum programs such as PTA, open house, and other social entertainment planned by the school staff." "Because they feel powerless to change what they do not like about the schools," concludes Ogbu (p. 175), "Burghersiders do not participate in PTA and other school affairs, and parents do not go to the teachers, the principals, the superintendent, or the school board to ask for a change."

The secret, suggest both Roland Barth (1990) and Thomas Sergiovanni (1996), is in large part lodged once again within the role of the building principal. Long seen authoritatively as a "knower," and as a buffer for other "knowers" (i.e., teachers) in the school, the principal must strive to serve the school "under a burden of presumed competence" (p. 70). Being a knower in a decidedly uncertain profession is a heavy burden. Change the image, suggests Barth, and change one's conception of oneself as a principal from *knower* to *learner* (perhaps "head learner"). Learners recognize that they do not have all the answers; and they realize that they can usually profit most from many rather than few sources of instruction. The best school, offer Barth and Sergiovanni, might be the school wherein teachers, parents, pupils, and administration have managed to become "a community of learners" or, alternatively, an "inquiring community" (see also Greene, 1994). Such a community would be responsive rather than guided, open rather than constrained, participatory rather than representational, and active rather than passive.

SUMMARY

The individual school is the focal point of community relations. While representatives of the community serve the school district as its formal policymaking body, it is nevertheless at the schoolsite where the *real* work of community and parental engagement goes on—where the educator stops "Old Molly," dismounts, and turns reluctantly to face the grim-visaged parents of "that Jensen boy."

By no means have the individual schools ignored parents and the interests and concerns of parents. And, the schools have always recognized that without the support of parents, particularly in the discipline and control of young learners, the teacher's job is far from professionally ideal. Nevertheless, the tradition of parental involvement over the years has tended toward an arms-length distancing of parent from professional rather than an active partnership. Acts of guiding parents, constraining their depth of involvement, seeking their representation, and asking for their support have tended to define "involvement." Alternatively, a recently emerging paradigm of school-community relations suggests a more responsive (particularly listening) approach to parents, an open school, an encouragement of participative rather than representational parental involvement, and a transition toward an active partnership in learning.

Interestingly, the proponents of more active partnerships now warn that without *much greater* attention to parental involvement, the public schools may be in danger of failing to "win back" an increasingly "estranged public" (Bradley, 1996b, p. 1).

Exercise
ANALYZING PARENTAL INVOLVEMENT PRACTICES

1. As a class project, survey through interviews and/or questionnaires the parent-involvement practices of a sample of schools. Choose schools representing a range of districts and communities.
2. Make a list and briefly describe every form of parental involvement represented in each school (e.g., open houses, newsletters, PTA activities, the use of parent volunteers).
3. Attempt to categorize the activities on each list in terms of the traditional versus emergent forms of involvement shown in Table 9.2. What problems of definition and categorization do you encounter? Do some activities defy categorization—for what reasons?
4. Analyze the categorized activities. Do schools differ from "open" to "guided" or "constrained"? Are some schools evidencing combinations of both traditional and emergent parent-involvement types?

Suggested Activities

1. Observe (as an ethnographer) a group gathering of parents and educators in a local school (e.g., an open house, a PTA meeting, a "coffee," an honors society induction, a student performance, an advisory council meeting). What interactions occur between teachers and parents? Are there many? Few? How would you describe the tone of these interactions? Relaxed? Standoffish? Strained?

2. Ask a few veteran teachers to recall any memorably difficult parent interactions over the course of their careers. Record the teachers' stories of these incidents, including their opinions of how these incidents might have influenced them professionally.

3. You are an elementary or secondary teacher interested in encouraging the parents of your pupils to visit your classroom at their convenience, observing school in session. Draft a persuasive letter to go to the parents of your pupils, attempting to make them feel warmly welcome and genuinely wanted as a classroom visitor and observer.

4. Divide the community-relations class into four groups, one for each form of parental involvement identified in Table 9.2. Discuss ways in which "guided" parental involvement could become "responsive," "constrained" remade into "open," and so on. Consider the professional gains and losses that would accompany these transitions.

5. Consider Roland Barth's challenge to principals to become the "head learner" in their schools. Just what does this mean, in behavioral terms, for principals? What differences might there be in principals' daily interactions with teachers, parents, students, and other staff members?

SUGGESTED READINGS

Atkin, Janet, and Bastiani, John. (1988). *Listening to Parents: An Approach to the Improvement of Home-School Relations.* London: Croom Helm, Ltd.

Barth, Roland S. (1990). *Improving Schools From Within: Teachers, Parents and Principals Can Make the Difference.* San Francisco: Jossey-Bass.

Booth, Alan and Dunn, Judith (eds.) (1996). *Family School Links: How Do They Affect Educational Outcomes?* Mahwah, NJ: Lawrence Erlbaum Associates.

Epstein, Joyce L. (1985, Winter). "Home and School Connections in Schools of the Future: Implications of Research on Parent Involvement," *Peabody Journal of Education* 62(2): 18–41.

Hoover-Dempsey, Kathleen V. and Sandler, Howard M. (1995, Winter). "Parental Involvement in Children's Education: Why Does It Make a Difference?" *Teachers College Record*, 97(2): 310–331.

Lareau, Annette. (1989). *Home Advantage: Social Class and Parental Intervention in Elementary Education.* London: Falmer.

Swap, Susan McAllister. (1987). *Enhancing Parent Involvement in Schools.* New York: Teachers College Press.

Chapter Ten

COMMUNITY RELATIONS IN SCHOOL-SITE MANAGEMENT

We have no thermometers comparable to achievement tests for measuring clients' satisfaction with their schools. Furthermore, such satisfaction tends to be a personal, not a collective, matter. The targets and routes for expressing personal dissatisfaction are elusive and obscure. Responsibility is diffused among teachers, principal, superintendent, and school board.
—John I. Goodlad, *Phi Delta Kappan*, 64(7) March, 1983, p. 469.

John Goodlad's comment that the routes to expressing satisfaction or dissatisfaction with the schools are "elusive and obscure" points to some important concerns in school organization and administration. Similarly, when responsibility in education is "diffused," and not easily targeted on any one official, there is a need to carefully investigate possible administrative constraints in "opening" the schools to their publics. Indeed, the politics-of-education literature indicates that a community's dissatisfaction with the public schools can sometimes build for years, unnoticed, until (with a flare-up) some conflict surfaces and administrative turnover occurs (Lutz and Iannaccone, 1978; Lutz and Merz, 1992).

Chapter 9 ended with a brief consideration of some ideas for organizing the school for parental involvement. A key suggestion was that redefined administrative attitudes—including the principal's conception of him- or herself as "learner" rather than "knower"— could be of significance in school improvement. This chapter pursues in greater depth the question of administering the school for improved community relations. It discusses separately some considerations for parental and community involvement in each of a number of key systems of school site-level administration.

FACILITIES MANAGEMENT

One of the most fascinating phenomena of the late 1980s and the 1990s has been an explosion in types of schools and school-enrollment alternatives. With roots in the "alternative-school movement" of the 1960s, the concept of the "magnet school" has become enormously popular in metropolitan areas (Metz, 1986; 1990). Usually with firm racial quotas, the magnet schools tend to offer some city school desegregation through voluntarism. Moreover, they offer pupils and parents an appealing and often innovative special focus—such as the performing arts, back-to-basics, mathematics and science, or modern language studies.

In a number of states, the options have been expanded statewide through the provision of highly competitive "specialty schools" for the most gifted and talented pupils (Nathan, 1990). More recently, a "charter school" movement has developed considerable momentum. Charter schools are typically released from state and local regulations in order to innovate in pedagogy or curricula. By 1996, twenty-five states allowed charter schools (Johnston, 1996). Other options (e.g., the "school without walls," the "alternative school," the "corporate community school," the "urban day school") have also proliferated under either public or private sponsorship (see Fiske, 1989; Olson, 1990a). There has also been increased experimentation with "privatization," whereby a public school is managed under contract by a for-profit organization (see Thomas, Moran, and Resnick, 1996).

Although not an experiment in differentiation by school type, the school "choice" movement has continued to gather momentum as a reform-minded effort toward consumer sovereignty (Boyd and Walberg, 1990; Clune and Witte, 1990; Chubb and Moe, 1990). Two of the most far-reaching, and most controversial, choice programs to date are those in Milwaukee, Wisconsin, and Cleveland, Ohio. Milwaukee has complied with a 1990 legislative mandate permitting a limited number of low-income families to transfer from public to private nonsectarian schools, carrying Milwaukee School District (public tax) resources with them (Olson, 1990a). Cleveland has extended this "voucher" initiative into the controversial arena of sectarian schooling. Originally favored by a few political conservatives, such choice options have lately gained widespread attention among and growing support from varying sectors of political opinion. The central appeal is the "marketplace" assumption behind choice, which is that schools will become more accountable to their publics and certainly more attentive to student needs if forced to compete for enrollments (Connell et al., 1982). Schools that do not perform well will "go under," as students leave to enter more productive educational environments (Elmore, 1986).

While many persons were originally worried about the possibility of adding to existing inequities of school attendance (particularly by race and social class), strategies for an opportunity-equalizing, regulated market system have softened some of this opposition (see Chubb and Moe, 1990; Moe, 1995). The great appeal to many reformers, well worth the danger of introducing disequalization, is that the consumer sovereignty wrapped around choice forces public education to place primary emphasis on improving the school site. A centralized, heavily bureaucratized system of school district management would likely be incompatible with the site-level flexibility and responsiveness needed under consumer demand. The appeal to educational reformers deepens, furthermore, under the argument that consumer-responsive schools will find that (a) parents are more satisfied with their child's school; thus (b) they will become more actively involved in the school' activities, and (c) will take more personal responsibility for their child's education (McDonnell, 1989).

One essential that can easily be lost, however, is that whatever the type of school (e.g., magnet or neighborhood) or its market characteristic (choice or assigned), it is what goes on *inside* the school facility that is the key to its effectiveness. As James Coleman (1987, p. 35) puts its, the school represents a *constructed* institution, one that should be "designed to complement the nonconstructed, spontaneous institution, the family."

This was a concept that early Americans understood fully. It is not by accident, observed David Tyack and Elisabeth Hansot (1982a), that our earliest schools resembled churches, with the steeple-like bell towers—for these buildings were at the center of the social life of their communities. It is also not hard to appreciate the action of a group of nineteenth-century Iowa farmers who used a team of oxen secretly one night to move the new schoolhouse a mile closer to their homes (Tyack, 1981). Nor is it difficult to understand the importance of town meeting after two meeting in one rural community to decide a series of such critical questions in the construction of their new schoolhouse as: "Was a well to be dug at the new site? Should a fence be built around the new schoolhouse? And should they build new privies, or move the old ones from the old site to the new?" (Fuller, 1982, p. 70).

To be sure, few magnet schools or "choice" schools or newly decentralized (site-based management) schools are likely to be built or rebuilt by their parent clientele. The evidence is that when they are, the "community-creating" effects of parent-teacher cooperation in school construction can be remarkable (Tiremand and Watson, 1984). But it should be fully understood, warns Ellen Goldring (1996), that the "type" of school (magnet or charter or neighborhood) matters little if parents and the public have not somehow become a "force" in the schools' environments. Parents must become "interwoven into the fabric of the institutional environments of schools" (Goldring, 1996, p. 51).

Most school facilities will, of course, be firmly in place (already "constructed") when they are reformed to encourage parent-community responsiveness. As facilities, they can reflect an earlier era in twentieth-century education that offered little "force" to parents and placed little value on community relations. In city environments, they may resemble the red brick or stone "factories" that marked early-twentieth-century school construction (Tyack and Hansot, 1982a). In both city and suburb, they may be large—multi-storied in the city and sprawling "shopping-mall" types in the suburbs. A late 1980s benefit of large size in some locales was a surplus of classrooms due to declining enrollments, with space transformed into computer labs, preschool or day-care programs, special education options, or resource rooms. A mid-1990s surge in school enrollments and/or attempts in many states to dramatically lower class sizes have now reduced the surplus of classrooms and therefore the options for more "responsive" facilities usage.

Furthermore, wherever located and however their classrooms have been apportioned, school facilities have retained a remarkable typicality and similarity through the years and across the nation. An office tends to be placed close to a main or front door. Signs direct the entrant in no-nonsense terms to report to this office as the first step in visitation. After entering the office, the visitor typically approaches a waist- or chest-high barrier separating school officialdom from pupils sent to the office, parents with requests or questions, the omnipresent textbook salesman, and other day-by-day intruders. From the office, long hallways (often lined with lockers or coathooks) lead toward egg-crate-fashion classrooms—each with a single, usually half-windowed door. No doors may guard the boys' and girls' restrooms (mirrors removed) spaced at intervals along each hall. Often, throughout the building there may be bright bulletin boards and slogans (e.g., "National Norms By '98"); but if a high school, the walls may be surprisingly barren (except for the trophy case).

Although a caricature, many schools fit this description of the facilities "atmosphere." This atmosphere, as Ronald Corwin and Kathryn Borman (1988) note, tends to convey a control orientation to the visitor—a sense that the school's decorum stands on a rather problematic disciplinary foundation. While control is certainly vital to any purposive gathering of young persons, an alternative way of viewing school facilities, suggests Florio-Ruane (1989), with perhaps differing results, might be to picture the school's facilities as an important part of a *cultural setting*.

What does it mean to think of the school's facilities and facilities management as a vital element in a *culture* of community relations? Perhaps a productive way to address this question is to borrow from Paula Kleine-Kracht (1990) the concept of "cultural linkages." A school's facilities assist mightily in the maintenance of bureaucratic and production linkages. The centrality of the principal's office, wide hallways, numbered classrooms, quick access to building exits, closed-off yet observable classrooms, a separate escape-from-it space (lounge) for teachers, and a large-group setting or two (gymnasium, cafeteria) are all common features of schools that serve administrative needs of safety, communication, control, ease of movement, and teacher professionalism and autonomy. Less readily recognized are the cultural linkages in a school's facilities. These are the shared meanings symbolized by the arrangement of a school's facilities (Kleine-Kracht, 1990; Smylie, 1991).

A first, not unexpected finding from the research literature is that size can be a strong predictor of a school's sense of community (Driscoll, 1990; Sergiovanni, 1996). By no means is a sense of community impossible in a large school, and by no means are small schools automatically close as communities. Nevertheless, the collegiality and commitment arising from the broadly shared values and shared feelings of membership in a "common agenda of activities," which are often used as defining characteristics of community, are not as common in large schools (Driscoll, 1990, p. 1). It is not size by itself that becomes the determinant, of course, but it is likely that enhanced opportunities for "frequent face-to-face interactions among students and adults" do occur in smaller environments (Driscoll, 1990, p. 1).

Beyond the key question of size, a second suggestion for facilities management is to use the available space in a manner that connotes community. Willis Hawley (1990, p. 225) offers an important objective in this regard, proposing that the school should engage actively in "reconciling the family and the school." Indeed, an innovative experiment in Miami has involved an actual placement of schools in or near parents' workplaces (e.g., near Miami-Dade County Airport for air traffic controllers).

Less radical options are available as well, however. To begin with, suggests Carl Marburger (1990, p. 81), try to communicate a message that the school is "open, helpful, and friendly." Marburger continues with the following suggestions:

- Post a "Parents and Visitors Are Welcome" sign on the front door
- Design a special parent lounge
- Schedule new family orientations and tours
- Have monthly parent-teacher luncheons
- Designate a special office or work area near the principal's office for the chairperson of the parent advisory council. [P. 87]

Many British schools have established special "Parents' Rooms" as part of their facilities. They have found this space allocation enormously practical for teacher-parent-pupil interactions, parent-volunteer networking, school-community socializing, and the coordination of parent-related communications. Increasingly common in the United States are "family centers" in the schools (Weiss, 1995). For example, a family center in a Clayton, Missouri, school provides a family resource library, family life classes, child-care information and referrals, health and nutrition education, individual counseling, and a drop-in resource (Weiss, 1995, p. 385).

Both Marburger and Joyce Epstein (1985) suggest that a powerful, modern-day use of space and equipment should be the establishment of computer linkages between school and home. Marburger (1990, p. 226) urges the use of computer-based telephone systems to provide "daily information to parents about student assignments." Indeed, a "Family Education Network" web site is now available with a variety of information sources and on-line discussion opportunities for parents (Trotter, 1996). Epstein observes that although not all families have home computers, the prevalence of both home and school computers is increasing rapidly—with, unfortunately, few connections between them. School computers tend to be used for only school programs and assignments; and home computers tend to be used for family entertainment or (increasingly) for family-directed education unrelated to the school curriculum. Epstein (1985, p. 27) suggests a number of "models" (with computers lent to families that lack their own) that will help merge school and home, including (a) a *basic skill s and drills model,* which uses home computers to "obtain extra learning time to practice and master basic skills"; (b) a *home enrichment model,* which goes "beyond the basics to explore problem solving and other higher order skills and projects"; and (c) a *home computer literacy model,* which teaches concepts and techniques of computing.

THE INCENTIVE SYSTEM

A central assumption behind the current interest in choice is that the incentives attached to a marketplace in public education can result in greater school effectiveness (Chubb and Moe, 1990). Parents will seek the best available schools for their children; and schools will be motivated by enrollment demand to become effective. This same argument suggests that as a public monopoly, the local school has had few incentives to improve. It is claimed that a market mechanism does exist for affluent American families who can afford to move to communities with exceptional schools. Nevertheless, for persons unable to afford the housing in high-quality school districts, there is no market, only the monopoly.

A similar marketplace ethic can be found *within* the public school. It is far more rewarding for teachers and administrators to give time and attention to "good" students and to students struggling hard to learn than to students who seem to lack motivation, interest, and

Figure 10.1

An Involvement Scale

−1	Alienation Zone	0	Commitment Zone	+1

Alienative
involvement
(high alienation)

Calculative
involvement
(mild alienation/
mild commitment)

Moral
involvement
(high commitment)

ability. Indeed, the adolescent act of dropping out of school can reflect an incentives-related "disenfranchisement" (Ianni, 1989) that may have begun in the earliest (kindergarden or prekindergarden) school experiences (see Rist, 1970). As discussed earlier in this volume, both administrators and teachers may discover that the rewards of organizational responsiveness and bureaucratic service exceed by far the personal and professional gains that result from parental involvement (Seeley and Schwartz, 1981). Although the rare note of thanks or word of praise from a parent is much treasured by teachers, contacts with parents more often stem from the less-than-rewarding problems of academic failure and pupil control. Finally, no matter how parent- or community-oriented a school principal may be, the incentives are extremely strong to buffer teachers from parents, back up teachers (right or wrong) in confrontations with parents, and protect teachers' professionalism from parents. Dissatisfied teachers will transfer to another school where their professionalism is more firmly recognized (Connell et al., 1982).

Amitai Etzioni (1980) has offered an incentives- and person-oriented model of the involvement of individuals in organizations. As depicted in Figure 10.1, Etzioni observes that persons will vary in the intensity of their involvement in an organization—from high-intensity (or moral) involvement, through a condition he labels "calculative involvement," to low-intensity (or alienative) involvement. The morally involved person feels a strong normative commitment to and identification with the organization. Conversely, the alienated person feels no commitment and no moral attachment. The calculative person may be on the borderline between mildly alienated and mildly committed—and thus, says Etzioni, may be especially sensitive to any inducements that are offered.

It is Etzioni's suggestion that organizations use rewards (and the power and control that stems from their use) in varying ways to obtain the compliance of individuals with organizational purposes. These rewards, if effective, will tend generally to "match" the individual's state of involvement. That is, with high-commitment individuals, effective rewards might be those in the *normative* domain, such as esteem, prestige, praise, symbols of high performance, and ritualistic ceremonies of collegial recognition. For highly alienated individuals, however, effective control may require the use of *coercive* mechanisms, such as physical sanctions or restraints, legalistic barriers, and a nonfulfillment of basic needs. Few individuals are at either extreme. Most persons operate at some level of calculative involvement; with these persons, compliance is achieved through *remunerative* channels—through the rewards and deprivations accompanying salaries, material resources, service provisions, information access, and the like.

Etzioni's theory can be applied productively to help us understand life in schools. For example, schools appear to differentiate their forms of control over students according to perceived differences in the "commitments" of their pupils. The problem student may be subjected to very close supervision and stick-to-the-rules discipline, while the high-achieving student in the same school may roam relatively freely and may assume quasi-staff positions of student leadership (see Carlson, 1964; also McPherson, Crowson, and Pitner, 1986).

The theory has not, however, been used to examine relationships between schools and their parental clientele. Nevertheless, it may be of value to speculate a bit from three different Etzioni-minded perspectives.

First, parents (like students) may find that the school makes assumptions about their degree of commitment to the school—and allocates its responsiveness accordingly. Annette Lareau (1989, p. 163), for example, observes that "teachers in communities with high levels of parent involvement devote a substantial amount of organizational resources to managing home-school relations." The teachers in such schools may even "take time away from teaching to coordinate, train, and make effective use of parents in the classroom" (Lareau, 1989, p. 163). On the other hand, the opposite scenario can just as easily occur. Mitchell Koza and Wayne Levy (1977–78) discovered that schools with little parental participation tend to devote or make available few of their resources to the parental community. Furthermore, such schools, surrounded by indications of little parental interest, are likely to attempt to instill participation by using such "coercive" measures as requiring parents to pick up pupil report cards.

With our increasing societal diversity and accompanying cultural differences between home and school, it is easy for school officials to misinterpret the commitments of parents. Commitment may initially need to be turned on its head, argues Valdés (1996). Indeed, parental commitment may need to start with evidence of the school's "appreciation and respect for the internal dynamics of the families and for the legitimacy of their values and beliefs" (Valdés, 1996, p. 203). For example, if presumably "uncommitted" parents are coerced into believing that raising "successful" children means giving up the childrearing practices they have long considered appropriate, the result may be to destroy any further opportunity for a close relationship.

A second Etzioni-driven speculation is that most parents (like most pupils) are likely to be neither highly committed nor highly alienated vis-à-vis their child's school. Rather they are more likely to be found in that category Etzioni (1980) labels "calculative" involvement—where remunerative rewards are most salient. To be sure, some communities might press for a direct-remuneration access to employment for neighborhood residents (e.g., as aides, security personnel, or clerks). More often, however, the type of remuneration expected by parents is less direct—perhaps some administrative and teacher compliance in the class placement or tracking of their children and in the disciplining of their children, or the school's policies on reporting home about their children. Parents can push vigorously and sometimes angrily for consideration (and a bit of special treatment) in these areas. However, school officials tend to be uneasy about such negotiating with parents. Certainly, many "special favors" are done (e.g., a transfer from Miss Jones's to Mrs. Smith's fourth-grade class). But in the main, the school prefers the safety of uniform, nonnegotiable rules, and no favors.

From the perspective of Etzioni's theory, the result tends to be an *incongruence* in the school's "compliance relationships" with parents, which results when the types of controls used by an organization are out of synch with commitment levels—when, for example, coercive controls are used with highly committed participants. Interestingly, parents are not unknown to volunteer and to participate actively in their child's school for the very reason that access to "special favors" is thereby enhanced. Conversely, the school can benefit if these parents will help "fight" for the school (e.g., at meetings of the school board) (Smrekar, 1996a).

Third, from Etzioni there is help in understanding differences between professional educators in their responses to the same sets of incentives and disincentives vis-à-vis parent relations. A scarce resource in schools, for example, is time. There is far too little time to cover the curriculum adequately, to individualize instruction, to plan, to complete paperwork, to join colleagues in committee work, and to relax a bit before beginning the next day's whirlwind. Patricia Hulsebosch (1988, p. 156) discovered that even with this time constraint, some "high-parent-involvement" teachers make an extra effort to contact parents (e.g., "before school, during lunch, after school; through phone calls, written notes, meetings and conferences"). In contrast, "low-parent-involvement" teachers complain of the heavy time lost in dealing with parents, an activity that detracts from the "real" work of teaching. Commented one of Hulsebosch's "low-involvement" subjects: "Probably one of the biggest nuisances that I can think of is the parents constantly dropping by and bothering you" (p. 158). Note that although administrators may find ways to add time to teachers' worklives, by no means will this resource benefit parents unless there is a corresponding change in "commitment" to parents.

THE COMMUNICATIONS SYSTEM

A *New York Times* article on August 16, 1989, heralded the "School Without a Principal" in Hill City, Minnesota. The article noted, "The Hill City school has not had a principal since last year, and the district is not looking for one." Indeed, a "share team" of representative teachers plus the school secretary manage the K-12 school of 330 pupils—and reportedly, "morale is better."

A similar-sounding organization is suggested by Brian Caldwell and Jim Spinks in the title of their book: *The Self-Managing School* (1988). While Caldwell and Spinks do not advocate principal-free schooling, their description of the characteristics of the self-managing school would fit well into the *New York Times*'s picture of Hill City. The self-managing school

- Integrates goal-setting policymaking, planning, budgeting, implementing, and evaluating
- Secures appropriate involvement of staff, students, and the community with clearly defined roles for government
- Focuses on the central functions of schools—learning and teaching. [Caldwell and Spinks, 1988, pp. 3–4]

Each of these idealized, even visionary, pictures contrasts mightily with traditional descriptions of managerial life in public schooling. Schools are better known, it is claimed, for their separation of goal setting from implementing and evaluation, for their fragmentation of effort and their ambiguities of "involvement" in decisionmaking, and for their tendencies to stray from the central functions of learning and teaching (see Boyd and Crowson, 1981; Boyd and Hartman, 1988).

Differences between the idealized and the real, scholars note, can often be traced (at least in part) to the characteristics of schools as managerial *communications systems*. Although integrated goal-setting and implementation and a wide involvement in decisionmaking may be desirable, the realities of classroom separation and inflexible scheduling in schools make communicative sharing a bit problematic. Van Cleve Morris and colleagues (1984), for example, talk of the frequent need for principals to conduct "peripatetic committee meetings," where the principal may discuss a problem with Miss Smith on the first floor, walk down the hall to check Smith's response with Mr. Jones, climb the stairs to confer with Mrs. Green, consult a bit with the librarian, then finally "go round again" at the end of the day to each person with a proposed "solution."

Other constraints on the free flow of communications in schools are found in loyalty and terminology differences that accompany the work roles of educators. These are cultural forces that have long thwarted collegial cooperation and involvement. Teachers are famous for a primary, unswerving loyalty to the children and an antipathy (indeed a closedness) toward communications that may reduce classroom time and autonomy—threatening, as Susan Moore Johnson (1989, p. 110) put it, to professionalize teaching by making "it something other than teaching." Similarly, the separateness and isolation found in schools can be reflected in constraints on the flow of communications caused by specialized terminology. The language of special education is not that of the regular classroom teacher: upper-elementary teachers use terms that differ from those used by lower-elementary teachers; departmental differences (e.g., between science and social studies) are found; and professional versus nonprofessional (e.g., maintenance, secretarial, cafeteria personnel) differences are important. For the parent, communication with the school can therefore mean weaving one's interpretive way through multiple systems rather than just one system of arcane attachments to and collections of verbal meaning. It can be a daunting assignment.

Well aware of the communications problems, public schools have probably given more attention to this aspect of improving parental involvement than to any other. Most school administrators and teachers are fully informed of the value of regular newsletters to the home, "good news" telephone calls to parents, wall calendars of school events, student-run newspapers, regularly scheduled parent-teacher conferences, and policy handbooks for parents. From the note home safety-pinned to Jimmie's shirt, to the care it takes to foster an active, well-attended PTA, public schools do think of home-school communication.

Nevertheless, something can be missing. *Channels* of communication are not a *system* of communications. If the ideals identified by Caldwell and Spinks in *The Self-Managing School* (1988) are to be realized, the school should emphasize systematically at least the values we discuss in the following paragraphs.

First, effective communications involves the key attribute of careful *listening*, in addition to a usual reporting of information. It is not easy for schools to listen. As Shirley Heck and C. Ray Williams (1984, p. 35) note, educators "are accustomed to being authority figures," and they may view probing questions or some clarification seeking as a threat to their authority. Moreover, as professionals, it is difficult for many educators to admit that they do not have answers to pedagogical questions; and similarly, they may be "afraid to ask for the advice and opinions of the parents with whom they are working" (Heck and Williams, 1984, p. 34). Listening also tends to take much more time than telling; and time is a commodity in constant shortage in schools. From the parents' perspective, the listening relationship is difficult because the parent may feel insecure in interaction with teachers, "on the spot" as the father or mother of a problematic child, or full of leftover anger from his or her own childhood experiences in school (Heck and Williams, 1984, p. 35). Nevertheless, listening, however much time it takes, is vital. One school superintendent in the Chicago area is famous for sitting at a card table at a local shopping mall on weekends, fielding questions and discussing the concerns of all comers. Other school administrators routinely place random, viewpoint-eliciting telephone calls to parents and community residents. Similarly, some classroom teachers use the telephone creatively or conduct home visits as ways to show their respect for parents' opinions. Whatever mode is used to communicate, Heck and Williams urge that the key is to "show genuine interest, avoid being defensive, and listen to what the parent is saying" (p. 35).

Second, effective communications finds a way to *broaden* the range and scope of participation in a school. From the smallest to the largest, schools are beehives of activity and movement within limited space and time. Communication failures frequently occur. An instrumental music teacher finds that her students are off on a day-long fieldtrip during the last rehearsal day prior to the spring Band Concert. Miss Jones schedules an exam; and it is only when just half her class of thirty shows up that she learns today is "picture-taking day" for the yearbook. Mr. Smith is asked why he hasn't submitted Form 2314 to the office, due last Tuesday. The office soon discovers that a third of the faculty failed to receive Form 2314 in their mailboxes.

A typical school year is full of such occurrences. Professionals' tempers can flare as important communications are missed, followed by inconvenience and embarrassment. One well-understood maxim in school administration is: "Everyone who needs to know, should know." The best administrators take care and spend extra time trying to ensure that communication failures occur infrequently. Inevitably there are a few breakdowns: The itinerant music teacher is not informed in advance of an upcoming field trip. But the best-run schools, appreciated by those who work within them, are efficient in their coordination of communications.

Less well understood in school management, however, is this additional dictum: "Even those persons who do not need to know, should know." Some schools experimenting with considerably broadened, rather than focused, patterns of communication are discovering previously untapped sources of pedagogical assistance. Bus drivers, cafeteria personnel, custodians, aides, secretaries, and school crossing guards will often join in with enthusiasm in programs of curriculum development; school goal- and direction-shaping; and caring for, rewarding, and socializing pupils (*New York Times*, 1989). Major benefits can be a much broadened sense of community throughout the school and a shared sense of "moral leadership" for the school (Sergiovanni, 1996).

Furthermore, suggest Heck and Williams (1984), the continued communicative involvement of retired teachers, volunteer parents, former students, and persons in supportive community roles (e.g., librarians, recreational directors) can create a strong helpful coterie of "ambassadors" for the school. Heck and Williams go on to observe:

The school can invite community service and professional groups in for mini-tours of the school facilities. These tours could bring community members up to date on programs and new equipment or just let them see "how things have changed since I was in school." All areas of the community should be included: business people, professionals, and nonparents. People who "talk for a living"—such as beauticians, barbers, and bartenders—should be included; they sometimes represent the single most effective grapevine system in any community. [P. 37–38]

THE TRAINING AND DEVELOPMENT SYSTEM

Advocates of both professional empowerment and parental involvement point out that those who perform both managerial and educative roles in schools may need to develop different qualities and different competencies. Therefore, a program of training or development may be an essential element of the larger administrative system (Raywid, 1990).

William Boyd(1989a, p. 10) argues that there are "at least three legs on the schoolhouse stool" in these reform-minded times. A parent leg is needed "to counterbalance the strong current thrusts toward managerial control and professional autonomy." Similarly, Arthur

Wise (1990, p. 405) notes the importance of promoting a "client-oriented" control of schools in this era of site autonomy and professional empowerment—and he emphasizes a "responsiveness of schools to their clientele" as the sine qua non of practitioner leadership.

Putting these ideas together, the argument is that (a) the third leg (a parent leg) of the schoolhouse stool is vital to today's education, but (b) the stool is in danger of toppling if increasingly autonomous educators do not promote a "client orientation" in their work, and (c) the protection of the third leg requires some careful professional training and development toward that end. State certification requirements, university offerings, and school district in-service programs are now fairly well supplied with community-relations and parental involvement seminars. However, seldom is a *protection* of the third leg of the stool the central feature of a training system. Just what does this mean as a training-and-development theme?

First, it means that training seeks ensurance that the cultural traditions of the local community will be recognized and respected by the school. In a comparative study of schools in their community contexts, for example, Colleen Capper (1990, pp. 22–23) speaks of the communities of "Deerfield" and "Dover." Deerfield responded to its Native American minority by employing "Native American language teachers to teach the native language to the elementary children." She notes further that "special Native American holidays were recognized in addition to the traditional school holidays in which children were dismissed from classes" (p. 22). By way of contrast, the community of "Dover" was experiencing a growing minority population and some racial tension. "Despite the much publicized racial tension," notes Capper, "school was held without ceremony on Martin Luther King Day" (p. 23).

Few schools are totally insensitive to the special cultural traditions, perspectives, language patterns, ceremonies, and values of their immediate clientele. Nevertheless, amid a new wave of immigration into and increased mobility within our nation, the public schools are facing a renewed diversity of cultures and a renewed challenge to find ways to make effective connections with this diversity (Hodgkinson, 1988; Pallas, Natriello, and McDill, 1989; Valdés, 1996).

Second, the protection of the parent leg of the stool involves a training of school administrators and teachers to regard parents as important "stakeholders" in the school. "Stakeholder" is a favorite term of political scientists to indicate those persons or groups who have a special interest in the outcome of a political issue or contest. As the quotation from John Goodlad in the epigraph to this chapter indicates, however, it is often difficult for stakeholders to determine just what outcomes are being produced by their schools and to pin down responsibility for the outcomes that do surface. On the other hand, the schools have trouble discovering when or if stakeholders are at all satisfied with the outcomes and responsibilities that are communicated.

In short, training for a stakeholder relationship with parents may involve training professional educators to (a) discover the *interests* (rather than the needs) of a parent community, (b) clarify the outcomes being provided to the stakeholder community, (c) pinpoint responsibility for these outcomes, and (d) discover whether there is a measure of satisfaction with any or all of the above. This is not at all an easy professional-development task, for educators themselves are most hesitant about clarifying outcomes (e.g., education is much more than a "test score") and are unsure themselves about who should bear "responsibility" (Miss Jones in grade two? Johnny's mother? Johnny's English and mathematics teachers? Peer influences?). At best, a productive sense of elusive stakeholder interests regarding, and their satisfactions with, school outcomes and accountabilities might arise out of a professional-development program that trains educators *with* stakeholders to gain common understandings.

Third, the protection of the entire schoolhouse stool may require a program of development recognizing the separate support provided by *each* leg. A discussion earlier in this book described the "professional distancing" that is characteristic of schooling. On its problematic side, such distancing can create a barrier between educator and parent. On its productive side, however, such distancing can steady the stool on three separate but mutually reinforcing legs. The task is to train both educators and parents to honor and complement the special autonomy of each "leg" without throwing an undue burden for the support of the stool on any one leg.

Hulsebosch (1988) suggests that a focus should be on the teacher, and that a training-and-development secret may lie in the inculcation of a strong sense of "professional identity" among teachers. Teachers with a weak identity, she finds, tend to have "strong negotiative reactions to those few occasions in which parents 'dared to question them' or 'confronted' them" (p. 270). Teachers with a strong professional identity, on the other hand, would dismiss such intrusions as just "a part of the job." Hulsebosch concludes:

Apparently teachers' "sense of responsibility" and "parents' sense of entitlement in demanding results from schools" is not enough to ensure that there will be collaboration between home and school. The specifics of the relationship between parents and teacher still remain to be resolved, and much of the control of that relationship still remains with the teacher. [Pp. 275–276]

In short, the probable answer to Goodlad's observation that responsibility has been nonproductively diffused in education is this: Under reform, the responsibility for a successfully steadied and supportive three-legged stool of schooling will likely follow the development of a strong professional identity in the individual teacher—an identity that includes a knowledge of craft, a vision of instructional ends, a commitment to children, and a freedom to pursue the highest standards of on-the-job accomplishment.

SUMMARY

The phrase "four walls of the school" is a metaphor for the historical separation between school and community. The school was literally to be walled-off administratively from the pressure of its publics. It is somewhat less widely recognized that the administrative and organizational systems of the school have tended historically to play a backup role to a four-walls separation. As "constructed institutions" (Coleman, 1987), the schools build facilities, incentives, communications, and training mechanisms over time that embody prevailing institutional values.

Thus, a change from a "closed" to an "open" relationship between the school and its community may necessitate some careful attention to that which B.B. Tye (1987) labels the "deep structures" of schooling—including a consideration of the size and space-usage effects of facilities, the commitment-reinforcing qualities of incentives, the importance of listening to and extending the range of communicators, and the integrative yet autonomy-protecting effects of training-and-development efforts.

Exercises
THE WALK AROUND

1. Take a team of observers into a sample of schools (both elementary and secondary).
2. Conduct a careful walking tour of each school, examining every visible aspect of the school's facilities—with an eye toward the cultural messages and the overall atmosphere conveyed by the school.
3. Compare the schools you observed. Do they differ in facilities usage? In atmosphere? Were there any unique facilities usages to be found? Do some school facilities appear to be more welcoming and responsive to outsiders than others? What are the specific differences?

Suggested Activities

1. If permitted by the participants, observe closely a number of one-on-one parent-teacher conferences. How much of the teacher's time is spent telling; how much listening? How would you describe the relationship between the teacher and parent during the conference?
2. Interview a range of support staff members at a school—custodians, cooks, clerks, aides. Ask the opinion of each vis-à-vis his or her role in the *instructional* program of the school. Is there a sense of involvement in instruction or is there a feeling of separateness and disinvolvement?
3. Assemble a file of unique cultural traits, habits, patterns, or viewpoints as discussed in the literature on a special minority group (e.g., Vietnamese, Native American, Mexican-American, Puerto Rican, Cambodian). Share your file and your findings with your classmates, discussing the pedagogical implications of cultural differences.
4. In one school to which you have access, test the hypothesis that the discipline and control system treats pupils of differing "commitments" in different ways. Do the "better" pupils enjoy more freedom of movement, less direct supervision, and more leeway in disruptive-type behavior than the academically "poorer" pupils?
5. Skills in successful listening are not easily developed. It is

often much easier to "tell" than to listen. With your class-mates, develop a list of questions and conversation-openers that teachers could draw on to get parents to "open up" about themselves and their children.

SUGGESTED READINGS

Caldwell, Brian J., and Spinks, Jim M. (1988). *The Self-Managing School.* London: Falmer.

Chubb, John E., and Moe, Terry M. (1990). *Politics, Markets, and America's Schools.* Washington, D.C.: The Brookings Institute.

Cibulka, James G., and Kritek, William J. (1996). *Coordination Among Schools, Families, and Communities: Prospects for Educational Reform.* Albany: State University of New York Press.

Epstein, Joyce L. (1985, Winter). "Home and School Connections in Schools of the Future: Implications of Research in Parent Involvement," *Peabody Journal of Education* 62(2): 18–41.

Marburger, Carl L. (1990). "Education Reform: The Neglected Dimension, Parent Involvement." In S. B. Bacharach (ed.), *Educational Reform: Making Sense of It All,* pp. 82–91. Boston: Allyn & Bacon.

Sergiovanni, Thomas J. (1996). *Leadership for the Schoolhouse: How Is It Different? Why Is It Different?* San Francisco: Jossey-Bass.

Chapter Eleven

SCHOOL OUTREACH

A new vocabulary is emerging. Collaboration, cooperation, compact, council, consortia, alliance, federation, and network are terms that apply to cross-sector and boundary-spanning structures springing up across the country even without federal or state mandates.
—Luvern L. Cunningham, "Educational Leadership and Administration: Retrospective and Prospective Views," 1990.

"The schools cannot do it alone." This is an old, old refrain in the educator's plea for help from the larger social and economic community. In the past, this plea translated into a seldom-realized cry for added school resources, more supportive parents, a less critical media, and more realistic expectations about what the public schools can do.

Recently, however, while the we-can't-do-it-alone message continues, a new emphasis on (and a new direction in) shared responsibility for education is emerging. The focus at this time is on service collaboration and cooperation between school and community, rather than simply on an adding *to* the schools *from* the community.

Interestingly, this new vocabulary of cooperation referred to by Cunningham (1990) is at present as likely to be found in the discourse of noneducators as it is in the speech of teachers and school administrators:

The Mayor's Office in Philadelphia has established an experimental "Family Services District" in West Philadelphia. The intent is to coordinate services for children, including schooling, as part of a "social service enterprise zone" in that part of the city. [Philadelphia Children's Network, 1990, p. 6]

At the state level in Pennsylvania, the Pennsylvania Chapter of the American Academy of Pediatrics has initiated an "Early Childhood Linkage System (ECELS)" to strengthen relationships between health professionals (in pediatrics, public health, dentistry, mental health, and nutrition) and early childhood educational programs. [*Pennsylvania Education*, 1990, p. 3]

The Kellogg Foundation supports a four-school partnership in Chicago between the University of Illinois at Chicago and the public schools. The University coordinates a provision of health services, social services, parent-education, and professional development for teachers as ingredients in a professionally integrated thrust in inner-city schooling. [Nucci, 1989]

The State University of New York (SUNY) at Albany coordinates a special university/philanthropist/school district program of enrichment for at-risk students—noting, in the process, that the "ability of government agencies, institutions of higher learning, and school districts to work collaboratively to help student success is critical to the success of intervention programs." [Koff and Ward, 1990, p. 224]

The new emphasis on coordination is rooted, as Cunningham (1990, p. 15) puts it, in

the realization that needs of children and youth are no longer satisfied by schools and schooling alone. Young people's problems often exhaust the resources of a single agency or a single set of professionals trained to work with this age group . . . These problems push beyond the boundaries of professional competence and of agency or institutional missions, thus making collaboration necessary.

The impetus derives heavily from a growing sense of urgency regarding the conditions of children in America. In an influential analysis in 1989, Michael Kirst assembled an impressive array of "social indicators" of the schooling, health, child-care, family life, child welfare, income support, delinquency, and child-abuse conditions of children in California. Similar analyses have since been undertaken in other states. In a closing address before the National Conference on School/College Collaboration (June 20, 1990), Kati Perry Haycock (Vice President of the Children's Defense Fund) offered some startling and disturbing summary statistics:

One in five American children—12 million in all—is living in poverty. Children are by far the poorest Americans and have grown poorer during the 1980's as our nation has grown richer.

    One in five children has no health insurance. Among industrialized nations, only the United States and South Africa fail to provide all children and families a basic floor of health protection.

    Every day in America, 69 babies die before one month of life, 107 die before their first birthday; 27 children die from poverty, 9 die from guns, 1,849 are abused, and 3,288 run away from home; 1,293 teenagers give birth, and 1,375 drop out of high school. [Haycock, 1990]

Similarly, Lonnie Wagstaff and Karen Gallagher (1990; p. 103) have observed:

The proportion of children living in poverty declined significantly during the 1960's, but has risen since 1970; in 1985, 20 percent of *all* children, 54 percent of children in female-headed families and 78 percent of black children in female-headed families lived in poverty.

Between 1960 and 1987, the number of families grew by 43 percent, while the number of families headed by females grew by 232 percent.

Living in a mother-only family increased the odds of dropping out of school by more than 122 percent among whites and by 30 to 55 percent among blacks and Hispanics.

Furthermore, the U.S. General Accounting Office estimated that between 80,000 and 400,000 children were likely to be homeless or doubled up, living with friends and extended family, on any given night in 1988 (Lewit and Baker, 1996).

In the face of evidence that the conditions of life for children are worsening, the responses of a number of policy analysts have paralleled those of Kirst and Milbrey McLaughlin (1990, p. 74), who have noted: "Given these societal changes, business as usual in children's services is not good enough." Two major problems that particularly constrain services to children, these authors continue, are (a) the rapidly growing underservice, and indeed declining support, that is provided the children of poor families; and (b) the existing fragmentation of delivery systems for children (a fragmentation that is no more than a "patchwork of solutions") (Kirst and McLaughlin, 1990, p. 75).

INTEGRATING CHILDREN'S SERVICES

Beyond the growing sense of a crisis in the care and development of children, the push to integrate services resides heavily in a renewed appreciation of the *ecological* relationship between schools, families, and neighborhoods (Andrews, 1987).

To be sure, the interweavings and interdependencies between family and community and formal education are long-acknowledged (even if not fully understood) phenomena. Less well recognized are the side effects and expected (but also unforeseen) consequences that interventions in one part of the ecological system have on the others

(Andrews, 1987, p. 154). Classroom teachers have long known that hungry children (and inadequately clothed and unhealthy children) are handicapped learners. Thus, many poverty-area public schools began taking steps years ago to provide breakfasts as well as other amenities (e.g., winter coats, boots, free innoculation services) to needy children. Of late, the schools have become even more assertive in identifying and protecting children from abusive parents.

Nevertheless, much remains unknown about the relationships among and the outcomes of ecological forces. For example, to what extent are the public schools heavily constrained by their immediate neighborhoods? And at the same time, to what extent can the public schools rise above neighborhood constraints?

In their study of community influences on school crime and violence in Chicago, Julius Menacker, Ward Weldon, and Emanuel Hurwitz (1989, p. 69) discovered that (a) "socially disorganized, crime-ridden neighborhoods produce socially disorganized, crime-ridden schools"; but (b) many schools nevertheless manage to provide havens of relative safety in some of the most crime-ridden areas of the city. The public schools accomplishing this "usually expand their services beyond ordinary educational activities in order to have a positive impact on the negative conditions fostered by the deleterious conditions of the community" (Menacker, Weldon, and Hurwitz, 1990, p. 77). One school, the authors report, "initiated a cooperative project with the police to clean out a hotel located near it that was used as a drug-dealing headquarters" (p. 77).

Other similar questions abound. For example, to what extent is school dropout prevention dangerously hampered by weak incentives for high school completion in many low-income communities? As Henry Levin (1984, p. 157) argues: "The poor employment and earnings prospects for high school graduates have reduced the incentives for high school completion for youth who have no reason other than future economic prospects to stay in school."

Much the same line of reasoning about interdependencies might be used to look into the ecological relationships between schools and neighborhood housing, economic development, transportation, library services, health services, and recreation programs. A fall 1990 investigation in Chicago discovered that the after-school and weekend programs of the city's parks department were little used by Chicago's children. Among the findings was evidence that "many park employees do little or nothing to advertise or promote their programs in the community, or to attract neighborhood children to the park. Many local schools do not have park brochures, and youth organizations in the city say children and teens are largely unaware of after-school activities available in the parks" (Stein and Rechtenwald, 1990, p. 18). Such underuse is even more problematic when there is the added consideration that overall city investments in programs and activities for children fall far short of comparable investments in suburbia (Littell and Wynn, 1989).

Beyond pointing to a new ecological awareness of the side effects of the interactions between school and community, the Chicago Parks Department example illustrates the *discontinuities* of care that can surround the education of children (Kirst and McLaughlin, 1990). Parks and recreation services can be no less educative and no less psychologically important to a child's development than the services of the local school. Nevertheless, there is seldom time or effort taken to coalesce human services into that which Mario Fantini (1983) has labeled a "network of learning environments." Rather, human services programs are more commonly characterized by (a) a lack of communication between persons from different agencies serving the same population of children; (b) differing, and sometimes contradictory, philosophies of care found in the distinctively separate programs of professional preparation; and (c) jurisdictional ("turf") barriers between differing types of services, usually grounded in separate sources of funding and sources of state regulation (Kirst and McLaughlin, 1990; Crowson and Boyd, 1993). The recognition anew is that school, family, and community are vitally interdependent and are equally important for the development and learning of children. The struggle is just how to bring this interdependence into an improved families, schools, and communities reality (Rigsby, Reynolds, and Wang, 1995).

A NEW OUTREACH

In their examination of the current discontinuities and fragmentation in human services delivery, Kirst and McLaughlin (1990, p. 77) ask an anguished question: "Who is there for the children?" Indeed, from the early nineteenth century on, the public ("common") schools often saw themselves in this role, as special protectors and socializers of children—forming virtues and good habits within a sinful world and amid numbers of irresponsible parents (Grubb and Lazerson, 1982; Spring, 1986). The phrase *in loco parentis* (in the place of a parent) came to represent, at least in part, a parent-replacement role for the public school—an institution "there for the children" when families fell into disarray (Grubb and Lazerson, 1982, p. 18).

However, through the twentieth century, the public school has become increasingly more realistic in its assumption of a parenting role—indeed leaning heavily over the years toward the claim that without some substantial help at home, the goal of educating children effectively is discouragingly unrealistic. It was not a large step from there to the realization that many families need help with their own educational preparation and school-support roles—thus the school should "reach out" to parents with programs to assist, train, and involve them in parenting practices that will improve their children's education.

Only recently has the reaching-out concept for the school acquired a newer and decidedly broadened meaning, for the understanding is that schools and parents are only contributing parts in a much larger network of learning environments (Fantini, 1983). In the terminology of Robert Sinclair and Ward Ghory (1983), the schools have now entered a "period of inclusion" in their definition of educative responsibilities—a definition that finds vital educational importance in close ties between the schools and other social service or community institutions (see also Kagan, 1989). Thus, there is considerable appeal to such notions as the experimental 'Schools Reaching Out Project" of the Institute for Responsive Education, for they promise to "rapidly redefine the traditional definitions and practices of 'parent involvement,' envisioning instead a comprehensive partnership between schools, families, and community agencies, organizations, and resources" (Davies, 1990). The organizing term, urges Joy Dryfoos (1994), should be a notion of "full-service schooling," where education is reconceptualized as a very broad base of professional services—all of which contribute interactively to the welfare and development of children.

This "comprehensive partnership" has yet to be fully developed theoretically; and the issues, and possibly some problems, in its implementation must still be clarified. Nevertheless, there is enough in the literature at present to suggest some key elements in a rationale for coordinated children's services, as well as some key questions or problems in their administration.

The "Mission" of School Outreach

Three values that surround the discussion to date of an integrated children's services approach to school-community relations are (1) the notion of a shared and coordinated *investment* in children (Hawley, 1990); (2) a renewed sense of the importance of both high-quality care and high-quality education in the *development* of children (Kagan, 1989); and (3) a belief that the various school, home, and community messages to children should be *mutually reinforcing* rather than confusing and discrepant (Ianni, 1989).

An Investment in Children. There is nothing new in conceptualizing children's services, and particularly education, as "investments" in the futures of children and even more in the future of the society. Individual parents have long considered education an important hedge against an uncertain future, and quite typically raise their children with such constant reminders as: "Be sure to stay in school if you hope to land a good job"; "Get an excellent education because they can never take that away from you"; or "You can't get anywhere in life if you don't work hard in school." Similarly, at the societal level, economists long ago discovered that a nation's varied investments in the formation of its "human capital" are strong predictors of economic growth and development.

What is changing, then, in the use of the investment construct is not a redefinition of its importance or an alteration in its orientation toward the future. Rather, the new investment perspective is an extension and enrichment of the construct. First, notes Hawley (1990), the widely varied services offered children should be viewed as a *set* of investment strategies—indeed as a set with both cross-service and longitudinal dimensions. There is a danger of little gain when investing in educational services for at-risk children without a complementary and shared-mission investment in many other services, including improved housing, health, nutrition, recreation, family stability, and community development (e.g., reduced crime, higher employment). Similarly, there may be little gain in investment in a remediation of early-in-life barriers to children's education (e.g., low birth weight, infant malnutrition) if the longitudinal follow up does not include continuing intervention "against the forces that will later impede their cognitive and social development" (Hawley, 1990, p. 219).

A second extension of the investment construct has been discussed earlier in this book, and finds its expression in a new array of "partnerships" between educators and the private sector. From business leaders' initiatives in establishing "community foundations" to support the public schools (Calvin and Keen, 1982); to a national organization (Cities in Schools, Inc.) to implement dropout prevention in public schools through coordinated health, educational, and social services; to clusters-of-schools partnerships involving corporate sponsorship—the result has been a new sense that investments in education far beyond the public purse and the public tax dollar are both necessary and adaptable to educational improvement. As public school officials have become increasingly sophisticated in tapping and productively using the many "investors" available to them, the schools have often discovered previously unnoticed "next-door" sources of productive effort and creativity. For example, volunteers' contributions of time and talent are on the rise in public schooling—at no (or at least low) cost to school districts. Sandra Tangri and Oliver Moles (1987) report that the state of Florida even provides statewide coordination and some matching-grant funding to spur school volunteer usage.

A third extension of the investment perspective recognizes that while the public school is an important *object* of investment to be sure, it is additionally an *investor* in its own right. This theme is illustrated clearly in a 1990 report and proposal from the Council of Chief State School Officers. The proposal suggests that state education departments should establish policies and provide assistance to local school districts to develop "family-support initiatives" (see Jennings, 1990, p. 8). Another notion is that the local school should now enter actively into community-development initiatives—perhaps playing the role of an "enterprise school" in assisting cooperative endeavors to bring new investment to bear upon distressed communities (Crowson and Boyd, 1997).

Such a proposal is a far cry from the administrator's wall-the-school-off philosophy of just a few decades ago. Furthermore, this new recognition of the school itself as an investor fits closely James Coleman's (1987) notion that today's families (in many communities) are heavily in need of a kind of support and assistance that amounts to an infusion of "social capital" into their neighborhoods. The public school, long in need of support from parents, should now realize, it is argued, that it has its own investor role as an "outreach" supplier of support *to* parents. As Coleman (1994, p. 31) has phrased it:

Now, confronting newly fragile families and weakened communities, schools find their task to be a different one: to function in a way that strengthens communities and builds parental involvement with children. The schools' very capacity to educate children depends upon the fulfillment of this task.

The Development of Children. "We cannot separate care and education," writes Sharon Kagan (1989, p. 112). Indeed, this necessary linkage between care and education in a developmental sense is at the heart of the Comer program of school-community relations and coordinated children's services. James Comer (1980, p. 31) observes:

For a student to arrive on the school's doorstep adequately prepared to learn and behave well at five years of age, the caretakers (usually parents) and others in the child's environment should have stimulated early development along important developmental lines—speech and language, thinking, emotional, social, and moral— and have taught and modeled the required behavior in a way that was helpful and rewarding.

Furthermore:

Children who have had difficult or bland pre-school developmental experiences more often do not acquire skills needed for school and success in later life. Some children receive adequate emotional support and psychological development prior to school but acquire ways which are different and disturbing to school people. Most schools have an expectation level geared to the societal majority. Children who show social and academic skills different from that of the majority are often considered bad or "dumb" or of low intelligence. Punishment is often used to correct "the bad." Low expectations are established for those perceived as "dumb," and a self-fulfilling prophecy is set in motion. [P. 34]

Thus, to rephrase it, there are "critical development pathways" (Comer, 1984) in the lives of children. School success depends heavily on a path of development that if missed can become a vicious circle and even a self-fulfilling prophecy of academic frustration and failure. Furthermore, some paths of home and family development fail to merge with the developmental expectations of the public school. Such "discontinuities," often cultural in origin (Ogbu, 1974, 1988), can evolve into anger, "rebellion, ambivalence, and apathy" (Comer,

1984, p. 327). If a school staff fails to understand its role in a developmental perspective, including the need to work toward bridging cultural gaps between home and school, the central-to-education tasks of imparting knowledge and building skills may be of problematic value.

Comer's (1984, p. 332) model of school improvement emphasizes an interactive mental health team, a teacher- and curriculum-improvement program with a child-development emphasis, a "parent program" stressing both the involvement of and assistance to parents, and a broadly "representative governance" approach to the operation of the school. Again, the conceptual driving force in the program is the idea that successful development (a) cuts across both home and school; (b) constitutes a critical "pathway" from home through school to adulthood; (c) binds academic progress with social, moral, and emotional development; and (d) binds *all* the resources in a school (including parents) into a common, interactive approach to child development. In his analysis, Comer often mentions the importance of a shared understanding of child development among school staff—and, concomitantly, the typical lack of adequate training for educators (and particularly for school administrators) in this important area of understanding (see Comer, 1980, pp. 223–224).

It is interesting, and indeed curious, that while schools are the most development-oriented of society's institutions, they are not well organized as child developers. They have had much difficulty historically in matching differences in the growth and maturation of children to grade level and classroom allocations of learners. For example, opinions have changed often, with the key question never quite resolved, as to whether a K–8, a middle-school, or a junior-high school arrangement of experiences for upper-elementary pupils is best developmentally. The articulation of year-to-year curricula toward steady educational growth has always been a problem for the schools, particularly in high school. And schools in most settings have been decidedly unsuccessful in bringing subject areas, such as English, mathematics, science, history, and physical education together in a common developmental focus.

Mutually Reinforcing Messages to Children. A third value surrounding the integrated children's services approach finds its basis in the confusions and complexities of modern life. The retail consumer of years past chose from a limited stack of brand-name items and perhaps agonized only over whether to purchase the "large economy size." Today's consumer faces an overwhelming display of both foreign and domestic brands, model numbers, extra-price options, colors, special "sales," and retail outlets. So confusing is it all that new occupations are emerging—to provide special, focused assistance to consumers (often via computers) in deciding which automobile, appliance, vacation package, home entertainment system, or insurance plan constitutes the "best buy."

In a similar vein, Kirst and McLaughlin (1990) suggest that the public school should now become a valued "broker" of services to families and children. Just as confusing as the retail consumer's choices are the options in most communities for health assistance, child care, job training and placement, family counseling, alcohol and drug abuse programs, tutorial assistance, housing and welfare help, teenage pregnancy and dropout programs, youth recreation, and food and nutrition assistance. Beyond a help-one-another network between families and kinfolk found in many neighborhoods, there is seldom an adequate communication through the community of the options available, the steps required to access services, and the benefits to be gained.

Therefore, similar to the consumer-helping professional would be "case managers" in the schools (Kirst and McLaughlin, 1990, p. 86). These persons would be familiar with the needs and conditions of families in the neighborhoods and also thoroughly familiar with the assistance services of public and private agencies. "The case manager does not take over for parents or tell them what to do," but does "coach the individual in identifying his or her own problem and course of action" (Kirst and McLaughlin, 1990, pp. 86–87).

Another thought-provoking idea on this brokering role is provided by Francis A.J. Ianni (1989). Beyond the confusion and complexity of merely identifying services and gaining access, families can be further confused by the tendencies of public and private agencies to work at cross-purposes, to provide overlapping services, and to deliver conflicting messages. The messages of the service delivery network, observes Ianni, should be "mutually reinforcing rather than disharmonious" (p. 105). Disharmony is especially likely, he continues, "when the home, the school, the workplace, and other social institutions present different standards of adulthood and different means of attaining it" (p. 7). Thus, here we find an important ingredient in the case manager's contribution to service delivery, for integrating service delivery can mean much more than a simple brokering—it may mean a brokering that finds and conveys a common mission and common community-relevant values across human-service categories.

Problems in School Outreach

Critics of a school outreach (toward coordinated service delivery and a creation of strengthened school-community linkages) might argue that the public school has not been notably successful in even a narrow definition of its role. How, then, does the community-relations reformer expect the public school to be any more successful in a broadened role? Furthermore, warns Seymour Sarason (1990, p. 95), the schools can be peculiarly "intractable" institutions in the face of reform—with power relationships heavily embedded in the organizational status quo, and with a power-related "baggage of implicit assumptions underlying practice."

Amid the current enthusiasm for reforming and even restructuring the schools, there has been curiously little attention given to the extreme difficulties of engendering change in school organization and service delivery (see Hannaway and Crowson, 1989; Crowson and Boyd, 1993). The difficulties and "intractabilities" are no less a challenge in the reform of school-community relations than in any other approaches to restructuring the schools. Among the key issues are (a) competing conceptions of responsibility for children: (b) institutional pressures on human service professionals; and (c) administrative and governance constraints, including training issues. As a summary, Table 11.1 lists the key points on both the "mission" and the "problems" sides of the outreach construct.

Private versus Public Responsibility for Children. Barry Franklin (1990) reminds us that educators moved long ago into school-based health and safety interventions (e.g., innoculations against infectious diseases, vision and hearing tests, school lunches). In the early days of these imposed services, conflicts sometimes resulted between parents and school officials—particularly in immigrant neighborhoods, where the services were seen to be "countering their traditional home grown remedies for childhood diseases" (Franklin 1990, p. 270). Indeed,

Table 11.1

The Interplay of Mission and Management in the Outreach Role of the School

Values in the Mission of School Outreach

1. An investment in children
2. The integrated development of children
3. The importance of mutually reinforcing messages to children

Problems in the Practice of School Outreach

1. Private versus public responsibility for children
2. Autonomy versus sharing for professionals
3. Leadership versus "deficiency" in school management

Franklin draws on some historical inquiry by W.J. Reese (1986) in noting an example from 1906, wherein "parents in New York City's Jewish and Italian neighborhoods were so outraged by the imposition of school-based medical inspection programs that they resorted to acts of civil disobedience to voice their opposition."

A growing sense of public responsibility for children developed in the nineteenth century and expanded during the twentieth, note W. Norton Grubb and Marvin Lazerson, while simultaneously the "model" American family has been considered free to raise its own children, privately, "relatively untouched by public institutions." As a sense of crisis in families has grown, the ideology of private responsibility has been in an increasingly "uneasy coexistence" with public responsibility (Grubb and Lazerson, 1982, p. 27). Consequently, "reformers have wavered between 'strengthening' the family and 'replacing' the family. . . . They have usually attempted a little of each" (p. 29).

One of the central problems in a newly professionalized effort to "reach out" from the schools into the community, and indeed into the lives of families, is this historically grounded tension between the privacy of the family and the public-regardedness of the school. Beyond the "you-didn't-do-your-job" recriminations of parents against educators and of educators against parents, the tension is affected by some very basic differences between educators and parents. Note Thomas Hoffer and James Coleman (1990, p. 128): The school is traditionally a far more impersonal and goal-directed institution than the family, and indeed mediates in its impersonality between the family and the larger society. That is, while the school represents a good deal of "caring" in its own way, it also represents the societal objectives of sorting, socializing, preparing, and remediating. Furthermore, in its impersonality and goal-directedness, the school tends to diversify and specialize—with guidance counselors, special educators, vocational educators, mathematics teachers, and coaches *each* applying a set of demands and sending sometimes conflicting messages to the home through the children (Hoffer and Coleman, 1990). That the tensions are still very much alive was fully in evidence in 1996—in the form of a "parental rights amendment" on the November ballot in Colorado. Although defeated, supporters of the initiative claimed the need to reaffirm the rights of parents to direct and control the upbringing, education, values, and discipline of their children (Samuelson, 1996).

In sum, the public school pursues a societal role that mediates between the family and society but also complements the family's adjustment to society. Furthermore, in fulfilling its role effectively, the school depends on the assistance of the family, and this too can lead toward "intrusion." The combination of role differentiation but also complementarity and dependency produces tensions—tensions that are much exacerbated by an unresolved conflict between an ideology of private responsibility versus public responsibility for children. As public officials attempt to integrate services for children, they can encounter much mutual distrust, past impersonality, reciprocal blame, and an unresolved allocation of "responsibility."

Coleman (1985) is perceptive in suggesting that the first carefully considered step in reaching out might advisedly be less a service-delivery innovation than an effort to help create "strong functional communities of families" in school-attendance neighborhoods. A strong community with close ties between families and across the generations ("intergenerational closure") "strengthens and supports parents in the school-related activities" (Coleman, 1985, p. 530).

Autonomy versus Sharing for Professionals. Sarason (1990) provides an important insight in noting that although our convention is to think of schools as places for children, in truth they are just as fundamentally places for adults—places where adults pursue careers, reach for professional fulfillment, and join in professional communion. Indeed, continues Sarason (1990, p. 162), a "workplace" atmosphere is so pervasive that it is even fully communicated to the children. Students, too, are workers; and school is a place to do labor.

As places for children, to be sure, but additionally as adults' workplaces, the schools take on the twin missions of child development and career development. Notoriously poor in providing the rewards important to some careers (e.g., high salaries, prestige, power, career advancement), the public schools have long attempted to compensate by providing their professionals with considerable autonomy, the security of tenure, relatively weak supervision, and some administratively backed authority over children. Some scholars have noted side effects to these "perks" that can work to the disadvantage of children—including the tenured protection of teacher inadequacy and an autonomy-related protection of teaching that favors some pupils while neglecting others. Other scholars note the motivational strength of professional autonomy, which often leads to the career-focused, pupil-centered commitment of the teacher (a long famous picture of the profession).

The key understanding is that enhanced school outreach, amid an effort to coordinate professional services to children, must account for workplace values as well as service-delivery values. Some of these values help to lead to the very fragmentation of services that the proponents of service coordination find problematic. For example, a separate professional identity, a separate program of training, and a separate literature of preparation divides the social worker from the health, educational, and urban planning professions. A continuation of this separateness is an important value in protecting job availability, the viability of university-based preparation, and the (often arcane) body of special terminology that defines each of the professions.

Additionally, the autonomy that each profession seeks is part, as Sarason (1990) notes, of an organizing feature of intense "power relationships." Autonomy is important not for its own sake but for the power and authority it conveys—a power to maintain a professional distance from one's clients while helping them, to work within the confines of administrative supervision but not under it, to avoid being overrun by one's more entrepreneurial co-workers. It is not by accident, claims Sarason (p. 79), that a beginning teacher's first and most critical test among colleagues is not proving whether he or she can teach. It is, rather, showing that he or she has the power to maintain classroom control, and not have to call on colleagues to come to the rescue.

Beyond the question of values are "institutional pressures" (Grubb and Lazerson, 1982, p. 120) on each grouping of service-delivery professionals—pressures that can conflict with the ethic of service as well as conflict with a goal of coordination. Each educator, for example (from special educator to physics teacher to foreign language instructor) seeks to maintain his or her clientele. A drop in foreign language enrollments or special education referrals or physics students has budgetary and even job-protection overtones. A coordination of services would likely be doomed if, similarly, the jobs and institutional resources of some educators and some health, social work, counseling, or law enforcement professionals were threatened in the process.

The problem, if not the solution, is nicely presented by Earl Schaefer (1983), whose model is reproduced in Figure 11.1.

Schaefer's model for parental and professional care and interaction indicates the separate domains of parent and family characteristics. Ideally, a "total system of child care" would evolve out of

Figure 11.1

A Model for Parent and Professional Care and Interaction

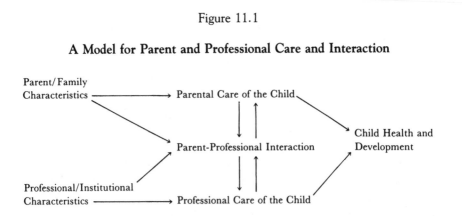

Source: Earl S. Schaefer, "Parent-Professional Interaction: Research, Parental, Professional, and Policy Perspectives." In R. Haskins and D. Adams (eds.), *Parent Education and Public Policy*. Norwood, N.J.: Ablex Publishing Co., 1983, p. 288.

interaction between parent and professional, which "feeds" back and forth to influence reciprocally both parent and professional (Schaefer, 1983, p. 289).

Little understood at this time, however, and distinctly under-researched as a set of service-delivery issues is the knowledge of just how professional and institutional characteristics (especially within a system of integrated professional services) and parent and family characteristics can be combined effectively to influence child development. How will institutional constraints on each member of a team of professionals affect the nature of interactions between parents and professionals? How can the coequal role of the parent, as depicted in Schaefer's model, be guaranteed in a program of professional integration? Conversely, how would many parents (particularly those wary of professionals) accept the suggestion of a coequal sharing of responsibility for child development that this model pictures? Do many parents already feel that they have "turned their children over" to too many experts? Certainly such a feeling was in evidence in November, 1996, in Colorado.

Leadership versus "Deficiency" in School Management. One of the central dilemmas in the delivery of professional services is that the highly trained service provider works with clients who tend to be much less knowledgeable than the service provider (Wise, 1990). Add more professionals to an integrated "team" of providers and the product can be an intimidating coterie of (occasionally smug) professionals secure in their own answers to the client's needs.

The intimidation that parents sometimes feel in the special education "staffing" can be an indication of a possible side effect of well-meaning efforts to improve services by coordinating them. If parents, families, and communities lose trust in the process, feel overwhelmed or manipulated and pressured beyond their own knowledge and understanding, the success of a parent-professional partnership to improve education is unlikely. They key question, then, is: "How can the state, the client, and the profession be assured that the appropriate services—those that best serve the client's needs—are being delivered?" (Wise, 1990, p. 406).

Comer (1980), Wagstaff and Gallagher (1990), and Cunningham (1990) all emphasize the importance of administrative leadership (from school site to central office) in answering this question. All also suggest that "business as usual" in school administration will not do; and that "tenacious leadership" (Cunningham, 1990, p. 145) in new directions will be necessary. While it is not at all clear yet (and this is a major part of the problem) just where or how tenacious leadership might proceed, there are at least some important hints of changed direction.

First, Wagstaff and Gallagher (1990, p. 110) warn that there is a "basic tension between school administrators and their constituencies." This tension "underlies the conflict between the community's need for school leadership that can lead and be trusted and the desire to have lay control of public education." While conflict is an oft-mentioned phenomenon in educational administration, historically the school administrator is better known for seeking to avoid or to control conflict rather than confront it. Elaborate organizational mechanisms may buffer the school district and its employees from environmental pressures (Hanson, 1981).

Similarly, at the school site, administrators may take special care to protect classroom teachers from conflict while simultaneously "socializing" parents with conflict potential into the procedures and folkways of the school (Morris et al., 1984). Internally, organizational features of the school—separate classrooms, infrequent meeting times, a pupil-control ideology, rule-centeredness, and a tight time schedule —are designed to minimize conflict. Surprisingly, there is also considerable feuding between faculty factions and departments and a deep undercurrent of potential conflict in many schools.

Curiously, a drive toward service-delivery collaboration and cooperation (and closer ties with families in the process) could significantly *increase* the potential for conflict. Professionals will not cooperate and will certainly not "partner" with parents easily. Seldom trained as politicians in the best sense of that word, many educational administrators may fail to appreciate how a willingness to take on conflict can lead to clearing the air, opening dialogue, and creatively accommodating differences. At least in part, one definition of "tenacious leadership" successfully applied may be the administrator's capacity to orchestrate positive outcomes for children, amid conflict, while avoiding the destructiveness of conflict gone hostile. Smylie and colleagues (1994) have documented the added tensions experienced by a group of principals in Chicago as they continued "gatekeeping" activities to minimize conflict while simultaneously opening their schools broadly to added services partnership and parent-directed activities.

Second, tenacious (even heroic) leadership in the promotion of school outreach may necessitate a careful attention to and an effort to combat some central "deficiencies" of schools as organizations (Boyd, 1990). As William Boyd's (1990) literature review notes, critics of schools as *workplaces* point out that the very structure of the school promotes isolation and discourages professional cooperation. Additionally, continues Boyd, critics of school *incentive* systems note that many of the rewards of schools (a) turn professionals inward toward their own classrooms rather than outward toward collegial cooperation; (b) promote a scratch-my-back reciprocity among colleagues rather than group or shared benefits; and (c) include such productivity-threatening "treaties" as an implicit agreement between teachers and administrators to exchange teacher cooperation in school management for weak classroom supervision by principals (see also Boyd and Hartman, 1988; Shapiro and Crowson, 1990).

Organizational deficiencies can be magnified as relatively untried experiments are attempted and as new roles and relationships must necessarily evolve. For example, space is typically at a premium in schools; and as indicated earlier, the traditional use of school space often reinforces its tendencies to separate professionals from clients. With a service-coordination experiment, a school's administration may discover that (a) it must negotiate a transfer of space from one much-valued purpose to another (and from one professional's "turf" to another), and (b) it must find a way to change that space from a closed-classroom atmosphere to an open, multiple-professional-use atmosphere (e.g., with added in-and-out access, individual professional offices as well as group decisionmaking space, and a client-welcoming arrangement of furniture). Thus, the special space and facilities needs of health and social service professionals may be quite foreign to school professionals. Alternatively, health and service professionals may enter schools with inadequate training in the sensitivities and perspectives of the elementary or secondary educational culture (Sarason, 1990). Activities and procedures that may seem natural to a health professional (e.g., a pullout for treatment) can easily be regarded as insensitive by teachers protective of their own classroom learning time with pupils.

Without some special leadership, then, that properly understands school change within its "social-institutional context," writes Sarason (1990, p. 122), there is little reason to expect that schools *will* change. Sarason continues:

> That context has structure, implicit and explicit rules, traditions, power rela-tionships, and purposes variously defined by its members. It is dynamic in that it is characterized by continuous activity and interchanges both within its boundaries and between it and its community surround. It is a context that can be described, but it is not a context that can be understood by what we ordinarily mean by description. It has covert as well as overt features. [P. 122]

Sarason goes on to observe that the person presumably leading a piece of change can be

> unaware how inadequately he knows the context. He or she assumes a degree of understanding the limits of which only become clear when implementation fails. They do not know the territory, although they have worked in it for a long time. [Pp. 122–123]

Third, there is an understandable myopia in the often-exciting world of educational change and experimentation—a myopia that directs the experimenter toward investigating the success of policy in influencing practice. It is assumed that the very essence of school reform, in all its many guises, is to be found in the impact of national, state, or local policy initiatives on the *practice* of schooling in districts, buildings, and classrooms. Policy (of course) is supposed to have an effect on practice.

Less fully understood is the finding that when reforms are imple-mented, evidence is frequently uncovered that practice has substan-tially influenced *policy* (see Darling-Hammond, 1990; Cohen and Ball, 1990). To begin with, the policy statement itself, and certainly its operationalization, may be predetermined by beliefs about what would be most acceptable to practice or most likely understood by practitioners. Also, policy in operation is mediated by practice and through the varying conceptual lenses of practitioners. Additionally, practice has a tendency over time to "take over" policy, often return-ing organizational patterns to traditions well in place before the policy changes were enacted.

The important administrative and leadership lesson to be learned from this may be twofold. First, as Oliver Moles (1990, 1991) suggests, an effective program of integrated services delivery should be *preceded* by a well-thought-through program of school outreach to parents—a reduction of "known barriers" well in advance of more sophisticated and more comprehensive efforts. Small things may well be in order, such as (a) some welcoming contact with parents early in each school year "to tell everyone about plans, procedures, and how they can assist student learning"; (b) personal contacts by teachers, from phone calls to home visits; and (c) a concerted effort by the school to listen to parents, as discussed in Chapter 10.

Second, preimplementation leadership will be needed in the training of school officials for interagency collaboration. It is not a natural part of the educational administrator's training or experience to work with a range of colleagues toward overcoming professional differences—to set aside one's own and the organization's time for collaboration, to devote school resources to a building of cooperation, or to see being a mediator or facilitator as part of one's own leadership role (Cunningham, 1990).

Furthermore, new programs often engender quite typical responses from school staffs that also call for administrative skills and perspectives untouched by most training programs. Staff members often see innovations as mere "add ons" that will have little overall impact and indeed do not deserve diversions of attention from their "real work." Similarly, educators often have a feeling that they have "been there" before, as the recipients of newly funded programs—and these, like most that have come and gone before, will be short lived. The schools have been besieged by fads, one after another, over the years. It is easy for staff members to become inured to them, to sense that "this too shall pass," and to feel further there is little sense in joining wholeheartedly in innovations if they are dependent on precarious levels of support.

In their evaluation of some demonstration projects for at-risk youth, staff from the Institute for Educational Leadership (1990, p. viii) noted that "few school staff are directly involved and, therefore, do not see themselves in any relationship to these programs. The translation of these programs into the basic mission of schools rarely occurs." In a comment on a key leadership requirement, the authors of this report continued: "We did not find any site where the administration had developed or was planning a formal strategy to help school staff understand how concepts and/or program elements of (these projects) were related to the totality of the school (p. viii). Thus, both training and planning are needed to blend practice effectively into innovative policy—but more importantly to help protect policy from the almost inevitable damages and redirections caused by practice.

Furthermore, increasingly it is also the totality of the community that must be a central element in the training and planning domain. Beyond "services" to children and families, the public schools are now encountering much broader issues and needs in community development and neighborhood revitalization. In an evaluation of one of the earliest and most ambitious efforts toward collaborated services (the "New Futures" initiative of the Annie E. Casey Foundation), White and Wehlage (1995) concluded that the project staff failed mightily in both understanding fully the social conditions in the communities they served and engaging the targeted communities cooperatively in solving their own problems.

SUMMARY

Schools and school districts under reform are increasingly turning the "old" direction of community and parental involvement in education around by engaging the schools and their professionals in programs of outreach toward the community. Although a form of public relations, to be sure, and requiring a close attention to skills in communication, the relationships tend now to go well beyond PR toward some "community-generating" endeavors between school and environment, toward a greater recognition of shared responsibilities for the welfare of children, and toward a "new vocabulary" of professional cooperation in the delivery of services to children.

In all of this, there is a renewed sense of the holistic or "ecological" forces that surround the educational lives of children plus the many opportunities for education-damaging discontinuities in their care. A new focus upon school outreach is developing, with a service-coordination flavor—a focus rooted in understandings of the importance of shared investments, integrated child development, and the value of mutually reinforcing interventions in the lives of children. In the experimental stage in communities across the country, such outreach programs are wrestling with problems of professional collaboration, with a clarified definition of purpose, and with the delineation of effective administrative leadership. There are in these endeavors many tensions and conflicts, and redefinitions of school "mission," that are now forcing themselves onto the public schools—with unanswered questions by the score as to how well the schools will adapt to partnerships with other service professionals, with parents, and with the community-at-large.

Exercise 11.1
PROFESSIONAL LANGUAGES

1. With help from practicing professionals (e.g., in health, social work, or education), identify a range of representative professional journals, one for each of a number of professional specialties.
2. Scan three or four representative journals for a recent article from each on a relatively common topic (e.g., job training, child development, crime prevention).
3. Read and compare the articles. Is there any evidence to be found of differing professional assumptions, terminology, perceptions of clientele needs, approaches to service delivery? Is there evidence of any shared or common understandings or conclusions?

Exercise 11.2
PLANNING AND ORGANIZING

Warren Bennis (1990, p. 150) advises: "Remember that change is most successful when those who are affected are involved in the planning."
1. Imagine that you wish to initiate a service-integration project in your traditional elementary school—a project involving the addition of persons trained in public health, social work, child psychology, and community organizing to the mix of educators in the school.
2. How would you organize the planning necessary to introduce this innovation? What issues and concerns in the implementation of this project will demand the closest planning attention?

Suggested Activities

1. With some classmates, make a list of some professional terms that tend to be unique to education (e.g., site-based management, cooperative learning, minimum competency testing, direct instruction). Share this list with a range of professionals in other fields—asking whether they know the terms and how they would define them.
2. Conduct a class debate on the issue of private versus public responsibility for the welfare and development of children. How does one find some "common ground" between these two perspectives?
3. "Shadow" (observe) a public-service professional other than an educator (e.g., a social worker, a public health nurse). What key similarities and differences are apparent in this person's job in comparison with a classroom teacher?
4. Observe, in sequence, an elementary teacher, a junior high teacher, a senior high teacher. Regarding the school's relationship to the *development* of children, What sense of continuity, but also of discontinuity, can be gleaned from these observations?
5. Interview a few veteran teachers, asking them to recall a number of educational "fads" in their own worklives. Ask their opinions of what happened to these past innovations. Were they poorly designed? Unworkable? Badly administered? Underfunded? Politically inept?

SUGGESTED READINGS

Bacharach, Samuel B. (ed.) (1990). *Education Reform: Making Sense of It All.* Boston: Allyn & Bacon.

Comer, James P., Haynes, Norris M., Joyner, Edward T., and Ben-Avie, Michael (eds.) (1996). *Rallying the Whole Village: The Comer Process for Reforming Education.* New York: Teachers College Press.

Dryfoos, Joy (1994). *Full-Service Schools.* San Francisco: Jossey-Bass.

Goodlad, John I. (ed.) (1987). *The Ecology of School Renewal.* Eighty-sixth Yearbook of the National Society for the Study of Education. Chicago: University of Chicago Press.

Kagan, Sharon Lynn (1993). *Integrating Services for Children and Families.* New Haven: Yale University Press.

Kirst, Michael (ed.) (1989). *The Conditions of Children in California.* Berkeley: Policy Analysis for California Education (PACE).

Mitchell, Bard, and Cunningham, Luvern L. (eds.) (1990). *Educational Leadership and Changing Contexts of Families, Communities, and Schools.* Eighty-ninth Yearbook of the National Society for the Study of Education, Part II. Chicago: University of Chicago Press.

Sarason, Seymour B. (1990). *The Predictable Failure of Educational Reform.* San Francisco: Jossey-Bass.

Chapter Twelve

TOWARD REFORM IN SCHOOL-COMMUNITY RELATIONS IN LARGE URBAN DISTRICTS

In August 1920, I came into Chicago on a train. Me and Carrie got off the train in Chicago and we took the streetcar into East Chicago, which was about thirty miles away. All I wanted was freedom. I thought, "I can make it anywhere!"

—Maggie L. Comer in *Maggie's American Dream*
by James P. Comer, 1988a, p. 34

Just arrived in Chicago. Up from the South. Running from an abusive stepfather. Still a teenager. The daughter of a Mississippi sharecropper. It never occurred to James Comer's mother, Maggie, that she might not be able to "make it anywhere." Indeed, in Comer's remarkable story of growing up in East Chicago, Indiana, Maggie Comer takes center stage as the irrepressible creator of a high-achieving, exceptionally strong black family—in a still-segregated America.

Secure in her marriage, her church, and her self-confidence, Maggie Comer guided four children toward educational accomplishment, adult success, and indeed, national prominence. It was face to face with the school band director before daughter Louise would be allowed to take music lessons with the white children. It was a harsh worklife in the steel mills for Hugh Comer and the drudgery of "day-work" for Maggie in order to provide a secure home, family dinners complete with memorable "family debates," and (when they were young) "toys with alphabetics on them" for the children.

For the children, it was also having to "deal with Mom," if the

263

"infamous pink letter" (an unsatisfactory warning note) reached home from school. James learned early that "good grades could save me from a lot of grief, at home and at school" (Comer, 1988, p. 111). It was the power of Maggie Comer's late-in-life reflection: "Even as a little barefoot girl back in the country, I had this dream. I had this gift from inside to want something. I thought to myself that if this one could do it, I could do it. And when I couldn't go on, I said my children would do it" (p. 227).

RESILIENCY AND SHARING

Maggie's American Dream reflects a changing focus in the examination of family effects on school achievement. As James Comer (1988) himself puts it, the story of the black family has for so long been targeted on "'the victims,' or worse, 'those who are not able or not trying.'" He continues: "An understanding of the strategies and strengths of the 'survivors' will tell us more about the obstacles and ways around them than an exclusive focus on 'the victims'" (p. xxiii). In her remarkable book *I've Known Rivers*, Sara Lawrence-Lightfoot (1994) similarly outlines an outstanding group of "storied lives"—a group of people, as she puts it, who are "not defeated by the abuses of racism that echo through their ancestry, their family histories, and their daily lives." Surrounded by a "world ... full of constant contradictions, ... [they] use them as a source of creative power" (p. 642).

Not at all limited to the minority family, but drawing its emphasis from such statements as Comer's and such insights as Lawrence-Lightfoot's, the new focus on family effects is on strength, competence, and success rather than deficiency, dependency, and defeat. The rediscovered construct is *resilience*—conveying an interest in the positive side of coping with the stressors and challenges of life and schooling rather than the negatives (see Werner and Smith, 1982; Mistune, 1986; Garmezy and Mistune, 1986). The resilient individual somehow overcomes obstacles to educational accomplishment, springing back from adversity, while others in similar circumstances may be defeated.

Not at all limited to the minority family, but drawing its emphasis from such statements as Comer's, the new focus in family effects is on strength, competence, and success rather than deficiency, dependency, and defeat. The recently rediscovered construct is *resilience*—conveying an interest in the positive side of coping with the stressors and challenges of life and schooling rather than the negatives (see Werner and Smith, 1982; Masten, 1986; Garmezy and Masten, 1986). The resilient individual somehow overcomes obstacles to educational accomplishment, springing back from adversity, while others in similar circumstances may be defeated.

Background

The roots of this switch from negative to positive thinking may go back a number of decades—particularly to an academic debate over the "culture-of-poverty" thesis that drove much of the 1960s Great Society legislation. With a strong intellectual foothold in the work of Oscar Lewis (e.g., *Five Families*, 1959; *Children of Sanchez*, 1961; *La Vida*, 1966), the culture-of-poverty thesis found, discouragingly, that the disadvantages, breakdowns, pathologies, and nonadaptations of direst poverty appear to be passed on generation after generation. The culture of poverty is just that—a contraculture all of its own with little "break-out" potential for its members. In education, such inquiry as that of Basil Bernstein (1961) seemed to support the thesis. Bernstein found poor mothers using a severely restricted conceptual language with their children, while middle-class mothers tended to employ a much richer and more elaborate language of the sort that would later be useful in school.

Lewis's work came under vigorous attack by persons who charged that his analysis (a) tended to blame the victims of poverty rather than its societal determiners and (b) found pathologies in the poverty culture but few strengths. Charles Valentine (1968), for example, took Lewis harshly to task for these weaknesses and for a methodological overconcentration on the side of family life that supported the culture-of-poverty thesis.

An early counterpoint to Lewis, much admired by his opponents, was Elliot Liebow's *Tally's Corner* (1967), a study of a group of unemployed men who gathered at a certain street-corner. Liebow found, in contrast to Lewis, a rich and varied culture—one strong in its bonds, its humor, and even its aspirations for improvement. What Liebow also found was an unresponsive, uncaring welfare, criminal justice, and employment system—working effectively to offer no hope, plus day-in and day-out messages of failure, to the men of Tally's Corner.

In education, similarly, Ray Rist's (1970) longitudinal study of a single classroom of kindergarten children found more sorting, allocating, and determining of life's chances (even at age five) by the *school* than was evidenced by the culture of the home. Indeed, Rist found a strong interactive effect, wherein children coming to school with the most visible external evidence of poverty origins (e.g., dirty and smelly clothes, hole-filled sneakers, poorly kept hair, the deepest of "ghetto dialects") were given the *least* amount of attention and understanding by their kindergarten teacher. From this start, differences in school achievement were "measurable" by second grade.

By no means has this debate over the positive versus the negative consequences of family culture been fully resolved. Nevertheless, there are some important contemporary developments. The first is that the deficit thesis behind the culture-of-poverty argument is no longer a viable interpretation. William Boyd (1989b, p. 26) put it succinctly:

In the 1960's disadvantaged children were thought to be "culturally deprived." Cultural deprivation provided a theory explaining that their problems in school stemmed from "deficits" in their family and cultural backgrounds. Today, "cultural deprivation" is viewed at best as an anthropological oxymoron, and at worst a racist concept. Consequently, it has been replaced generally by reference to "cultural differences."

The second contemporary interpretation, however, is that serious cultural discontinuities between home and school do in fact exist for many children (Ogbu, 1974, 1978, 1988). The seriousness of this for American schooling is reflected in the growing concentration of an underclass of poor families and at-risk children in the nation's cities—left behind by middle- and working-class families who have escaped the city, leaving behind whole neighborhoods to grow up without knowing a formally employed wage earner (Wilson, 1987, 1996). Even more discouraging, the cultural differences between home and school reflect discontinuities induced by origins of economic, political, and social exploitation (such as involuntary servitude) (Ogbu, 1974, 1978). Although no longer considered cultural "deficiencies," the recognition is that these differences are enormous barriers to school success for many poor children—and, indeed, more than barriers, they may even represent personal "costs" in succeeding (for example, having to "act white" in school in order to get ahead) (Fordham and Ogbu, 1986).

The third contemporary interpretation is that cultural differences are just that—differences. These differences are found in the ways people talk, move, live, establish relationships, raise their children, engage in play, decide what is good and what is bad, remember the past, and decide what is worth knowing. Without placing a positive or negative value on them, such differences should be regarded as the "cultural capital" belonging to each group of people—that is, the investments of skills, traditions, mores, beliefs, and behaviors passed on from generation to generation (Coleman, 1988a). Unlike the "deprivation" hypothesis of the 1960s, the cultural-capital model suggests that all cultures have capital and, indeed, that each cultural group has its own qualities and strengths. Moreover, there will be considerable variation *within* cultures in the styles of family life and in their attributes that lead to success in school (Clark, 1983). Capital is not always evenly distributed nor is the same type of capital found among all members of a cultural group. As an eye-opening aside here, it is only very recently, notes Kassie Freeman (1997), that there has been an understanding that cultural differences can be reflected in the decisions of minority students to attend college. Such considerations as whether college is truly an option, an "intimidation factor," and how much hope can I really trust in are key, perceived barriers for many African Americans.

Resiliency

In brief summary, a culture-of-poverty emphasis on the "pathologies" of the underclass has given way to an appreciation of the cultural differences, even the strengths, of all families. Nevertheless, America since the 1960s has increasingly isolated its poorest families in self-contained islands of blight, joblessness, violence, exploitation, inadequate health and other social services, poor schools, and all around despair. As indicated earlier in this volume, the "conditions of children" (and particularly poor children) in America are of nationally recognized concern. More children are poor today than at any time in the past three decades (Wilson, 1996). Beyond the poverty and isolation of the underclass, continuing discontinuities (Ogbu, 1974, 1978) between home and school in America persist as serious barriers to opportunity, to cultural understanding, and even to the very viability of the schools as public-benefit institutions.

There are two sides to the construct of resiliency. The term was used, prophetically (reflecting one side), as early as 1967, by Hylan Lewis in his foreword to *Tally's Corner*. Lewis (1967, p. x) wrote: "Dr. Liebow's penetrating analysis of the worlds of the streetcorner men goes a long way toward accounting for the survival and resiliency of these men—but at what cost!"

The "cost" referred to by Lewis is summarized later by Liebow (1967). By no means wrapped in a completely distinctive subculture with an integrity of its own, argues Liebow (p. 222), the men of Tally's Corner do seek "the goals and values of the larger society." Failing this, each of the men conceals "his failure from others and from himself as best he can" (p. 222). Summarizing, Liebow observes:

> If, in the course of concealing his failure, or of concealing his fear of even trying, he pretends—through the device of public fictions—that he did not want these things in the first place and claims that he has all along been responding to a different set of rules and prizes, we do not do him or ourselves any good by accepting this claim at face value. [P. 222]

If one side of resiliency is reflected in a turning inward, toward barest survival, the other side is reflected in a "Maggie-like" drive toward success in the face of adversity. The central question is: Why do some youngsters from deep-poverty backgrounds choose the "success" route—succeeding in school despite the surrounding conditions and school-community discontinuities? How do these individuals beat the odds? From the perspective of this brighter or positive side of the resiliency coin, the emphasis may well be on the strengths to be found in cultural differences among communities, the rich varieties of family life to be discovered in all cultures (Clark, 1983), and the types and varieties of cultural capital that are brought to the lives of a community's children—often by mentorship-oriented "wizards" (observe McLaughlin, Irby, and Langman, 1994), who are to be found in the more active and the most committed of community organizations.

Both sides of the resiliency construct are important. In their successful proposal to establish a National Center for Education in the Inner Cities, the research staff at Temple University concluded:

> In spite of all the difficulties of urban life, many children who live there grow up to

healthy adulthood, often strengthened in commitments to humane purposes by the challenging experiences they have faced. We must study both the successes and failures of students and schools in the inner city and, from the insights revealed in such studies, seek ways to magnify what can be made positive in the lives of inner-city children and youth. [Center for Education in the Inner Cities, 1990, p. 2]

Sharing

An important correlate of the change in emphasis—from patholo-gies to strengths and from defeat to resiliency—is the notion that if the local community offers its own "capital," then it behooves the local school to *share* its child development responsibilities with the community.

Indeed, this was the thinking behind the "radical" reform of local school governance in Chicago. Beginning in 1989–90, significant powers over budgets, curricula, and personnel were granted elected Local School Councils for each of the city's 540 schools. These governing councils were dominated by parents and community rep-resentatives, with the minority composed of teachers and administra-tors. The "radical" assumption was that these parents and community people—from the poorest to the wealthiest and from the least educated to the most sophisticated neighborhoods in the city— would be able to act responsibly and to draw on the strengths and the capital of the surrounding community in order to run (and even improve) their own schools. Fears that political corruption, misman-agement, and debilitating conflict would newly characterize the Chi-cago schools had, by the second (1990–91) year of reform, not been realized—despite the confusion of a successful lawsuit that challenged and forced changes in the method of voting for Local School Council members. Indeed, the staying power of Chicago's grassroots reform has been remarkable, and, despite many changes in structure (in-cluding a Mayor's-office "takeover" of the schools), the emphasis upon the community and upon local governance in Chicago has continued through the 1990s.

As with the construct of resiliency, there are two sides to the "sharing" coin. One side is ably expressed by Seymour Sarason (1990, p. 39), who says that no longer should "the educational community accept full responsibility for dealing with educational problems, most of which by their very nature are exacerbated by forces beyond the school. . . . Just as the medical community does not accept respon-sibility for cancer caused by smoking, pollution, food additives, and scores of other possible carcinogens, ... the educational community cannot accept responsibility for problems originating in the larger society." Sarason concludes, forcefully, that "educators must assume leadership in relationship to diverse community groups and institutions, in a way that makes clear that responsibility is shared" (p. 39). He is also, however, a very strong advocate for sharing and has argued that "the existing governance structure of school systems should be abolished"—in favor of full-fledged parental involvement and control (Sarason, 1995, p. 161).

The other side of the same coin would suggest, Chicago style, that no longer are effective city schools the unique provinces of professional educators. The community offers strengths, perspectives, energy, its own capital, and resilient families as valuable resources. In terms paralleling Sarason's analogy, the conclusion may be that no longer should parents and the community leave full responsibility for schooling in the hands of educators. The parental community (even the poverty community) "knows enough" and has the strength to be an effective partner in a shared instructional endeavor.

THE CONSEQUENCES OF REFORM

In parallel to this new emphasis on the strengths of urban communities and the cope-with-it resiliency of many, even deepest poverty, families is a serious concern over the isolation and multigenerational failure of many members of the urban underclass to move beyond barest survival, perhaps toward attaining the additional "cultural capital" necessary to improved school achievement. Both the strengths and the deficits sides of these parallel perspectives are the source of a new interest today in a greater sharing of responsibility between educators and parents. Such thoughts constitute the theory behind such far-reaching changes in the governance of school as the school-reform experiment in Chicago. But Chicago is by no means alone. Receiving national attention as well have been parental-involvement and school-community "partnership" programs in Indianapolis, New York, San Diego, Houston, Boston, Milwaukee, and Los Angeles (see, for example, Epstein, 1991; Chrispeels, 1991; Warner, 1991; and Davies, 1991). Once the most "radical" of reforms, Chicago's effort may pale by comparison against even more recent experiments in Cleveland and Milwaukee, wherein parents are given voucher-style controls over their choice of schools.

Counterposed against questions of theory are important conse-
quences-of-reform questions for practice. Underexplored to date are
important issues in the grassroots' politics and administration of
city programs that follow this new theory of shared strength and
responsibility. Interestingly, while connecting-to-the-community is a
value of renewed importance across urban America, there has simultaneously been a growing intervention of "the city" into the public
schools. Mayor Daley has "taken over" the Chicago schools. Similar
moves have occurred in Cleveland, Boston, and Los Angeles (Hendrie,
1997).

Typically, this intervention strives not to return the educational
system to overcentralized control but, instead, to bring the resources
of the entire city to bear on school improvement—while continuing to work to strengthen individual neighborhoods and foster grassroots involvement. Included in this initiative is often an accompanying
neighborhood revitalization or community-development press—extending well beyond the local school to include the notion that
jobs, neighborhood-level investments, added health-care resources,
improvements in housing, better law enforcement, and the like all
go together *with* gains from the revitalization of the schools.

There are important issues of administration and practice growing
out of these ideas and actions for reform. Events to date in such
cities as Chicago can be used as guides to an informed consideration of improved urban school-site administration, under reform.
Specifically, there are central issues of power and politics, of role
definition and allocating responsibility, of organizational learning,
and of "creating" parent-school communities (amid the larger environment of a city itself on the move).

Power and Politics. Much of the traditional parental involvement
in schools—in its major forms of PTA-style volunteerism, parent-
teacher conferences, advisory councils, community-opinion surveys,
and even paraprofessional employment—has been without a transfer
of significant power. To be sure, parents have never been power*less*.
School administrators and teachers feel vulnerable to both individual
and collective parental displeasure. In city schools, there was often a
special fear that parents might take a dispute "public"—either to
higher levels of the educational bureaucracy or outward to the media.
Also, most schools have always had some powerful parents— who can
be depended on for good advice or for opinion-guiding leadership in
the community (Morris et al., 1984).

Because of the emphasis placed on parental involvement in such federal programs as Chapter 1 and in many similar state programs, urban schools have also become increasingly sophisticated in their methods of parental communication, in the building of home-school relationships (e.g., home visits, phone calls, parent resource centers), and in the management of mandated parental advice (D'Angelo and Adler, 1991). Nevertheless, while these contacts have produced a greater educator sensitivity to parental interests and needs, the Chapter 1 and like-minded initiatives have not been famous for redirecting school power.

Indeed, studies of the urban principalship by Dale Mann (1976) and others (e.g., Morris et al., 1984; Crowson and Porter-Gehrie, 1980) found most school-site administrators to be fairly adept manipulators of advisory councils, able handlers of dissatisfied and even disruptive parents, and bufferers of teachers and classrooms from instruction-wasting interruptions. Mann discovered that far more New York City principals saw themselves as the communicator of school system policies and procedures *to* parents than as the conduit of local concerns *from* parents to the schools and the upper bureaucracy.

One question, then, is to what extent a new "sharing" between school and community can be found in changed power relationships. It would appear that this would certainly be the case in Chicago, with the onset of far-reaching reform permitting parent-dominated councils to hire or fire all of the city's school principals. Half of the city's schools decided whether to replace or retain their principal in the first year of reform, half in the second. The power of the community to change principals was real; it survived a Court challenge from the Chicago Principals' Association; and it communicated symbolically that indeed a significant change in school governance for Chicago was at hand.

Intriguingly, among the 276 Chicago schools involved in a hiring decision in 1990, the report was that 82 percent retained their current principal (awarding a three-year contract), while the remainder (18 percent) decided to try someone new (Steinberg and Robinson, 1990). Contrary to the prediction of many, there was no evidence of a racial criterion—white principals were as likely to be retained as fired in black schools, and black principals were as likely to be retained as fired in white schools. There were some unsupported charges that a number of the city's majority-Hispanic neighborhoods were opting for an Hispanic administrator to replace either a white or black principal (see Robinson, 1990). There were also some very heated turnovers— with a split in the community, considerable media attention, and sidewalk demonstrations in occasional support of a "popular" principal who had been fired (O'Donnell, 1990). In the years since, there has been a bit of a disturbing fall-off in the numbers of people willing to serve in the Local School Councils and a small increase in the reported cases of local misuses of power (e.g., by principals, by community representatives, or by both).

Nevertheless, most of the evidence for Chicago reform is that the power shifts in most of Chicago's schools have gone remarkably smoothly (see Chicago Panel on Public School Policy and Finance, 1990). Some critics have suggested that this is because most of the city's savvy principals quickly found a way to dominate their councils; others, less critical, have suggested that the majority of the principals quickly adapted to an effective working relationship *with* the councils. Very likely many examples of both could be found.

What hadn't yet become evident in Chicago by the mid 1990s was whether the decentralizing reform to the communities would translate into a decided improvement in the academic quality of the schools. Indeed, some hundred ninety of Chicago's schools were "put on probation" by Chicago's chief executive officer in 1996. Fear that quality improvement was not happening had prompted the mayor's intervention in 1995—and an accompanying tightening of accountability, of central-office efficiency, of expenditure controls, and of close administrative oversight for the entire city. As of 1997, concerns had not materialized that all of this would repoliticize the school system and destroy the city's gains in community control. However, despite a remarkably positive "report card" on the takeover, by 1997, the jury was still out in Chicago on just how much "real" reform was underway inside the schools; and at least a third of the city's schools remained on probation.

If the sense of "real" reform is that shifts in power should ultimately be reflected in changes *inside* the schools, Chicago's case was decidedly too early in its progress, by the beginning of 1997, to be instructive. We may, however, glean some interesting insights and guidelines from an analysis of similar developments in Australia (Watkins, 1990).

In 1983, the government of Victoria, Australia, changed a 1975 act that established Local School Councils—altering them from advisory bodies to governing councils for each of Victoria's public schools. Peter Watkins (1990) studied six of these councils for a year; his analysis suggests three foci in determining whether the shared "power" is indeed influencing the schools.

First, suggests Watkins (p. 323), there should be evidence of a sense of shared *responsibility*. Indeed, in schools where council influence was working, there was a problem coping with the "rush of responsibility"—council members *with* educators joined in shared worries over curricula, finances, personnel, pupil progress, getting the work done, and so on. Where responsibility is not shared—where each set of actors either claims responsibility for itself or blames the other side for responsibility unfulfilled—there can be little sharing of power.

Second, relatedly, one should find evidence of a shared council agenda. Watkins (1990, p. 318) draws on research by T.W. Hammond (1986) in noting "that the structure of the agenda plays an important role in the distribution of power and responsibility, allowing for certain policies to be facilitated, while passage of others is made more difficult." Some early observations of Chicago's reforms suggested that many principals adroitly accomplished that which local school district superintendents have long been famous for—a good deal of agenda control. What finds its way on the agenda, and even more vitally what gets left off (Bachrach and Baratz, 1962), are key indications of the give and take to be expected between school and community.

Third, beyond the agenda itself, suggests Watkins (1990), one should find evidence of a discussion and *debate* on agenda issues. It is not unusual or unlikely for Local School Council members to feel intimidated, ignorant, and helpless in the face of pedagogical terminology, state and federal rules, the "expert" opinions of educators, and the limits on debate imposed by time deadlines (e.g., "this plan must be approved tonight or we lose our funding"). Conversely, when debate does occur, the educators claim they must often sit through hours of trivia, small-minded complaints, and ill-founded decisions. In a personal conversation, for example, one Chicago principal complained bitterly of his council's decision to spend a sizable budget allotment on graduation gowns for the school's kindergarten classes. Instructive here was the principal's admission that he had not felt free to debate the matter with the council; through debate he may have been able either to reach an understanding of the council's perspective or to change it. Watkins noted that because parents do not feel confident debating issues of education policy and the curriculum, they often go back to issues they do feel comfortable with such as discipline, dress, facilities, and deportment.

Role and Responsibilities. There has already been much discussion of roles in this book; and, indeed, the point should be clear that the delineation of role has been a key stumbling block over the years in improving school-community relations. Parenting is the special province of the home, but a province often (and increasingly) in need of help from other institutions in society. School-teaching is a profession with special training and licensure, but a profession often (and increasingly) in need of focused, educational help from parents. The school is an institution separate from the community; yet it is a reflection of and extremely dependent on the community. The educator has a clear pedagogical role to fulfill but finds that this role usually requires supportive assistance from the health, safety, welfare, psychology, nutrition, recreation, and job-training professions.

Education-related roles overlap, and are filled with ambiguity. The "story" of public schooling has spanned from colonial times to the present conflict when one party or another seems to be overstepping the bounds of either parent or pedagogue. As the present-day reform movement appears to be moving toward both professional empowerment and an enhanced school-community partnership, old, unresolved questions and conflicts of role are encountered anew. One of the best and most often referenced efforts to date to identify a "model" of school-family role connections has been offered by Joyce Epstein (1987a, 1987b, 1988). Epstein's model has the attraction of suggesting separate types of role involvement for parents and school authorities but also a *sharing* of roles between home and school. As summarized by Chapman (1991, p. 357), Epstein's model includes:

- Basic obligations of families, including health, safety, and a positive home environment;
- Basic obligations of schools, including communication with parents regarding their child's programs and progress;
- Parent involvement at school, including volunteer activities and support for sports, student performances, and other activities;
- Parent involvement in learning activities at home, including supervising homework and helping children work on skills that will help them learn in the classroom; and

- Parent involvement in governance, decision making, and advocacy, including participation in parent/teacher organizations and in various decision-making and advisory roles. [Chapman, 1991, p. 357]

Chicago's reform mandates the final, governance portion of Epstein's model; and with varying degrees of intensity, the city's schools have become increasingly attentive as well to the other elements. Nevertheless, the question of role definition under reform is a major unresolved issue in most large urban environments like Chicago's—environments filled with role-confusion problems. The basic obligations of families are often not being fulfilled, and the resources of society, including the schools, have been far from adequate compensation. The basic obligations of schools in communicating with parents are hampered by an annual full-population student turnover in many schools and by deep cultural and language diversities and discontinuities. Getting parents involved has so bedeviled city schools ("only the parents of the high achievers seem to show up") that many urban educators either have given up or just give lip service to the idealized hope of heavy parental participation. While many experiments in "outreach" to involve parents in supporting learning at home are in operation and are exciting, the numbers of participating parents remain small. In short, the specific behaviors and roles needed to fulfill the promise of Epstein's model are yet to be worked out in many large urban environments.

However, exciting experimentation in redefining roles *is* underway. One of the most promising has been the "Schools Reaching Out" project of The Institute for Responsive Education (Davies, 1991). Another collection and description of promising programs has been assembled by Heather Weiss and the Harvard Family Research Project (1995). For example, consider the role redefinitions, as described either by Davies (1991) or by Weiss (1995), involved in the following:

(a) A parent center at the Ellis School in Boston—offering ESL and GED classes; sponsoring breakfasts for fathers; helping parents with access to social service, housing, and health agencies; recruiting parent volunteers for teachers; organizing clothing exchanges; and so on.
(b) The Addison County Parent/Child Center in Vermont—using parents actively as volunteers in all aspects of a childcare

program, parent training, an alternatives-for-teens program, and family outreach. Parent volunteers participate in every dimension, from transportation to teaching to home visits, to leadership, management, and support (Weiss, 1995).

(c) "Action research teams" "to involve teachers directly in studying home/school/community relations and in devising actions to improve their own practices" (Davies, 1991, p. 380).

One outcome of the "action research team" can be a clarification of role for the classroom teacher vis-à-vis parental involvement. Note, in this regard, William Firestone's (1990, p. 174) observation that one central barrier to teacher commitment is "role ambiguity or lack of clarity about what one's responsibilities or acceptable courses of action are."

Organizational Learning. Schools are, naturally, places for individuals to learn. Additionally, schools as organizations are themselves "learners," although there is some debate on this point. Some scholars claim that to talk of organizations as learners comes uncomfortably close to treating organizations as living things. People learn, and organizations are only groupings of people—not learners themselves. Other scholars, however, claim that while organizational learning may occur through individuals, there is something more, something collective, that "lives on" in every organization—long after particular individuals have come and gone. Organizations have collective memories; they develop belief structures, world views, and ideologies. They learn. They can also fail or refuse to learn (Hedberg, 1981).

The importance of this topic to our discussion is evident in the arguments that (a) organizations most often learn through changes in their environments, (b) the environment often (although not always) "shocks" the organization into some learning, and (c) organizations engage in learning that seeks a better fit with the environment (Hedberg, 1981). The Chicago school reform can most assuredly be seen as a bit of a "shock" to a system that was well adapted to top-down, bureaucratic decisionmaking; to advice, but not governance, from parents and the community; and to a long tradition of distancing the inner workings of the school from all outsiders (Wong and Rollow, 1990).

What are the Chicago Schools and other urban systems under reform learning from such environmental shocks? Without drawing

What are the Chicago schools and other urban systems under reform learning from such environmental shocks? For one thing, Chicago and other systems that decentralized may now realize that the "shock" of this reform may have gone a bit too far. As mentioned, Chicago has recentralized to some extent under mayoral leadership; and in early 1997, New York City recentralized significant authority into the hands of its chancellor, for the first time since decentralization reform in 1969 (Hendrie, 1997). Without drawing more heavily at this point on the rapidly expanding literature on reform implementation, we can at least speculate that much of the organizational "learning" in Chicago and elsewhere is somewhere between these two "extreme" forms of environmental shock versus a longer-term reassessment and a gradual adaptive fit. On the one hand, many schools may be effectively incorporating the decentralizing reform into their long-established standard operating procedures. In this case, administrators may be buffering the school staff from the governing council, may be educating the council into adopting a hands-off role vis-à-vis the school, or may be effectively redirecting the attention and energies of the council away from vital areas of intervention in the school. One of the central tasks of Chicago's Local School Councils in their first full year of reform was to fashion "school-improvement plans." Indications about the school-improvement plans are that only a few have been truly creative (Chicago Panel on Public School Policy and Finance, 1990).

On the other hand, many schools may be effectively reorienting the internal dynamics of their buildings in ways that reflect a changed consciousness of the environmental press. A newsworthy example was the report of council-pressured decisions by the Gompers Middle School in Chicago to adopt school uniforms, paint and reroof the building, print curriculum guides for parents to help their children learn, and establish a "drop-everything" period each day when everyone from pupils to teachers to janitors is expected to stop to read (Johnson, 1990).

In the first instance, the learning (or nonlearning) of the school consists of the protection of a pedagogical and procedural status quo. In the second instance, the learning that takes place can be far more difficult and far more upsetting to members of the organization—for it often changes mightily the prereform use of time, expectations of behavior, individual autonomy, communications patterns, and incentives. Peter Senge (1990) labels the first form "adaptive" learning, or coping, while the second form is a more constructive "generative" learning. It is this second form of learning, claims Hedberg (1981), that eventually awards an organization *more power* over its environment. Indeed, Roland Barth (1990, p. 152) observes that a school that has been able to change, with its community, toward its own redesigned and reintegrated "vision" of itself can enjoy a good measure of "diplomatic immunity" from the severest strains of its environment.

There is, unfortunately, no "magic key" for those persons who would wish to facilitate organizational learning. Hedberg (1981) suggests the importance of promoting experimentation—of rewarding a new curiosity in the organization and of course thereby discouraging the complacency of times past. Senge (1990, p. 9) emphasizes the value of a "principle of creative tension"—using the tension, and indeed the "shock" of reform, as a positive step toward comparing current reality with "where we want to be" as an organization. Both Senge and, much earlier, Chester Barnard (1938), emphasize the importance of a "teacher" in a learning organization—a leader (perhaps a principal) who is him- or herself a learner and who can guide the school toward becoming a learning community (see also McPherson, Crowson, and Pitner, 1986). In like manner, Howard Gardner (1995) notes the power of a very creative and attention-grabbing "story" or narrative—a message that clearly captures the minds and the enthusiasm of members and even the audience of an organization.

Creating Community. There has already been much discussion in this book of the outreach role of the school and of the school's potential as a community-creating resource for its neighborhood. Interestingly, there has been little analysis to date that turns this relationship on its head—that is, that asks whether the neighborhood can be influential in creating a greater sense of community *within* the school. Indeed, the perspective generally is that increased school-community ties tend to create a potential for added within-organization conflict, role ambiguity, and change-related stress. The assumptions are that the school may eventually be better off as a community-responsive institution but that it will first have to undergo some difficult adjustments and some tension-producing activities.

As of early 1991, there was insufficient evaluative evidence to judge the extent to which Chicago's school reform had been accompanied by heavily increased or decreased tensions *within* the schools. To be sure, in a number of the nearly one-in-five instances of principal nonretention, the change in principals did reportedly disrupt school programs and staff and student activities. Some of the nonretained principals had served their schools for twenty years or more. The schools were *their* schools, displaying the traits and personalities of these long-tenured principals.

On the other hand, there is some evidence that many of the governing councils in Chicago in the first year of reform took pains, sagaciously, to skirt the edges of deep intervention in their schools or to allay staff fears of "revolution" rather than fuel them. A "Local School Council Awards Program" (1990), summarizing admittedly the "best" of council actions for year one of Chicago's reform, listed the following council efforts: (a) persuaded local businesses to adopt their school, (b) started a Community Assistance Fair, (c) obtained computers for the school, (d) opened a Family Resource Center, (e) pressured "downtown" to repair and paint the school, (f) developed an after-school sports program, (g) launched a library-card drive among students and parents, and (h) offered English as a Second Language and GED programs to parents. Many of the other actions, interestingly, could be interpreted as efforts to support and encourage school staff members rather than change them—including increasing the traditionally meager allotment of funds to teachers for classroom use; compensating teachers for attending professional meetings; paying teachers extra for in-service participation; enlisting parents, community members, and former students to help with school security; and initiating a range of student-attendance incentives.

This is not to say that the award-winning councils in Chicago's first year of reform avoided entirely the decisionmaking that might lead to within-school tensions. Some councils decided to (a) fully reorganize the curriculum, (b) establish new textbook selection committees, (c) reinstate homerooms, (d) bring university personnel in for added teacher training, (e) organize a "Parent/Community Volunteer Team" to patrol the school and its grounds, and (f) add a number of new programs and staff members to the mix of personnel in the school (e.g., full-day kindergarten, art and music classes, speech therapy, a preschool program, a computer-education program) (Local School Council Awards Program, 1990).

The evidence thus far in Chicago's school reform is that much of this rather cautious intervention *from* the community has continued. The more energetic of the city's Local School Councils vigorously take action to improve the schools but are careful, for the most part, to address issues of school support (e.g., physical plant improvements, parental involvement, overcrowding, security, attendance) rather than fundamental change. Furthermore, although a number of the councils engage in *some* interventions into curriculum, staff development, and programs, the councils are also active in consensus building and the development of linkages.

It is within this reform context of an opportunity for vigorous decisionmaking, with an accompanying chance for either supportive or damaging intervention, that a role for the building principal less than adequately considered thus far becomes important. Although recently a voluminous literature has accumulated on the responsibilities of the principal in promoting school effectiveness, much less attention has been paid to what Terrence Deal and Kent Peterson (1990) label "the principal's role in shaping school culture." Table 12.1 summarizes Deal and Peterson's suggestion that building principals can indeed shape the culture of their schools and can indeed perform the vital role of creating a within-organization sense of community, amid reform. Deal and Peterson explain the importance of the community-creating role of the principal as follows:

Principals are often told that cultural leadership is the art of fusing a personal vision with a school that needs direction. This requires *both* a principal who knows what he or she wants *and* a community of faculty, parents, students, and staff who believe they need a new direction to solve existing problems. [P. 14]

As indicated in Table 12.1, Deal and Peterson suggest five culture-shaping roles for the building principal. A *symbolic* role builds on the principal's appreciation and "reading" of the school culture—its history and traditions, its collective memories, its beliefs and values. Then, from the location and accessibility of the office, to gestures and facial expressions, to sets of daily routines, to the many formal and informal communications of each day, the principal "signals" to the organizational community a value-laden sense of direction for the school.

Similarly, the principal plays the roles of "potter," "poet,"

Table 12.1

The Principal's Role in Shaping School Culture

Role	*Behavior*
1. The principal as *symbol*	1. Affirms values through office arrangements, personal dress and demeanor, focus of time and attention, verbal and written "signals" of appreciation or censure.
2. The principal as *potter*	2. Shapes values through ceremonies, slogans, rituals, symbols, and celebrations of heroes/heroines.
3. The principal as *poet*	3. Uses language (e.g., words, metaphors, ideas, stories, acronyms) to convey the school's "best image of itself."
4. The principal as *actor*	4. Uses school as a "stage," with its social dramas orchestrated to "reaffirm or redirect cultural values and beliefs."
5. The principal as *healer*	5. Uses transitions (e.g., retirements, holidays, graduations, reductions in force, deaths) as a drawing-people-together opportunity.

Adapted from T.E. Deal and K.D. Peterson, *The Principal's Role in Shaping School Culture*. Washington, D.C.: U.S. Department of Education, Office of Educational Research and Improvement, September 1990, pp. 20–30.

"actor," and "healer." A *potter* tries to shape newly developing and shared values through such devices as celebrations of school "heroes," value-celebrating rituals, and value-displaying ceremonies. A *poet* communicates in subtle ways (e.g., through stories, mottos, ideas, and just plain talk) the school's shared "image of itself." An *actor* finds drama in the culture of the school, using its events, its routines, and even its conflicts and crises as a stage and an opportunity to "reaffirm or redirect the values and beliefs of the school." Finally, a *healer* uses change and transition (from a retirement to a death to a budget reduction to a holiday) as a chance to solidify the school's "collective experience"—the experience of community, of "drawing-together," that characterizes an effectively shared school culture (Deal and Peterson, 1990).

Interestingly, from their first year on, many of Chicago's award-winning councils must have had an intuitive grasp of the importance of the Deal and Peterson (1990) perspective—for among the practices of selecting and evaluating principals highlighted in the Local School Council Awards Program (1990) were the following:

- Council members from the De Witt Clinton Elementary School asked "that candidates for principal outline their philosophies, plans and goals for the school"; and the council involved "teachers and parents in assessing the responses."
- The council of the John C. Haines Elementary School established "major criteria for selecting a principal that includes sensitivity to the culture and nature of the community."
- Council members from the Beasley Academic Center visited "the finalists' current schools before selecting a principal."
- Both the Haines and Beasley Schools invited finalists "to a public forum for presentations and questions."

SUMMARY

In this concluding chapter, we turn our attention a bit more specifically to the reform of school-community relations in large-city schools. We frequently use the early-in-reform case of public schooling in Chicago as illustration. Chicago presents a case of decentralized, grassroots' governance—through parent and community controlled councils—among each of the city's hundreds of schools. This is now, however, a case leavened with a rebalancing of the grassroots against city hall.

The chapter began with the discussion of a perspective (a theory of sorts) on city schooling that differs markedly from the "urban pathologies" approach of years past. While recognizing fully the extremely difficult conditions of childhood and of life in the inner cities, and recognizing too the discontinuities between home and school that persist, the changed emphasis nevertheless is on the deep strengths of families, communities, and individuals—and the *resiliency* of many individuals who "beat the odds" to achieve educational and occupational goals. A vital corollary of the resiliency perspective is the notion that the strengths of communities and families should be the source of a new sense of *sharing* between home and school, including as in Chicago a sharing in the actual governance of schools.

To date, there has not been a deep accumulation of experience, or of research and evaluation, on the *practice* of a shared responsibility for urban education. Four issues of importance addressed in this chapter concern basic questions of power relationship, of role definition, of organizational learning, and of school cohesiveness or community. Decentralized governance and parental involvement can fall far short of a meaningful sharing of power for a school's improvement agenda, the debates around that agenda, and the sense of common responsibility for fulfilling that agenda. Similarly, (a) the definitions of roles for both educators and parents remain in flux, and are yet to be thoroughly worked out as both parents and teachers find ways to capitalize on the special strengths of one another; (b) the organizational context itself needs to learn positive, even resilient, responses to the "shocks" of reform-minded change in its operating environment; and (c) the school itself, internally, needs to be led creatively to a new cultural sense of itself as a shared-with-parents community of successful learning.

Much of this chapter, like much of this book, goes beyond the hard-and-fast knowledge that is now available on the successes, consequences, and pitfalls of reformed school-community relations. Most of the reform-minded discussion is just too new. The results are still not in on such "radical" ventures as Chicago's decentralization reform; and they are certainly not in on the rebalancing of top-down and bottom-up that is underway in Chicago, as well as New

York, Cleveland, and elsewhere. Therefore much of this book has the flavor of "what should be" or "here's what to look for" rather than "here are some well-researched results and answers." It has been the purpose of this book to raise issues and to suggest administrative as well as policy directions rather than to convey "solutions." We hope its readers will find the discussion at least somewhat helpful in grappling with their own leadership questions, as they engage anew in struggles toward a more productive partnership between school and community.

Exercise
DEFINING ROLE OBLIGATIONS

In cooperation with colleagues or classmates, draft a parent and teacher handbook, along the lines of the model of school-family role connections suggested by Joyce Epstein (1987a, 1987b, 1988).

This handbook should offer specific suggestions for parents and teachers in fulfilling each of the following categories of "role connection" between home and school.
1. The basic education-related obligations of families.
2. The basic family-related obligations of schools.
3. Parental involvement at school, including school governance.
4. Parental involvement in learning at home.

Share the draft of your handbook with other parties. What, particularly, are the implications of the handbook for school administrators?

Suggested Activities

1. Read some thought-provoking ethnographies that highlight cultural differences (as well as ties) between home and school. Excellent examples are Susan U. Phillips, *The Invisible Culture*, 1983; J.A. Hostelter and G.E. Huntington, *Children in Amish Society*, 1971; Alan Peshkin, *God's Choice*, 1986; and John Ogbu, *The Next Generation*, 1974. Discuss, around these books, the concept of "discontinuity" between home and school. Additionally, consider the special strengths of each culture that could be used as resources for learning by the school.

2. Conduct a "life-history" interview with a senior citizen. As this person recounts his or her life—his or her story of growing up, going to school, working, perhaps marriage and children, then retirement—look for indicators of a special "resiliency" in this person's life. What stresses are recounted, and how were they overcome?

3. Observe a meeting of a school advisory council. What appears to be the agenda? Is there a hidden agenda? Who seems to be in control of the agenda? Is there discussion and debate? What conclusions can you draw about the advisory function of the council from your single observation?

4. While there is much interest in organizational learning, the more intriguing question is why organizations don't learn. Observe a school during its workday and interact informally with as many professionals and staff members as possible. Try to gain from your investigation a sense of what might be hardest to change in the school: certain attitudes? Time schedules? Allocations of space? The school's "paper trail"?

5. Shadow a building principal for at least two working days. Keep a record of as much "culture shaping" in the work of this principal as it is possible to discern. What values, for example, seem to be communicated in the principal's dress, speech, office arrangements, and time usage? What values and beliefs seem to hold center stage at times of crisis or conflict? What rituals, symbols, and stories exist?

SUGGESTED READINGS

Comer, James P. (1988). *Maggie's American Dream: The Life and Times of a Black Family.* New York: New American Library.

Davies, Don (1991, January). "Schools Reaching Out: Family, School, and Community Relationships for Student Success," *Phi Delta Kappan* 72(5): 376–382.

Deal, Terrence E., and Peterson, Kent D. (1990, September). *The Principal's Role in Shaping School Culture.* Washington, D.C.: U.S. Department of Education, Office of Educational Research and Improvement.

Epstein, Joyce L. (1987). "Toward a Theory of Family-School Connections: Teacher Practice and Parent Involvement." In K. Hurrelman, F-X Kaufman, and F. Losel (eds.), *Social Intervention: Potential and Constraints*, pp. 121–136. New York: de Gruyter.

Epstein, Joyce L. (1991, January). "Paths to Partnership: What We Can Learn from Federal, State, District, and School Initiatives," *Phi Delta Kappan* 72(5): 344–349.

Garmezy, N., and Masten, A.M. (1986). "Stress, Competence and Resilience: Common Frontier for Therapists and Psycho-pathologists," *Behavior Therapy* 17: 500–521.

Halpern, Robert (1995). *Rebuilding the Inner City.* New York: Columbia University Press.

Lawrence-Lightfoot, Sara (1994). *I've Known Rivers: Lives of Loss and Liberation.* New York: Penguin Books.

McLaughlin, Milbrey W., Irby, M. I., and Langman, J. (1994). *Urban Sanctuaries.* San Francisco: Jossey-Bass.

Ogbu, John U. (1978). *Minority Education and Caste: The American System in Cross-Cultural Perspective.* New York: Academic Press.

Werner, E.E., and Smith, R.S. (1982). *Vulnerable but Invincible: A Study of Resilient Children.* New York: McGraw-Hill.

BIBLIOGRAPHY

Academic Development Institute (1990a). *Alliance for Achievement: Building the Value-Based School Community*. Chicago: Academic Development Institute.

Academic Development Institute (1990b, February). "The Role of the Parent in Student Achievement," A Research Report 1(1). Chicago: Academic Development Institute.

Adler, A. (1957). *Understanding Human Nature*. New York: Premier Books.

Agger, R.E., and Goldstein, M.N. (1971). *Who Will Rule the Schools: A Cultural Class Crisis*. Belmont, Calif.: Wadsworth.

Alexander, K., and Pallas, A. (1983). "Private Schools and Public Policy: New Evidence on Cognitive Achievement in Public and Private Schools," *Sociology of Education* 56: 170–182.

Anderson, C.A. (1974). "Potentialities for Popular Participation in Planning." In *Participatory Planning in Education*, pp. 273–280. Paris: The Organization for Economic Co-operation and Development.

Andrews, R.L. (1987). "The School-Community Interface: Strategies of Community Involvement." In J.I. Goodlad (ed.), *The Ecology of School Renewal*, Eighty-sixth Yearbook of the National Society for the Study of Education, pp. 152–169. Chicago: University of Chicago Press.

Arnez, N.L. (1981). *The Besieged School Superintendent: A Case Study of School Superintendent-School Board Relations in Washington, D.C., 1973–1975*. Washington, D.C.: University Press of America.

Astuto, T.A., and Clark, D.C. (1992). "Challenging the Limits of School Restructuring and Reform," in A. Lieberman (ed.), *The Changing Contexts of Teaching*, pp. 90–109. Chicago: University of Chicago Press.

Atkin, J., and Bastiani, J. (1988). *Listening to Parents: An Approach to the Improvement of Home-School Relations*. London: Croom Helm.

Bacharach, S.B. (ed.) (1990). *Education Reform: Making Sense of It All*. Boston: Allyn & Bacon.

Bachrach, P., and Baratz, M. (1962). "The Two Faces of Power," *American Political Science Review* 56: 947–952.

Baker, B.L. (1989). *Parent Training and Developmental Disabilities*. Washington, D.C.: American Association on Mental Retardation.

Bailyn, B. (1960). *Education in the Forming of American Society*. New York: Random House.

Barnard, C.I. (1938). *The Functions of the Executive*. Cambridge, Mass.: Harvard University Press.

289

Barth, R.S. (1990). *Improving Schools From Within: Teachers, Parents and Principals Can Make the Difference.* San Francisco: Jossey-Bass.

Barton, P.E. (1983). *Partnerships Between Corporations and Schools.* Research Report Series. Washington, D.C.: National Commission for Employment Policy.

Baum, H.S. (1986). "Politics in Planners' Practice." In B. Checkoway (ed.), *Strategic Perspectives in Planning Practice*, pp. 25–42. Lexington, Mass.: Lexington Books.

Becker, H.S. (1961). "The Teacher in the Authority System of the Public School." In A. Etzioni (ed.), *Complex Organizations: A Sociological Reader*, pp. 243–251. New York: Holt, Rinehart & Winston.

Becker, W.C. (1971). *Parents Are Teachers: A Child Management Program.* Champaign, Ill.: Research Press.

Beckhard, R., and Harris, R. (1977). *Organizational Transitions.* Reading, Mass.: Addison-Wesley.

Behrman, R.E. (eds.) (1992, Spring). "School-Linked Services," *The Future of Children* 2(1).

Bellah, R.N.; Madsen, R.; Sullivan, M.; Swidler, A.; and Tipton, S.M. (1985). *Habits of the Heart: Individualism and Commitment in American Life.* Berkeley: University of California Press.

Bennis, W. (1990). *Why Leaders Can't Lead: The Unconscious Conspiracy Continues.* San Francisco: Jossey-Bass.

Bernstein, B. (1961). "Social Class and Linguistic Development: A Theory of Social Learning." In A.H. Halsey, J. Floud, and C.A. Anderson (eds.), *Education, Economy, and Society*, pp. 288–314. New York: The Free Press.

Blase, J.J. (1989, November). "The Micropolitics of the School: The Everyday Political Orientation of Teachers Toward Open School Principals," *Educational Administration Quarterly* 25(4): 377–407.

Bledstein, B.J. (1978). *The Culture of Professionalism.* New York: W.W. Norton.

Blumberg, A. (1985). *The School Superintendent: Living with Conflict.* New York: Teachers College Press.

Booth, A., and Dunn, J. (eds.) (1996). *Family School Links: How Do They Affect Educational Outcomes?* Mahwah, N.J.: Lawrence Erlbaum Associates.

Boyd, W.L. (1989a, Summer). "Balancing Competing Values in School Reform: The Politics of Perestroika." Chapter prepared for inclusion in J. Chapman and J. Dunstan (eds.), *Democracy and Bureaucracy: Tensions in Australian Government Schooling.* Australian College of Education.

Boyd, W.L. (1989b, October). "What Makes Ghetto Schools Work or Not Work?" Invited paper prepared for conference on The Truly Disadvantaged, sponsored by the Social Science Research Council and Northwestern University, Evanston, Illinois.

Boyd, W.L., and Crowson, R.L. (1981). "The Changing Conception and Practice of Public School Administration." In D.C. Berliner (ed.), *Review of Research in Education*, Volume 9, pp. 311–373. Washington, D.C.: American Educational Research Association.

Boyd, W.L., and Hartman, W.T. (1988). "The Politics of Educational Productivity." In D.H. Monk and J. Underwood (eds.), *Distributing Education Resources Within Nations, States, School Districts, and Schools.* Cambridge, Mass.: Ballinger.

Boyd, W.L., and Walberg, H.J. (eds.) (1990). *Choice in Education: Potential and Problems.* Berkeley, Calif.: McCutchan.

Boyte, H.C. (1984). *Community Is Possible: Repairing America's Roots*. New York: Harper & Row.

Bradley, A. (1996a, November 6). "Divided We Stand: What Has Come Between the Public and Its Schools?" *Education Week* 16 (10): 31-35.

Bradley, A. (1996b, November 20). "A Lesson in Winning Back an Estranged Public," *Education Week* 16(12): 1, 20-21.

Bremer, J., and von Moschzisker, M. (1971). *The School Without Walls: Philadelphia's Parkway Program*. New York: Holt, Rinehart & Winston.

Bronfenbrenner, U. (1974, August). "The Origins of Alienation," *Scientific American* 231(1): 60.

Brown, L.D. (1986). "Participatory Research and Community Planning." In B. Checkoway (ed.), *Strategic Perspectives on Planning Practice*, pp. 123–137. Lexington, Mass.: Lexington Books.

Browne, W.P. (1980). *Politics, Programs, and Bureaucrats*. Port Washington, N.Y.: Kennikat Press.

Bryk, A.S.; Deabster, P. Easton, J; Lupescu, S.; and Thum Y. (1994). "Measuring Achievement Gains in the Chicago Public Schools, *Education and Urban Society*, 306-319.

Bryson, J.M. (1988). *Strategic Planning for Public and Nonprofit Organizations: A Guide to Strengthening and Sustaining Organizational Achievement*. San Francisco: Jossey-Bass.

Bunker, B.B. (1989). "Leading School Systems Through Transitions." In J.J. Mauriel (ed.), *Strategic Leadership for Schools*, pp. 261–286. San Francisco: Jossey-Bass.

Cain, G.G., and Goldberger, A. (1983). "Public and Private Schools Revisited," *Sociology of Education* 56: 208–218.

Caldwell, B.J., and Spinks, J.M. (1988). *The Self-Managing School*. London: Falmer Press.

Callahan, R.E. (1962). *Education and the Cult of Efficiency*. Chicago: University of Chicago Press.

Calvin, A.D., and Keen, P. (1982, October). "Community Foundations for Public Schools," *Phi Delta Kappan* 64(2): 126–127.

Campbell, R.F., et al. (1987). *A History of Thought and Practice in Educational Administration*. New York: Teachers College Press.

Campbell, R.F.; Cunningham, L.L.; Nystrand, R.O.; and Usdan, M.D. (1990). *The Organization and Control of American Schools*, sixth edition. Columbus, Ohio: Charles E. Merrill Pub. Co.

Capper, C.A. (1990, April). "Exploring Community Influences on Leadership and Reform: A Micro-level and Macro-level Analysis of Poverty and Culture." Paper presented at the annual meeting of the American Educational Research Association, Boston.

Carew, J.V., and Lightfoot, S.L. (1979). *Beyond Bias: Perspectives on Classrooms*. Cambridge, Mass.: Harvard University Press.

Carlson, R.O. (1964). "Environmental Constraints and Organizational Consequences: The Public School and Its Clients." In D.E. Griffiths (ed.), *Behavioral Science and Educational Administration*, Sixty-third Yearbook of the National Society for the Study of Education, Part II, pp. 262–278. Chicago: University of Chicago Press.

Carlson, R.V., & Awkerman, G. (eds.) (1991). *Educational Planning: Concepts, Strategies, Practices.* New York: Longman.

Carter, L. (1984, August-September). "The Sustaining Effects Study of Compensatory and Elementary Education," *Educational Researcher*, pp. 4–7.

Cattermole, J., and Robinson, N. (1985, September). "Effective Home/School Communication—From the Parents' Perspective," *Phi Delta Kappan* 67(1): 48–50.

Cavazos, L.F. (1989). *Educating Our Children: Parents and Schools Together.* A Report to the President. Washington, D.C.: Department of Education.

Center for Education in the Inner Cities (1990, June). A Technical Proposal. Philadelphia: Temple University Center for Research in Human Development and Education.

Central Advisory Council for Education (1967). *Children and Their Primary Schools* ("Plowden Report"). London: HMSO.

Cervone, B.T., & O'Leary, K. (1982, November). "A Conceptual Framework for Parent Involvement," *Educational Leadership*, pp. 48–49.

Chapman, W. (1991, January). "The Illinois Experience: State Grants to Improve Schools Through Parent Involvement," *Phi Delta Kappan* 72(5): 355–358.

Checkoway, B. (ed.) (1986). *Strategic Perspectives on Planning Practice.* Lexington, Mass.: Lexington Books.

Chicago Panel on Public School Policy and Finance (1990, October). "Chicago School Reform: Second-Year Marks of Success," *Panel Update* 7(2): 1, 7.

Chrispeels, J.H. (1991, January). "District Leadership in Parent Involvement," *Phi Delta Kappan* 72(5): 367–371.

Chubb, J.E., and Moe, T.M. (1988). "No School Is an Island: Politics, Markets, and Education." In W.L. Boyd and C.T. Kerchner (eds.), *The Politics of Excellence and Choice in Education.* New York: Falmer Press.

Chubb, J.E., and Moe, T.M. (1990). *Politics, Markets, and America's Schools.* Washington, D.C.: Brookings Institution.

Cibulka, J.G., and Kritek, W.J. (1996). *Coordination Among Schools, Families, and Communities: Prospects for Educational Reform.* Albany: State University of New York Press.

Cicourel, A., and Kitsuse, J. (1963). *Educational Decision Makers.* Indianapolis: Bobbs-Merrill.

Clark, R. (1983). *Family Life and School Achievement: Why Poor Black Children Succeed or Fail.* Chicago: University of Chicago Press.

Clune, W.H., and Witte, J.F. (eds.) (1990). *The Theory of Choice and Control in Education.* London: Falmer Press.

Cohen, D.K., and Ball, D.L. (1990, Fall). "Policy and Practice: An Overview," *Educational Evaluation and Policy Analysis* 12(3): 347–353.

Coleman, J.S. (1985, April). "Schools and the Communities They Serve," *Phi Delta Kappan* 66(8): 527–532.

Coleman, J.S. (1987, August-September). "Families and Schools," *Educational Researcher* 16(6): 32–38.

Coleman, J.S. (1988a). "Social Capital in the Creation of Human Capital." *American Journal of Sociology* 94 (Supplement): S95–S120.

Coleman, J.S. (1988b, April). "Statement Before the Select Education Subcommittee of the Education and Labor Committee of the House of Representatives." Washington, D.C.

Coleman, J.S. (1994). "Parental Involvement: Implications for Schools," in R.J. Yinger and K.M. Borman (eds.), *Restructuring Education: Issues and Strategies for Communities, Schools, and Universities*, pp. 19-31. Cresskill, N.J.: Hampton Press.

Coleman, J.S., and Hoffer, T. (1983). "Response to Tauber-James, Cain-Goldberger and Morgan," *Sociology of Education* 56: 219–234.

Coleman, J.S., and Hoffer, T. (1987). *Public and Private Schools: The Impact of Communities*. New York: Basic Books.

Coleman, J.S.; Hoffer, T.; and Kilgore, S. (1982a). "Achievement and Segregation in Secondary Schools: A Further Look at Public and Private School Differences," *Sociology of Education* 55: 162–182.

Coleman, J.S.; Hoffer, T.; and Kilgore, S. (1982b). "Cognitive Outcomes in Public and Private Schools," *Sociology of Education* 55: 65–76.

Coleman, J.S.; Hoffer, T.; and Kilgore, S. (1982c). *High School Achievement*. New York: Basic Books.

Comer, J.P. (1980). *School Power: Implications of an Intervention Project*. New York: The Free Press.

Comer, J.P. (1984, May). "Home-School Relationships as They Affect the Academic Success of Children," *Education and Urban Society* 16(3): 323–337.

Comer, J.P. (1986, February). "Parent Participation in the Schools," *Phi Delta Kappan* 67(6): 442–446.

Comer, J.P. (1987, March). "New Haven's School-Community Connection," *Educational Leadership*, pp. 13–16.

Comer, J.P. (1988). *Maggie's American Dream: The Life and Times of a Black Family*. New York: New American Library.

Comer, J.P. (1988, November). "Educating Poor Minority Children," *Scientific American* 259(5): 42–48.

Comer, J.; Haynes, N.; and Joyner, E. (1996). "The School Development Program," in J. Comer, N. Haynes, E. Joyner, and M. Ben-Avie (eds.), *Rallying the Whole Village: The Comer Process for Reforming Education*, pp. 1-26. New York: Teachers College Press.

Comer, J.P.; Haynes, N.M.; Joyner, E.T.: and Ben-Avie, M. (eds.) (1996). *Rallying the Whole Village: The Comer Process for Reforming Education*. New York: Teachers College Press.

Connell, R.W.; Ashenden, S.K.; and Dowsett, G.W. (1982). *Making the Difference: Schools, Families and Social Division*. Sydney, Aus.: George Allen & Unwin.

Constitution, Glenview Public Schools, Glenview, Illinois (1989). An agreement between the Glenview Education Association and the Board of Education of the Glenview Public Schools, 1989–1992.

Conway, J.A.; Jennings, R.E.; and Milstein, M.M. (1974). *Understanding Communities*. Englewood Cliffs, N.J.: Prentice-Hall.

Cooper, B.S. (1990, April). "A Tale of Two Cities: Radical School Restructuring in London and Chicago." Paper presented at the annual meeting of the American Educational Research Association, Boston.

Cooper, M. (1988). "Whose Culture Is It, Anyway?" In A. Lieberman (ed.), *Building a Professional Culture in Schools*, pp. 45–54. New York: Teachers College Press.

Cope, R.G. (1978). *Strategic Policy Planning*. Littleton, Colo. The Ireland Educational Corporation.

Corwin, R.G., and Borman, K.M. (1988). "School as Workplace: Structural Constraints on Administration." In N.J. Boyan (ed.), *Handbook of Research on Educational Administration*, pp. 209–237. New York: Longman.

Craft, M.; Raynor, J.; and Cohen, L. (eds.) (1980). *Linking Home and School: A New Review*, third edition. London: Harper and Row.

Crain, R.L. (1969). *The Politics of School Desegregation*. Garden City, N.J.: Anchor Books.

Cremin, L.A. (1979). "Family-Community Linkages in American Education: Some Comments on the Recent Historiography." In H.J. Leichter (ed.), *Families and Communities as Educators*, pp. 119–140. New York: Teachers College Press.

Cremin, L.A. (1988). *American Education: The Metropolitan Experience, 1987–1980*. New York: Harper and Row.

Cronin, J.M. (1973). *The Control of Urban Schools: Perspective on the Power of Educational Reformers*. New York: The Free Press.

Crowson, R.L. (1974). "State Authority and Local Autonomy: An Assessment of Intergovernmental Relations in Education." Ph.D. dissertation, The University of Chicago.

Crowson, R.L. (1987, August). "The Local School District Superintendency: A Puzzling Administrative Role," *Educational Administrative Quarterly* 23(3): 49-69.

Crowson, R.L, and Boyd, W.L. (1993, February). "Coordinated Services for Children: Designing Arks for Storms and Seas for Unknown," *American Journal of Education* 101(2): 140-179.

Crowson, R.L., and Boyd, W.L. (1996). "Implications of Restructuring and Site-Level Decentralization Upon District-Level Leadership," in M. Barber and R. Dann (eds.), *Raising Educational Standards in the Inner Cities: Practical Initiatives in Action*, pp. 145-168. London: Wellington House.

Crowson, R.L., and Boyd, W.L. (1997). "New Roles for Community Services in Educational Reform," in A. Hargreaves (ed.), *International Handbook of Educational Change*. Toronto: Ontario Institute for Studies in Education.

Crowson, R.L.; Boyd, W.L.; and Mawhinney, H.B. (eds.) (1996). *The Politics of Education and the New Institutionalism: Reinventing the American School*. London: Falmer Press.

Crowson, R.L., and Hannaway, J. (1989). "Introduction and Overview: The Politics of Reforming School Administration." In J. Hannaway and R.L. Crowson (eds.), *The Politics of Reforming School Administration*, pp. 1–12. New York: Falmer Press.

Crowson, R.L., and Porter-Gehrie, C. (1980, Winter). "The Discretionary Behavior of Principals in Large-City Schools," *Educational Administration Quarterly* 16(1): 45–69.

Cuban, L. (1985). "Conflict and Leadership in the Superintendency," *Phi Delta Kappan* 67(1): 28–30.

Cubberly, E.P. (1909). *Changing Conceptions of Education*. Boston: Houghton Mifflin.

Cunningham, L.L. (1990). "Reconstituting Local Goverment for Well-Being and Education." In B. Mitchell and L.L. Cunningham (eds.), *Educational Leadership and Changing Contexts of Families, Communities, and Schools*, Eighty-ninth Yearbook of the National Society for the Study of Education, Part II, pp. 135–154. Chicago: University of Chicago Press.

Dahl, R.A. (1960). *Who Governs?* New Haven: Yale University Press.

D'Angelo, D.A., and Adler, C.R. (1991, January). "Chapter 1: A Catalyst for Improving Parent Involvement," *Phi Delta Kappan* 72(5): 350–354.

Darling-Hammond, L. (1988). "Policy and Professionalism." In A. Lieberman (ed.), *Building a Professional Culture in Schools*, pp. 55–77. New York: Teachers College Press.

Darling-Hammond, L. (1990, Fall). "Instructional Policy Into Practice: The Power of the Bottom Over the Top," *Educational Evaluation and Policy Analysis* 12(3): 233–241.

Davies, D. (1981). "Citizen Participation in Decision Making in the Schools." In D. Davies (ed.), *Communities and Their Schools*, pp. 83–119. New York: McGraw-Hill.

Davies, D. (ed.) (1981). *Communities and Their Schools*. New York: McGraw-Hill.

Davies, D. (1990, April 17). "Can Urban School Politics and Practices Be Changed to Parent Involvement Initiatives?" Paper presented at the annual meeting of the American Educational Research Association, Boston.

Davies, D. (1991, January). "Schools Reaching Out: Family, School, and Community Partnerships for Student Success," *Phi Delta Kappan* 72(5): 376–382.

Davis, A.; Gardner, B.B.; and Gardner, M.S. (1941). *Deep South.* Chicago: University of Chicago Press.

Deal, T.E., and Peterson, K.D. (1990, September). *The Principal's Role in Shaping School Culture.* Washington, D.C.: U.S. Department of Education, Office of Educational Research and Improvement.

Delagado-Gaitan, C. (1994). "Spanish-Speaking Families' Involvement in Schools," in C. Fagnano and B. Werber (eds.), *School, Family and Community Interaction: A View From the Firing Lines*, pp. 85-98. Boulder, Colo.: Westview Press.

Devaney, K., and Sykes, G. (1988). "Making the Case for Professionalism," in A. Lieberman (ed.), *Building a Professional Culture in Schools*, pp. 3-22. New York: Teachers College Press.

Dewey, J. (1897). "My Pedagogic Creed," *School Journal* 54: 77-80.

Dewey, J. (1956). *The School and Society.* Chicago: University of Chicago Press.

Dollard, J. (1937). *Class and Caste in a Southern Town.* New Haven: Yale University Press.

Dornbusch, S.M., and Wood, K.D. (1989). "Family Processes and Educational Achievement." In W.J. Weston (ed.), *Education and the American Family: A Research Synthesis*, pp. 66-95. New York: New York University Press.

Dreikers, R., and Soltz, V. (1964). *Children: The Challenge.* New York: Hawthorn.

Driscoll, M.E. (1989). "The School as a Community." Ph.D. dissertation. Department of Education, The University of Chicago.

Driscoll, M.E. (1990). "The Formation of Community in Public Schools: Findings and Hypotheses," *Administrator's Notebook* 34(4): 1-4.

Driscoll, M. E.; Boyd, W.L.; and Crowson, R. (1996). *Collaborative Services Initiatives: A Report of a National Survey of Program Directors* (Report No. 96-7). Philadelphia: Temple University, National Center on Education in the Inner Cities.

Dryfoos, J. (1994). *Full-Service Schools.* San Francisco: Jossey-Bass.

Easton, D. (1965). *A Framework for Political Analysis.* Englewood Cliffs, N.J.: Prentice-Hall.

Edwards, V., and Redfern, A. (1988). *At Home in School.* London: Routledge.

Elmore, R.F. (1986). *Choice in Public Education.* Santa Monica, Calif.: RAND Corporation.

Emmons, C.; Comer, J.; and Haynes, N. (1996). "Translating Theory in Practice: Comer's Theory of School Reform," in J. Comer, N. Haynes, E. Joyner, and M. Ben-Avie (eds.), *Rallying the Whole Village: The Comer Process for Reforming Education,* pp. 27-41. New York: Teachers College Press.

Epstein, J.L. (1982). *Student Reactions to Teacher Practices of Parent Involvement* (Report P-21). Baltimore, Md.: Johns Hopkins University, Center for Research on Elementary and Middle Schools.

Epstein, J.L. (1985, Winter). "Home and School Connections in Schools of the Future: Implications of Research on Parent Involvement," *Peabody Journal of Education* 62(2): 18-41.

Epstein, J.L. (1987a). "Toward a Theory of Family-School Connections: Teacher Practices and Parent Involvement," In K. Hurrelman, F-X Kaufman, and F. Losel (eds.), *Social Intervention: Potential and Constraints,* pp. 121-136. New York: de Gruyter.

Epstein, J.L. (1987b). "What Principals Should Know About Parental Involvement," *Principal* 66: 6-9.

Epstein, J.L. (1988). "How Do We Improve Programs of Parent Involvement?" *Educational Horizons* 66: 58-59.

Epstein, J.L. (1991, January). "Paths to Partnership: What We Can Learn from Federal, State, District, and School Initiatives," *Phi Delta Kappan* 72(5): 344-349.

Epstein, J.L. (1992). "School and Family Partnerships," in M. Alkin (ed.), *Encyclopedia of Educational Research,* pp. 1139-1151. New York: Macmillan.

Epstein, J.L. (1994). "Theory to Practice: School and Family Partnerships Lead to School Improvement and Student Success," in C. Fagnano and B. Werber (eds.), *School, Family and Community Interaction: A View from the Firing Lines,* pp. 39-54. Boulder, Colo.: Westview Press.

Espe-Sherwindt, M, and Kerlin, S.L. (1990, April). "Early Intervention with Parents with Mental Retardation: Do We Empower or Impair?" *Infants and Young Children* 2(4): 21–28.

Essert, P.L., and Howard, R.W. (1952). *Educational Planning by Neighborhoods in Centralized Districts.* New York: Bureau of Publications, Teachers College, Columbia University.

Etzioni, A. (1980). "Compliance Structures." In A. Etzioni and E.W. Lehman (eds.), *A Sociological Reader on Complex Organizations,* third edition, pp. 87–100. New York: Holt, Rinehart and Winston.

Family Study Institute (1990, February). "The Role of the Parent in Student Achievement." A Report of the Family Study Institute 1(1). Chicago.

Fantini, M. (1968). "Community Control and Quality Education in Urban School Systems." In H.M. Levin (ed.), *Community Control of Schools,* pp. 40–75. Washington, D.C.: The Brookings Institution.

Fantini, M. (1983). "From School System to Educative System: Linking the School with Community Environments." In R.L. Sinclair (ed.), *For Every School a*

Community: Expanding Environments for Learning. Boston: Institute for Responsive Education.

Fantini, M. (1986). *Regaining Excellence in Education.* Columbus, Ohio: Charles E. Merrill Co.

Fantini, M., and Sinclair, R. (eds.) (1985). *Education in School and Nonschool Settings.* Chicago: National Society for the Study of Education.

Firestone, W.A. (1977, February). "The Balance of Control Between Parents and Teachers in Co-op Free Schools," *School Review* 85(2): 264–286.

Firestone, W.A. (1990). "The Commitments of Teachers: Implications for Policy, Administration, and Research." In S.B. Bacharach (ed.), *Advances in Research and Theories of School Management and Educational Policy,* Volume 1, pp. 151–183. Greenwich, Conn.: JAI Press.

Fiske, E.B. (1989, December 6). "Corporate-Style Management Is What Schools Need, An Executive Says. So He Starts a School." *New York Times.*

Florio-Ruano, S. (1989). "Social Organization of Classes and Schools. In M.C. Reynolds (ed.), *Knowledge Base for the Beginning Teacher,* pp. 163–172. Oxford: Pergamon Press.

Fordham, S. (1988). "Racelessness as a Factor in Black Students' Success: Pragmatic Strategy or Pyrrhic Victory?" *Harvard Educational Review* 58(1): 54–58.

Fordham, S., and Ogbu, J.U. (1986). "Black Students' School Success: Coping with the Burden of 'Acting White.'" *Urban Review* 18(3): 176–206.

Franklin, B.M. (1990, July-September). "'Something Old, Something New, Something Borrowed . . .': A Historical Commentary on the Carnegie Council's Turning Points," *Journal of Education Policy* 5(3): 265–272.

Freeman, K. (1997). "Mixing Culture and Capital: African American High School Students' Consideration of the Value of Higher Education," *Review of Higher Education.*

Friedman, J. (1973). *Retracking America.* New York: Doubleday.

Fuller, W.E. (1982). *The Old Country School: The Story of Rural Education in the Middle West.* Chicago: University of Chicago Press.

Gamble, C. (1996, November 20). "S.C. Uses 'Hard Talk' in Effort to Reconnect Public Schools," *Education Week* 16(12): 13.

Gardner, H. (1995). *Leading Minds: An Anatomy of Leadership.* New York: Basic Books.

Garmezy, N, and Masten, A.S. (1986). "Stress, Competence and Resilience: Common Frontier for Therapists and Psychopathologists," *Behavior Therapy* 17: 500–521.

Garmezy, N; Masten, A.S., and Tellegen, A. (1984). "The Study of Stress and Competence in Children: A Building Block for Developmental Psychopathology," *Child Development* 55: 97–111.

Garmezy, N., and Rutter, M. (1985). "Acute Reactions to Stress." In M. Rutter and L. Hersov (eds.), *Child and Adolescent Psychiatry: Modern Approaches,* second edition, pp. 152–176. Oxford, Eng.: Blackwell Scientific Publications.

Garmezy, N., and Rutter, M. (eds.) (1983). *Stress, Coping, and Development in Children.* New York: McGraw-Hill.

Garmezy, N., and Tellegen, A. (1984). "Studies of Stress-Resistant Children: Methods, Variables, and Preliminary Findings." In F. Morrison, C. Lord, and

D. Keating (eds.), *Advances in Applied Developmental Psychology*, Volume 1, pp. 231–287. New York: Academic Press.

Getzels, J.W. (1979). "The Communities of Education." In H.J. Leichter (ed.), *Families and Communities as Educators*, pp. 95–118. New York: Teachers College Press.

Ginott, H. (1965). *Between Parent and Child*. New York: Macmillan.

Gittell, M. (1968). "The Balance of Power and the Community School." In H.M. Levin (ed.), *Community Control of Schools*, pp. 115–137. Washington, D.C.: Brookings Institution.

Glenn, C.L., Jr. (1988). *The Myth of the Common School*. Amherst: University of Massachusetts Press.

Glickman, C.D. (1990, September). "Pushing School Reform to a New Edge: The Seven Ironies of School Empowerment," *Phi Delta Kappan* 27(1): 68–75.

Goldberg, A.S. (1979). "Concluding Remark." In G.L. Immegart and W.L. Boyd (eds.), *Problem-Finding in Educational Administration*, pp. 270–273. Lexington, Mass.: Lexington Books.

Goldring, E.B. (1986, Spring). "The School Community: Its Effects on Principals' Perceptions of Parents," *Educational Administration Quarterly* 22(2): 115–132.

Goldring, E.B. (1990, April). "How Do Principals Survive with Parental Involvement? A Public Choice Theory Analysis." Paper presented at the annual meeting of the American Educational Research Association, Boston.

Goldring, E.B. (1996). "Environmental Adaptation and Selection: Where Are the Parents and the Public? In R.L. Crowson, W.L. Boyd, and H.B. Mawhinney (eds.), *The Politics of Education and the New Institutionalism*, pp. 43-53. London: Falmer Press.

Goodlad, J.I. (1981). "Education, Schools, and a Sense of Community." In D. Davies (ed.), *Communities and Their Schools*, pp. 331–354. New York: McGraw-Hill.

Goodlad, J.I. (1985). "Rethinking What Schools Can Do Best." In M. Fantini and R. Sinclair (eds.), *Education in School and Nonschool Settings*. Eighty-fourth Yearbook of the National Society for the Study of Education. Chicago: University of Chicago Press.

Goodlad, J.I. (ed.) (1987). *The Ecology of School Renewal*. Eighty-sixth Yearbook of the National Society for the Study of Education. Chicago: University of Chicago Press.

Gordon, I.J. (1976). "Towards a Home-School Partnership Program." In I.J. Gordon and W.F. Breivogel (eds.), *Building Effective Home-School Relationships*, pp. 1–20. Boston: Allyn & Bacon.

Gordon, I.J., and Breivogel, W.F. (1976). *Building Effective Home-School Relationships*. Boston: Allyn & Bacon.

Gordon, T. (1970). *P.E.T.: Parent Effectiveness Training*. New York: Wyden.

Gove, S.K., and Wirt, F.M. (eds.) (1976). *Political Science and School Politics*. Lexington, Mass.: Lexington Books.

Grant, G. (1988). *The World We Created at Hamilton High*. Cambridge, Mass.: Harvard University Press.

Greene, M. (1994). "From Social Discord to Learning Community." In R.J. Yinger and K. M. Borman (eds.), *Restructuring Education: Issues and Strategies for Communities, Schools, and Universities.* Cresskill, N.J.: Hampton Press.

Greenstein, J. (1983). *What the Children Taught Me: The Experience of an Educator in the Public Schools.* Chicago: University of Chicago Press.

Gregory, T.B., and Smith, G.R. (1987). *High Schools as Communities: The Small School Reconsidered.* Bloomington, Ind.: Phi Delta Kappan Educational Foundation.

Griffore, R.J., and Boger, R.P. (eds.) (1986). *Child Rearing in the Home and School.* New York: Plenum Press.

Grotberg, E. (1983). "Integration of Parent Education Into Human Service Programs." In R. Haskins and D. Adams (eds.), *Parent Education and Public Policy*, pp. 324–330. Norwood, N.J.: Ablex.

Grubb, W.N., and Lazerson, M. (1982). *Broken Promises: How Americans Fail Their Children.* New York: Basic Books.

Gutman, A. (1987). *Democratic Education.* Princeton, N.J.: Princeton University Press.

Gutman, A. (1989). "Democratic Theory and the Role of Teachers in Democratic Education." In J. Hannaway and R. Crowson (eds.), *The Politics of Reforming School Administration*, pp. 183–199. New York: Falmer Press.

Haertel, E.; James, T.; and Levin, H. (eds.) (1987). *Comparing Public and Private Schools, Volume 2: School Achievement.* New York: Falmer Press.

Hallinger, P., and Murphy, J. (1986). "The Social Context of Effective Schools." *American Journal of Education* 94(3): 328–355.

Halpern, R. (1995). *Rebuilding the Inner City.* New York: Columbia University Press.

Halpern, S.C., and Lamb, C.M. (1982). *Supreme Court Activism and Restraint.* Lexington, Mass.: Lexington Books.

Hammond, T.W. (1986). "Agenda Control, Organizational Structure and Bureaucratic Politics," *American Journal of Political Science* 30: 379–420.

Hannaway, J., and Crowson, R. (eds.) (1989). *The Politics of Reforming School Administration.* New York: Falmer Press.

Hanson, E.M. (1981). *Educational Administration and Organizational Behavior.* Boston: Allyn & Bacon.

Hanushek, E. (1994). *Making Schools Work: Improving Performance and Controlling Costs.* Washington, D.C.: The Brookings Institution.

Hasenfeld, Yeheskel (ed.) (1992). *Human Services as Complex Organizations.* Newbury Park, Calif.: Sage Publications.

Haskins, R., and Adams, D. (eds.) (1983). *Parent Education and Public Policy.* Norwood, N.J.: Ablex.

Havighurst, R.J., et al. (1962). *Growing Up in River City.* New York: John Wiley & Sons.

Hawkins, R.B., Jr. (1985). "A Strategy for Revitalizing Public Education." In J.H. Bunzel (ed.), *Challenge to American Schools: The Case for Standards and Values*, pp. 29–46. New York: Oxford University Press.

Hawley, W.D. (1990). "Missing Pieces of the Educational Reform Agenda: Or, Why the First and Second Waves May Miss the Boat." In S.B. Bacharach (ed.), *Education Reform: Making Sense of It All*, pp. 213–233. Boston: Allyn & Bacon.

Hawley, W.; Rosenholtz, S.; Goodstein, H.; and Hasselbring, T. (1984). "Good Schools: What Research Says About Improving Student Achievement," *Peabody Journal of Education* 61(4).

Haycock, K.P. (1990, June 20). "Partnerships for America's Children." Closing Plenary Address, National Conference on School/College Collaboration, Chicago.

Haynes, N.; Comer, J.; and Hamilton-Lee, M. (1988a). "The Effects of Parental Involvement on Student Performance." *Educational and Psychological Research* 8(4): 291–299.

Haynes, N.; Comer, J.; and Hamilton-Lee, M. (1988b). "The School Development Program: A Model for School Improvement," *Journal of Negro Education* 57(1): 11–21.

Heck, S.F., and Williams, R. (1984). *The Complex Roles of the Teacher*. New York: Teachers College Press.

Hedberg, B. (1981). "How Organizations Learn and Unlearn." In P.C. Nystrom and W.H. Starbuck (eds.), *Handbook of Organizational Design*, Volume 1, pp. 3–27. Oxford: Oxford University Press.

Henderson, A. (ed.) (1981). *Parent Participation—Student Achievement: The Evidence Grows*. Columbia, Mary.: National Committee for Citizens in Education.

Henderson, A. (1987). *The Evidence Continues to Grow: Parent Involvement Improves Student Achievement*. Columbia, Md.: National Committee for Citizens in Education.

Hendrie, C. (1997, January 15). "Crew Packs Arsenal of New Powers in N.Y.C." *Education Week* 16(16): 1, 28.

Henry, M. (1996). *Parent-School Collaboration: Feminist Organizational Structures and School Leadership*. Albany: State University of New York Press.

Hess, G.A., Jr. (1989, October). "School Improvement Plans Are the Key to Reform," *Panel Update*, Newsletter of the Chicago Panel on Public School Policy and Finance 6(3).

Hess, G.A., Jr. (1996). *Restructuring Urban School: A Chicago Perspective*. New York: Teachers College Press.

Heyns, B.L., and Hilton, T.L. (1982). "Cognitive Tests for High School and Beyond: An Assessment," *Sociology of Education* 55: 89–102.

Hiner, N.R. (1989). "'Look into Families': The New History of Children and the

Hodgkinson, H.L. (1988). "Facing the Future: Demographics and Statistics to Manage Today's Schools for Tomorrow's Children," *The School Administrator* 8(45): 25–31.

Hoffer, T.B., and Coleman, J.S. (1990). "Changing Families and Communities: Implications for Schools." In B. Mitchell and L.L. Cunningham (eds.), *Educational Leadership and Changing Contexts of Families, Communities, and Schools*. Eighty-ninth Yearbook of the National Society for the Study of Education, Part II, pp. 119–134. Chicago: University of Chicago Press.

Hollingshead, A.B. (1949). *Elmtown's Youth*. New York: John Wiley & Sons.

Holmes, M., and Wynne, E.A. (1989). *Making the School an Effective Community*. New York: Falmer Press.

Holt, J. (1983, February). "Schools and Home Schoolers: A Fruitful Partnership," *Phi Delta Kappan* 64(6): 391–394.

Holt, M. (1987). *Judgment, Planning and Educational Change*. London: Harper & Row.

Hoover-Dempsey, K.V., and Sandler, H.M. (1996, Winter). "Parental Involvement in Children's Education: Why Does It Make A Difference?" *Teachers College Record* 97 (2): 310-331.

Hooyman, N.R. (1981). "Strategies of Citizen Participation." In J.F. Jones and R.S. Pondy (eds.), *Social Development: Conceptual, Methodological and Policy Issues*, pp. 108-138. New York: St. Martin's Press.

Hopfenberg, W., et al. (1993). *The Accelerated Schools Resource Guide*. San Francisco: Jossey-Bass.

Hulsebosch, P.L. (1988). "Significant Others: Teachers' Perspectives on Parent Involvement." Ph.D. dissertation, University of Illinois at Chicago.

Hunter, F. (1953). *Community Power Structure*. Chapel Hill, N.C.: University of North Carolina Press.

Ianni, F.A.J. (1989). *The Search for Structure: A Report on American Youth Today*. New York: The Free Press.

Illich, I., et al. (1977). *Disabling Professions*. London: Marion Boyars Publishers.

Institute for Educational Leadership (1990, August). "Final Report: The Implementation of the WAVE." Prepared for 70001 Training and Employment Service. Washington, D.C.

Janowitz, M. (1967). *The Community Press in an Urban Setting*, second edition. Chicago: The University of Chicago Press.

Jennings, L. (1990, February 14). "States Should Require Schools to Craft Family-Support Plans, Chiefs Propose," *Education Week*, p. 8.

Johnson, K. (1990, October 30). "School Councils Draw a Good Preliminary Review," *USA Today*, p. 6D.

Johnson, S.M. (1989). "Schoolwork and Its Reform." In J. Hannaway and R. Crowson (eds.), *The Politics of Reforming School Administration*, pp. 95–112. New York: Falmer Press.

Johnson, S.M., and Nelson, N.C.W. (1987, April). "Teaching Reform in an Active Voice," *Phi Delta Kappan* 68(8): 591–598.

Johnston, R.C. (1996, December 4). "In '96 Sessions, Charter Laws Keep Spreading," *Education Week* 16 (4): 14, 19.

Jones, B.L., and Maloy, R.W. (1988). *Partnerships for Improving Schools*. New York: Greenwood Press.

Kaestle, C.F. (1983). *Pillars of the Republic: Common Schools and American Society, 1780–1860*. New York: Hill and Wang.

Kagan, S.L. (1989, October). "Early Care and Education: Beyond the Schoolhouse Doors," *Phi Delta Kappan* 71(2): 107–112.

Kagan, S.L. (1990, December). "Readiness 2000: Rethinking Rhetoric and Responsibility," *Phi Delta Kappan* 72(4): 272–279.

Kagan, S.L. (1993). *Integrating Services for Children and Families*. New Haven: Yale University Press.

Kahne, J. (1996). *Reframing Educational Policy: Democracy, Community, and the Individual*. New York: Teachers College Press.

Kaufman, P.W. (1984). *Women Teachers on the Frontier*. New Haven: Yale University Press.

Kaufman, R. (1988). *Planning Educational Systems: A Results-Based Approach*. Lancaster, Penn.: Technomic Publishing AG.

Kaufman, R. (1991). "Asking the Right Questions: Types of Strategic Planning." In R.V. Carlson and G. Awkerman (eds.), *Educational Planning: Concepts, Strategies, Practices*, pp. 177-199. New York: Longman.

Kemerer, F.R. (1995, September). "The Constitutionality of School Vouchers," *West's Education Law Reporter* 101(1): 17-36.

Kerbow, D., and Bernhardt, A. (1993). "Parental Intervention in the School: The Context of Minority Involvement," in B. Schneider and J. Coleman (eds.), *Parents, Their Children, and Schools*, pp. 115-146. Boulder, Colo.: Westview Press.

Kidder, T. (1989). *Among Schoolchildren*. Boston: Houghton Mifflin.

Kilgore, S. (1983). "Statistical Evidence, Selectivity Effects and Program Placement: Responses to Alexander and Pallas," *Sociology of Education* 56: 182–186.

Kindred, L.W.; Bagin, D.; and Gallagher, D.R. (1984). *The School and Community Relations*, third edition. Englewood Cliffs, N.J.: Prentice-Hall.

Kirst, M. (1984). *Who Controls Our Schools?*. New York: Freeman & Co.

Kirst, M. (ed.) (1989). *The Conditions of Children in California*. Berkeley: Policy Analysis for California Education (PACE).

Kirst, M.W., and McLaughlin, M. (1990). "Rethinking Policy for Children: Implications for Educational Administration." In B. Mitchell and L.L. Cunningham (eds.), *Educational Leadership and Changing Contexts of Families, Communities, and Schools*. Eighty-ninth Yearbook of the National Society for the Study of Education, Part II, pp. 69–90. Chicago: University of Chicago Press.

Kleine-Kracht, P. (1990). "The Cultural Effect of Administrative Duties: The Case of Classroom Observation," *Administrator's Notebook* 34(3): 1–4.

Kochen, F.; Allen, P.; and Foster, G. (1990). "Family School Community Partnership Program," *Politics of Education Bulletin* 17(1): 1ff.

Koff, R.H., and Ward, D. (1990, November). "Philanthropy, the Public Schools, and the University: A Model for At-Risk Youth," *Phi Delta Kappan* 72(3): 223–226.

Koteen, J. (1989). *Strategic Management in Public and Non-Profit Organizations*. New York: Praeger.

Koza, M.P., and Levy, W. (1977–78). "School Organization and Community Participation," *Administrator's Notebook* 26(9): 1–4.

LaNoue, G.R., and Smith, B.L.R. (1973). *The Politics of School Decentralization*. Lexington, Mass.: Lexington Books.

Lareau, A. (1989). *Home Advantage: Social Class and Parental Intervention in Elementary Education*. London: Falmer Press.

Lareau, A. (1994). "Parent Involvement in Schooling: A Dissenting View," in C. Fagnano and B. Werber (eds.), *School, Family and Community Interaction: A View from the Firing Lines*, pp. 61-74. Boulder, Colo.: Westview Press.

Lawrence-Lightfoot, S. (1994). *I've Known Rivers: Lives of Loss and Liberation*. New York: Penguin Books.

Lazzarda, M.; Miller, K.; and Wolfe, S. (1989). "Developing Teacher Leadership Roles: Experiences and Reflections of Three Teachers," *ERS Spectrum* 7(4): 40–43.

Leichter, H.J. (ed.) (1979). *Families and Communities as Educators*. New York: Teachers College Press.

Leichter, H.J. (1979). "Families and Communities as Educators: Some Concepts of Relationship." In H.J. Leichter (ed.), *Families and Communities as Educators*, pp. 3–94. New York: Teachers College Press.

Leler, H. (1983). "Parent Education and Involvement in Relation to the Schools and to Parents of School-Aged Children." In R. Haskins and D. Adams (eds.), *Parent Education and Public Policy*, pp. 141–180. Norwood, N.J.: Ablex Publishing Co.

Lemann, N. (1991, January 13). "Four Generations in the Projects," *New York Times Magazine*, pp. 16–21+.

Levin, H.M. (ed.) (1968). *Community Control of Schools*. Washington, D.C.: Brookings Institution.

Levin, H.M. (1984, Summer). "About Time for Educational Reform," *Educational Evaluation and Policy Analysis* 6(2): 151–163.

Lewis, H. (1967). "Foreword." In E. Liebow, *Tally's Corner: A Study of Negro Streetcorner Men*. Boston: Little Brown.

Lewis, O. (1959). *Five Families*. New York: Basic Books.

Lewis, O. (1961). *The Children of Sanchez*. New York: Random House.

Lewis, O. (1966). *La Vida*. New York: Random House.

Lewit, E.M., and Baker, L.S. (1996). "Homeless Families and Children," *The Future of Children* 6(2): 146-158.

Lieberman, A. (ed.) (1988). *Building a Professional Culture in Schools*. New York: Teachers College Press.

Liebow, E. (1967). *Tally's Corner: A Study of Negro Streetcorner Men*. Boston: Little Brown.

Lightfoot, S.L. (1978). *Worlds Apart*. New York: Basic Books.

Lightfoot, S.L. (1984). *The Good High School*. New York: Basic Books.

Lipsky, M. (1976). "Toward a Theory of Street-Level Bureaucracy." In W.D. Hawley, et al. (eds.), *Theoretical Perspectives on Urban Politics*, pp. 196–213. Englewood Cliffs, N.J.: Prentice-Hall.

Lipsky, M. (1980). *Street-Level Bureaucracy: Dilemmas of the Individual in Public Services*. New York: Russell Sage Foundation.

Littell, J., and Wynn, J. (1989). *The Availability and Use of Community Resources for Young Adolescents in an Inner-City and a Suburban Community*. Chicago: Chapin Hall Center for Children.

Little, J.W. (1993, Summer). "Teachers' Professional Development in a Climate of Educational Reform," *Educational Evaluation and Policy Analysis* 15(2): 129-152.

Local School Council Awards Program (1990). *Local School Councils Ideas and Successes.* Chicago School Reform: Year One. Chicago: Illinois Bell, The Ameritech Foundation, and the Chicago Public Schools Alumni Association.

Lombana, J.H. (1983). *Home-School Partnerships*. New York: Grune and Stratton.

Long, N. (1958, November). "The Local Community as an Ecology of Games," *American Journal of Sociology* 64: 251-261.

Louis, K.S., and Kruse, S.D. (1995). *Professionalism and Community: Perspectives on Reforming Urban Schools.* Thousand Oaks, Calif.: Corwin Pres.

Lutz, F.W., and Iannaccone, L. (1978). *Public Participation in Local Schools: The Dissatisfaction Theory of American Democracy*. Lexington, Mass.: Lexington Books.

Lutz, F.W., and Merz, C. (1992). *The Politics of School/Community Relations*. New York: Teachers College Press.

Lynd, R.S., and Lynd, H.M. (1929). *Middletown*. New York: Harcourt, Brace and Co.

Lynd, R.S., and Lynd, H.M. (1937). *Middletown in Transition*. New York: Harcourt Brace Jovanovich.

McCaffery, J.L. (1989). "Making the Most of Strategic Planning and Management." In R.E. Cleary, N. Henry, and Associates (eds.), *Managing Public Programs: Balancing Politics, Administration and Public Needs*, pp. 193–210. San Francisco: Jossey-Bass.

McCarty, D., and Ramsey, C. (1971). *The School Managers: Power and Conflict in American Public Education*. Westport, Conn.: Greenwood Publishing.

McDonnell, L.M. (1989, September 5–7). "Restructuring American Schools: The Promise and the Pitfalls." Paper commissioned for Education and the Economy: Hard Questions, Hard Answers. A conference sponsored by the Institute on Education and the Economy, Teachers College, Columbia University.

McLaughlin, M.W.; Irby, M.I.; and Langman, J. (1994). *Urban Sanctuaries: Inner-City Youth and Neighborhood Organizations*. San Francisco: Jossey-Bass.

McLaughlin, M., and Shields, P. (1987, October). "Involving Low-Income Parents in the Schools: A Role for Policy," *Phi Delta Kappan*, pp. 156–160.

McLaughlin, M.W., and Yee, S.M. (1988). "School as a Place to Have a Career." In A. Lieberman (ed.), *Building a Professional Culture in Schools*, pp. 23–44. New York: Teachers College Press.

Macleod, F. (ed.) (1989). *Parents and Schools: The Contemporary Challenge*. London: Falmer Press.

McPartland, J., and McDill, E. (1982). "Control and Differentiation in the Structure of American Education," *Sociology of Education* 55: 77–88.

McPherson, R.B. (1988, Summer). "Superintendents and the Problem of Delegation," *Peabody Journal of Education* 65(4): 113–130.

McPherson, R.B.; Crowson, R.L.; and Pitner, N.J. (1986). *Managing Uncertainty: Administrative Theory and Practice in Education*. Columbus, Ohio: Charles E. Merrill.

Maddaus, J. (1990). "Parental Choice of School: What Parents Think and Do," *Review of Research in Education* 16: 267–296.

Maeroff, G. (1983). *School and College Partnerships in Education*. Princeton, N.J.: Carnegie Foundation for the Advancement of Teaching.

Maeroff, G. (1988, March). "A Blueprint for Empowering Teachers," *Phi Delta Kappan* 69(7): 472–477.

Malcolm, D.J. (1927). *The Letters of a County School Superintendent to His Daughter*. Chicago: Benj. H. Sanborn.

Malen, B., and Ogawa, R. (1988). "Professional-Patron Influences on Site-Based Governance Councils: A Confounding Case Study." *Educational Evaluation and Policy Analysis* 10(4): 251–270.

Malen, B., and Ogawa, R. (1990). "Decentralizing and Democratizing the Public Schools—A Viable Approach to Reform?" In S.B. Bacharach (ed.), *Education Reform: Making Sense of It all*, pp. 103–119. Boston: Allyn & Bacon.

Malen, B.; Ogawa, R.; and Kranze, J. (1990). "What Do We Know About School-Based Management? A Case Study of the Literature and a Call for Research." In W. Clune and J. Witte (eds.), *Choice and Control in American Education, Volume 2: The Practice of Choice, Decentralization, and School Restructuring*, pp. 289–342. New York: Falmer Press.

Manley-Casimir, M. (1989). "Conscience, Community Mores and Administrative Responsibility: A Prologue," *Administrator's Notebook* 33(4): 1–4.

Mann, D. (1976). *The Politics of Administrative Representation.* Lexington, Mass.: Lexington Books.

Mann, D. (1987, October). "Business Involvement and Public School Improvement, Part I," *Phi Delta Kappan* 69(2): 123–128.

Mansbridge, J.J. (1983). *Beyond Adversary Democracy.* Chicago: University of Chicago Press.

Marburger, C.L. (1990). "Education Reform: The Neglected Dimension, Parent Involvement." In S.B. Bacharach (ed.), *Education Reform: Making Sense of It All*, pp. 82–91. Boston: Allyn & Bacon.

Markel, G.P., and Greenbaum, J. (1979). *Parents Are to Be Seen and Heard.* San Luis Obispo, Calif.: Impact Publishers.

Marockie, H., and Jones, H.L. (1987). "Reducing Dropout Rates Through Home-School Communication," *Education and Urban Society* 19(2): 200–205.

Masotti, L.H. (1967). *Education and Politics in Suburbia: The New Trier Experience.* Cleveland, Ohio: The Press of Western Reserve University.

Masten, A.S. (1986, August). "Patterns of Adaptation to Stress in Middle Childhood." Paper presented at the annual meeting of the American Psychological Association, Washington, D.C.

Mauriel, J.J. (1989). *Strategic Leadership for Schools.* San Francisco: Jossey-Bass.

Mayberry, M.: Knowles, J.G.; Ray, B.; and Marlow, S. (1995). *Home Schooling.* Thousand Oaks, Calif.: Corwin Press.

Mazzoni, T.L. (1987). "The Politics of Educational Choice in Minnesota." In W.L. Boyd and C.T. Kerchner (eds.), *The Politics of Excellence and Choice in Education*, pp. 217–230. New York: Falmer Press.

Mazzoni, T., and Sullivan, B. (1990). "Legislating Educational Choice in Minnesota: Politics and Prospects." In W.L. Boyd and H.J. Walberg (eds.), *Choice in Education: Potential and Problems*, pp. 149–176. Berkeley, Calif.: McCutchan.

Melcher, B.H., and Kerzner, H. (1988). *Strategic Planning: Development and Implementation.* Blue Ridge Summit, Penn.: Tab Books, Inc.

Menacker, J. (1987). *School Law: Theoretical and Case Perspectives.* Engelwood Cliffs, N.J.: Prentice-Hall.

Menacker, J. (1989, July). "Activist Conservatism in the Driver's Seat," *Urban Education* 24(2): 199–214.

Menacker, J.; Weldon, W.; and Hurwitz, E. (1989, September). "School Order and Safety as Community Issues," *Phi Delta Kappan* 71(1): 39–40, 56.

Menacker, J.; Weldon, W.; and Hurwitz, E. (1990, April). "Community Influences on School Crime and Violence," *Urban Education* 25(1): 68–80.

Metz, M.H. (1986). *Different by Design: The Context and Character of Three Magnet Schools.* London: Routledge, Kegan Paul.

Metz, M.H. (1990). "Magnet Schools and the Reform of Public Schooling." In W.L. Boyd and H.J. Walberg (eds.), *Choice in Education: Potential and Problems*, pp. 123–147. Berkeley, Calif.: McCutchan Publishing.

Meyer, J.W., and Rowan, B. (1977, September). "Institutional Organizations: Formal Structure as Myth and Ceremony," *American Journal of Sociology* 83: 340–363.

Miller, R., and Buttram, J.L. (1991). "Collaborative Planning: Changing the Game

Rules." In R.V. Carlson and G. Awkerman (eds.), *Educational Planning: Concepts, Strategies, Practices*, pp. 279–294. New York: Longman.

Minar, D.W. (1966, December). "The Community Basis of Conflict in School System Politics," *American Sociological Review* 31(6): 822–834.

Mintz, S. (1989). "The Family as Educator: Historical Trends in Socialization and Transmission of Content Within the Home." In W.J. Weston (ed.), *Education and the American Family: A Research Synthesis*, pp. 96–121. New York: New York University Press.

Minzey, J.D. (1981). "Community Education and Community Schools." In D. Davies (ed.), *Communities and Their Schools*, pp. 269–295. New York: McGraw-Hill.

Mitchell, B., and Cunningham, L.L. (eds.) (1990). *Educational Leadership and Changing Contexts of Families, Communities and Schools*. Eighty-ninth Yearbook of the National

Moe, T. (1995). "School Choice and the Creaming Problem." In T.A. Downs and W.A. Testa (eds.), *Midwest Approaches to School Reform*. Chicago: Federal Reserve Board.

Moles, O.C. (1982, November). "Synthesis of Recent Research on Parent Participation in Children's Education," *Educational Leadership*, pp. 44–47.

Moles, O.C. (1987). "Who Wants Parent Involvement? Interest, Skills and Opportunities Among Parents and Educators," *Education and Urban Society* 19(2): 137–145.

Moles, O.C. (1990). "Effective Parent Outreach Strategies." Paper prepared for parent involvement seminars, California State Department of Education.

Moles, O.C. (1991). "Collaboration Between Schools and Disadvantaged Parents: Obstacles and Openings." In N. Chawkin (ed.), *Minority Parents and the Schools*. Albany, N.Y.: SUNY Press.

Moore, M.D. (1988). "Resolving Conflict and Establishing Community." In M.O. Jones, M.D. Moore, and R.C. Snyder (eds.), *Inside Organizations: Understanding the Human Dimension*, pp. 261–269. Newbury Park, Calif.: Sage Publications.

Morgan, W.R. (1983). "Learning and Student Life Quality of Public and Private School Youth," *Sociology of Education* 56: 187–202.

Morris, V.C.; Crowson, R.L.; Porter-Gehrie, C.; and Hurwitz, E., Jr. (1984). *Principals in Action: The Reality of Managing Schools*. Columbus, Ohio: Charles E. Merrill.

Mortimore, P.; Summons, P.; Stoll, L.; Lewis, D.; and Ecob, R. (1988). *School Matters*. Berkeley: University of California Press.

Muller, C. (1993). "Parent Involvement and Academic Achievement: An Analysis of Family Resources Available to the Child," in B. Schneider and J. Coleman (eds.), *Parents, Their Children, and Schools*, pp. 77-114. Boulder, Colo.: Westview Press.

Muller, C., and Kerbow, D. (1993). "Parent Involvement in the Home, School and Community," in B. Schneider and J. Coleman (eds.), *Parents, Their Children, and Schools*, pp. 13-42. Boulder, Colo.: Westview Press.

Murnane, R. (1984). "Comparisons of Public and Private Schools: Lessons from the Uproar," *The Journal of Human Resources* 19: 263-277.

Murphy, J., and Hallinger, P. (eds.) (1993). *Restructuring Schooling: Learning from Ongoing Efforts*. Newbury Park, Calif.: Corwin/Sage.

Nathan, J. (1989, December). "Helping All Children, Empowering All Educators: Another View of School Choice," *Phi Delta Kappan* 71(4): 304-307.

Nathan, J. (1990). "Progress, Problems, and Prospects of State Educational Choice Plans." In W.L. Boyd and H.J. Walberg (eds.), *Choice in Education: Potential and Problems,* pp. 263-287. Berkeley, Calif.: McCutchan.

National Center for the Accelerated Schools Project. (1991a). "What Are Accelerated Schools?" *Accelerated Schools* 1(1). Stanford, Calif.: Stanford University.

National Center for the Accelerated Schools Project. (1991b). "Getting Started." *Accelerated Schools* 1(2). Stanford, Calif.: Stanford University.

New York Times. (1989, August 16). "School Without a Principal."

Noell, J. (1982). "Public and Catholic Schools: A Reanalysis of 'Public and Private Schools,'" *Sociology of Education* 55: 123–132.

Nucci, L. (1989). "The Nation of Tomorrow." A proposal submitted to the Kellogg Foundation. Chicago: University of Illinois at Chicago, College of Education.

Nunnery, M.Y., and Kimbrough, R.B. (1971). *Politics, Power, Polls, and School Elections.* Berkeley: McCutchan.

Ochoa, A.M., and Mardirosian, V. (1990, April). "Parents as Equal Collaborators of Their Children's Education: Towards Transformational Empowerment." Paper presented at the annual meeting of the American Educational Research Association, Boston.

O'Donnell, M. (1990, March 1). "Mass Protests Greet Ouster of Principals," *Chicago Sun Times,* pp. 1, 4–5.

Ogawa, R.T., and Studer, S.C. (1996, April). "A Cost Study of Bridging and Buffering Family-School Relations." Paper presented at the annual meeting of the American Educational Research Association, New York City

Ogbu, J.U. (1974). *The Next Generation: An Ethnography of Education in an Urban Neighborhood.* New York: Academic Press.

Ogbu, J.U. (1978). *Minority Education and Caste: The American System in Cross-Cultural Perspective.* New York: Academic Press.

Ogbu, J.U. (1988). "Diversity and Equity in Public Education: Community Forces and Minority School Adjustment and Performance." In R. Haskins and D. MacRae (eds.), *Policies for America's Public Schools: Teachers, Equity and Indicators,* pp. 127–170. Norwood, N.J.: Ablex Pub. Co.

Olmsted, P., and Rubin, R. (1983). "Parent Involvement: Perspectives from the Follow Through Experience." In R. Haskins and D. Adams (eds.), *Parent Education and Public Policy,* pp. 112–140. Norwood, N.J.: Ablex.

Olson, L. (1990a, September 12). "Milwaukee's Choice Program Enlists 391 Volunteers," *Education Week* 10(2): 1, 14-15.

Olson, L. (1990b, April 4). "Parents as Partners: Redefining the Social Contract Between Families and Schools," *Education Week,* pp. 17-24.

The Organization for Economic Co-operation and Development (1974). *Participatory Planning in Education.* Paris: OECD.

Otterbourg, S.D. (1986). *School Partnerships Handbook.* Englewood Cliffs.: N.J.: Prentice-Hall, Inc.

Page, L.A. (1996, August). "Beliefs and Practices of Home Schoolers About Responsibility in a Democracy." Unpublished doctoral dissertation, Department of Educational Leadership, Peabody College, Vanderbilt University, Nashville, Tenn.

Page, A.L., and Clellend, D.A. (1978, September). "The Kanawha County Textbook Controversy: A Study of the Politics of Life Style Concern," *Social Forces* 57(1): 265–281.

Pallas, A.M.; Natriello, G.; and McDill, E.L. (1989). "The Changing Nature of the Disadvantaged Population: Current Dimensions and Future Trends," *Educational Researcher* 18(5): 16–22.

Patterson, G.R., and Guillon, E.M. (1971). *Living with Children: New Methods for Parents and Teachers*. Champaign, Ill.: Research Press.

Pellegrini, D.S.; Masten, A.S.; Garmezy, N.; and Ferrarese, M.J. (1987). "Correlates of Social and Academic Competence in Middle Childhood," *Journal of Child Psychology and Psychiatry* 5: 699–714.

Pennsylvania Education (1990, September 28). "Public/Private Partnership to Improve Early Childhood Programs," pp. 9–10.

Perlman, B.; Gueths, J.; and Weber, D.A. (1988). *The Academic Intrapreneur*. New York: Praeger.

Peshkin, A. (1978). *Growing Up American: Schooling and the Survival of Community*. Chicago: University of Chicago Press.

Peshkin, A. (1986). *God's Choice: The Total World of a Fundamentalist Christian School*. Chicago: University of Chicago Press.

Peshkin, A. (1990). "The Relationship Between Culture and Curriculum: A Many Fitting Thing." In P. Jackson (ed.), *Handbook of Research in Curriculum*.

Peshkin, A. (1995). "The Complex World of an Embedded Institutional: Schools and Their Constituent Publics." In L.C. Rigsby, M.C. Reynolds, and M.C. Wang (eds.), *School-Community Connections: Exploring Issues for Research and Practice*, pp. 229-258. San Francisco: Jossey-Bass.

Peters, B.G. (1978). *The Politics of Bureaucracy: A Comparative Perspective*. New York: Longman.

Pfeffer, J., and Salancik, G.R. (1978). *The External Control of Organizations: A Resource Dependence Perspective*. New York: Harper & Row.

Philadelphia Children's Network (1990, October 31). "Philadelphia's Child-Serving System: An Approach to System Change." A Family Service District Proposal, Philadelphia.

Pulliam, J.D. (1987). *History of Education in America*, fourth edition. Columbus, Ohio: Charles E. Merrill.

Purkey, S.C., and Smith, M.S. (1983). "Effective Schools: A Review." *Elementary School Journal* 83(4): 427–452.

Ravitch, D. (1974). *The Great School Wars, New York City, 1805–1973: A History of the Public Schools as Battleground of Social Change*. New York: Basic Books.

Raywid, M.A. (1990). "Rethinking School Governance." In R.F. Elmore (ed.), *Restructuring Schools: The Next Generation of Educational Reform*, pp. 152–205. San Francisco: Jossey-Bass.

Reed, S., and Sautter, C. (1990, June). "Children of Poverty: The Status of 12 Million Young Americans," *Phi Delta Kappan* 71(10): K1–K12.

Reese, W.J. (1986). *Power and the Promise of School Reform: Grass-Roots Movement During the Progressive Era*. Boston: Routledge and Kegan Paul.

Reich, R.B. (1991). "Secession of the Successful," *New York Times Magazine*, Sunday, February 2.

Reynolds, A.J. (1989). "Early Schooling of Children at Risk." Ph.D. dissertation, College of Education, University of Illinois at Chicago.

Rich, D. (1987a). *Schools and Families: Issues and Actions.* Washington, D.C.: National Education Association.

Rich, D. (1987b). *Teachers and Parents: An Adult to Adult Approach.* Washington, D.C.: National Education Association.

Rigsby, L.C.; Reynolds, M.C.; and Wang, M.C. (eds.) (1995). *School-Community Connections: Exploring Issues for Research and Practice.* San Francisco: Jossey-Bass.

Rist, R.C. (1970). "Student Social Class and Teacher Expectancies: The Self-fulfilling Prophecy in Ghetto Education," *Harvard Educational Review* 40: 411–451.

Robinson, T. (1990, March 28). "Hispanics Hit Hardest in Firings of Principals," *Chicago Sun Times,* p. 7.

Rogers, C. (1951). *Client-Centered Therapy.* Boston: Houghton Mifflin.

Rosenholtz, S.J. (1989). *Teachers' Workplace: The Social Organization of Schools.* New York: Longman.

Rossman, G.B.; Corbett, H.D.; and Firestone, W.A. (1988). *Change and Effectiveness in Schools: A Cultural Perspective.* Albany: State University of New York Press.

Rutter, M.; Maughan, B.; Mortimore, P.; and Ouston, J. (1979). *Fifteen Thousand Hours.* Cambridge: Harvard University Press.

Ryan, C. (1976). *The Open Partnership: Equality in Running the Schools.* New York: McGraw-Hill.

Salganik, L., and Karweit, N. (1982). "Voluntarism and Governance in Education," *Sociology of Education* 55: 152–161.

Samuelson, R.J. (1996, November). "Sounds Great, Won't Work," *Newsweek* 49.

Sarason, S.B. (1971). *The Culture of the School and the Problem of Change.* Boston: Allyn & Bacon.

Sarason, S.B. (1983). *Schooling in America: Scapegoat and Salvation.* New York: The Free Press.

Sarason, S.B. (1990). *The Predictable Failure of Educational Reform.* San Francisco: Jossey-Bass

Sarason, S.B. (1995). *Parental Involvement and the Political Principle: Why the Existing Governance Structure of Schools Should Be Abolished.* San Francisco: Jossey-Bass.

Saxe, R.W. (1984). *School-Community Relations in Transition.* Berkeley: McCutchan.

Sayre, W.S., and Kaufman, H. (1965). *Governing New York City: Politics in the Metropolis.* New York: W.W. Norton & Co.

Schaeffer, E.S. (1983). "Parent-Professional Interaction: Research, Parental, Professional, and Policy Perspectives." In R. Haskins and D. Adams (eds.), *Parent Education and Public Policy,* pp. 283-303. Norwood, N.J. Ablex.

Schlechty, P.C., and Ingverson, D.W. (1987, April). "A Proposed Incentive System for Jefferson County Teachers," *Phi Delta Kappan* 68 (8): 585-590.

Schneider, B. (1993). "Parents, Their Children and Schools: An Introduction," in B. Schneider and J. Coleman (eds.), *Parents, Their Children, and Schools,* pp. 1-12. Boulder.: Westview Press.

Schneider, B., and Coleman, J. (eds.) (1993). *Parents, Their Children, and Schools.* Boulder, Colo.: Westview Press.

Scott-Jones, D. (1994). "African American Families and Schools: Toward Mutually

Supportive Relationships," in C. Fagnano and B. Werber (eds.), *Schools, Family and Community Interaction: A View from the Firing Lines*, pp. 75-84. Boulder, Colo.: Westview Press.

Seay, M.F. (1953). "The Community School: New Meaning for an Old Term." In N.B. Henry (ed.), *The Community School*. Fifty-second Yearbook of the National Society for the Study of Education, Part II. Chicago: University of Chicago Press.

Sebring, P.; Bryk, A.; Roderick, M.; Camburn, E.; Luppescu, S.; Thum, Y.M.; Smith, B.; and Kahne, J. (1996). *Charting Reform in Chicago: The Students Speak*. Chicago: Consortium on Chicago School Research.

Seeley, D.S. (1982, November). "Education Through Partnership," *Educational Leadership*, pp. 42–43.

Seeley, D., and Schwartz, R. (1981). "Debureaucratizing Public Education: The Experience of New York and Boston." In D. Davies (ed.), *Communities and Their Schools*, pp. 59–81. New York: McGraw-Hill.

Senge, P.M. (1990, Fall). "The Leader's New York: Building Learning Organizations," *Sloan Management Review*, pp. 7–23.

Sergiovanni, T.J. (1996). *Leadership for the Schoolhouse: How Is It Different? Why Is It Important?* San Francisco: Jossey-Bass.

Sergiovanni, T.J.; Burlingame, M.; Coombs, F.D.; and Thurston, P.W. (1980). *Educational Governance and Administration*. Englewood Cliffs, N.J.: Prentice-Hall.

Serviovanni, T.J.; Burlingame, M.; Coombs, F.D.; and Thurston, P.W. (1980). *Educational Governance and Administration*. Englewood Cliffs, N.J.: Prentice-Hall.

Shakeshaft, C. (1987). *Women in Educational Administration*. Newbury Park, Calif.: Sage Publications.

Shapiro, J.Z., and Crowson, R.L. (1990). "Rational Choice Theory and Administrative Decision Making: Implications for Research in Educational Administration." In S.B. Bacharach (ed.), *Advances in Research and Theories of School Management and Educational Policy*, pp. 279–301. Greenwich, Conn.: JAI Press.

Sharrock, A. (1980). "Research on Home-School Relations." In M. Craft, J. Raynor, and L. Cohen (eds.), *Linking Home and School: A New Review*, third edition, pp. 87–106. London: Harper & Row.

Sinclair, R.L. (ed.) (1983). *For Every School a Community: Expanding Environments for Learning*. Boston: The Institute for Responsive Education.

Sinclair, R.L., and Ghory, W.J. (1983). "Expanding Environments for Learning: The Making and Breaking of Learning Boundaries." In R.L. Sinclair (ed.), *For Every School a Community: Expanding Environments for Learning*. Boston: The Institute for Responsive Education.

Slavin, R.; Madden, N.; Karweit, N.; Dolan, L.; and Wasik, B. (1992). *Success for All: A Relentless Approach to Prevention and Early Intervention in Elementary Schools*. Arlington, Va.: Educational Research Service.

Slavin, R.; Madden, N.; Dolan, L.; Wasik, B.; Ross, S.; Smith, L.; and Dianda, M. (1996). "Success for All: A Summary of Research," *Journal of Education for Students Placed at Risk*, 1. Reprinted in Slavin, R. (1996). *Education for All*, pp. 83–109. Lisse: Swets & Zeitlinger Publishers.

Smrekar, C. (1994, April). "The Character and Content of Family-School Interactions in a School-Linked Integrated Services Model." Paper presented at the annual meeting of the American Educational Research Association, New Orleans.

Smrekar, C. (1996a). *The Impact of School Choice and Community: In the Interest of Families and Schools.* Albany: State University of New York Press.

Smrekar, C. (1996b). "The Kentucky Family Resource Centers: The Challenge of Re-making Family-School Interactions." In J.G. Cibulka and W.J. Kritek (eds.), *Coordination Among Schools, Families, and Communities: Prospects for Educational Reform,* pp. 3-25. Albany: State University of New York Press.

Smylie, M.A. (1991). "Organizational Cultures of Schools: Concept, Content, and Change." In S. Conley and B. Cooper (eds.), *The School as a Work Environment: Implications for Reform.* Needham Heights, Mass.: Allyn & Bacon.

Smylie, M.A.; Crowson, R.L.; Chou, V.; and Levin, R.A. (1994, August). "The Principal and Community-School Connections in Chicago's Radical Reform," *Educational Administration Quarterly* 30(3): 342-364.

Smylie, M.A., and Denny, J.W. (1989, March). "Teacher Leadership: Tensions and Ambiguities in Organizational Perspective." Paper presented at the annual meeting of the American Educational Research Association, San Francisco.

Spring, J. (1986). *The American School, 1642–1985* New York: Longman.

Spring, J. (1976). *The Sorting Machine: National Educational Policy Since 1945.* New York: McKay.

Stake, R.E. (1986). *Quieting Reform: Social Science and Social Action in an Urban Youth Program.* Urbana: University of Illinois Press.

Stein, S., and Recktenwald, W. (1990, November 11). "City Parks Are No Place to Play," *Chicago Tribune,* pp. 1, 18.

Steinberg, L. (1989). "Communities of Families and Education." In W.J. Weston (ed.), *Education and the American Family: A Research Synthesis,* pp. 138–168. New York: New York University Press.

Steinberg, N., and Robinson, T. (1990, March 14). "Shouts Erupt Over Firing of Principal at Burns School," *Chicago Sun Times,* p. 3.

Strauss, A. (1979). *Negotiations: Varieties, Contexts, Processes, and Social Order.* San Francisco: Jossey-Bass.

Substance (1990, April). A Monthly Journal for the Chicago Schools 15(6): 6.

Sumption, M.R., and Engstrom, Y. (1966). *School-Community Relations: A New Approach.* New York: McGraw-Hill.

Swap, S.M. (1987). *Enhancing Parent Involvement in Schools.* New York: Teachers College Press.

Swap, S.M. (1993). *Developing Home-School Partnerships: From Concepts to Practice.* New York: Teachers College Press, Columbia University.

Talbert, J.E. (1988). "Conditions of Public and Private School Organization and Notions of Effective Schools." In T. James and H. Levin (eds.), *Comparing Public and Private Schools, Vol. I: Institutions and Organizations.* New York: Falmer Press.

Tangri, S., and Moles, O. (1987). "Parents and the Community." In V. Richardson-Koehler (ed.), *Educator's Handbook: A Research Perspective,* pp. 519–550. New York: Longman.

Taueber, K.E., and James, D. (1983). "Racial Segregation Among Public and Private Schools: A Response," *Sociology of Education* 56: 204–207.

Thomas, W.B.; Moran, K.J.; and Resnick, J. (1996). "Intentional Transformation in a Small School District: The Turner School Initiative." In R.L. Crowson, W.L. Boyd, and H.B. Mawhinney (eds.), *The Politics of Education and the New Institutionalism*, pp. 115-126. London: Falmer Press.

Thompson, J.D. (1967). *Organizations in Action*. New York: McGraw-Hill.

Tiebout, C. (1956, October). "A Pure Theory of Local Expenditures," *Journal of Political Economy* 64: 416–424.

Tireman, L.S., and Watson, M. (1948). *A Community School in a Spanish-Speaking Village*. Albuquerque: University of New Mexico Press.

Tocqueville, A. (1848). *Democracy in America*, edited by J.P. Mayer. Garden City, N.Y.: Doubleday & Co., 1969.

Tregoe, B.B.; Zimmerman, J.W.; Smith, R.A.; and Tobia, P.M. (1989). *Vision in Action: Putting a Winning Strategy to Work*. New York: Simon & Schuster.

Trotter, A. (1996, September 25). "New Web Site Seeks to Help Parents Make the Home-School Connection," *Education Week* 16(4): 11.

Trubowitz, S.; Fibkins, J.D.; Longo, P.; and Sarason, S. (1984). *When A College Works With a Public School: A Case Study of School-College Collaboration*. Boston: Institute for Responsive Education.

Tyack, D.B. (1981). "Governance and Goals: Historical Perspectives on Public Education." In D. Davies (ed.), *Communities and Their Schools*, pp. 11–31. New York: McGraw-Hill Book Co.

Tyack, D.B. (1974). *The One Best System: A History of American Urban Education*. Cambridge, Mass.: Harvard University Press.

Tyack, D., and Hansot, E. (1982a, April). "Hard Times, Hard Choices: The Case for Coherence in Public School Leadership," *Phi Delta Kappan* 63(8): 512.

Tyack, D., and Hansot, E. (1982b). *Managers of Virtue: Public School Leadership in American, 1820-1980*. New York: Basic Books.

Tye, B.B. (1987). "The Deep Structure of Schooling." *Phi Delta Kappan* 69(4): 281–284.

United States Department of Education (1984). *Partnerships in Education*. Washington, D.C.: U.S. Government Printing Office.

Valentine, C.A. (1968). *Culture and Poverty: Critique and Counter-Proposals*. Chicago: University of Chicago Press.

Valdés, G. (1996). *Con Respeto: Bridging the Distances Between Culturally Diverse Families and Schools*. New York: Teachers College Press.

Vidich, A.J., and Bensman, J. (1968). *Small Town in Class Society: Class, Power and Religion in a Rural Community*. Princeton, N.J.: Princeton University Press.

Wagstaff, L.H., and Gallagher, K.S. (1990). "Schools, Families, and Communities: Idealized Images and New Realities." In B. Mitchell and L.L. Cunningham (eds.), *Educational Leadership and Changing Contexts of Families, Communities, and School*. Eighty-ninth Yearbook of the National Society for the Study of Education, Part II, pp. 91–117. Chicago: University of Chicago Press.

Walberg, H.J. (1984, February). "Families as Partners in Educational Productivity," *Phi Delta Kappan*, pp. 397–400.

Walberg, H.J. (1986). "Home Environment and School Learning: Some Quantitative Models and Research Synthesis." In R.J. Griffore and R.P. Boger (eds.), *Child Rearing in the Home and School*, pp. 105–120. New York: Plenum Press.

Walberg, H.J., et al. (1989, June). "Restructuring the Nation's Worst Schools," *Phi Delta Kappan* 70(10): 802–806.

Walde, A.C., and Baker, K. (1990, December). "How Teachers View the Parents' Role in Education," *Phi Delta Kappan* 72(4): 319–322.

Walker, D. (1975). "Curriculum Development in an Art Project." In W.A. Reid and D. Walker (eds.), *Case Studies in Curriculum Change*. London: Routledge and Kegan Paul.

Waller, W. (1932). *The Sociology of Teaching*. New York: Wiley.

Wang, M.; Haertel, G.; and Walberg, H. (1990). "What Influences Learning? A Content Analysis of Review Literature." *Journal of Education Research* 84(1): 30–43.

Warner, I. (1991, January). "Parents in Touch: District Leadership for Parent Involvement," *Phi Delta Kappan* 72(5): 372–375.

Warner, W.L., and Lunt, P.S. (1941). *The Social Life of a Modern Community*. New Haven: Yale University Press.

Warren, R.L. (ed.) (1973). *Perspectives on the American Community*, second edition. Chicago: Rand McNally.

Watkins, P. (1990, October-December). "Agenda, Power and Text: The Formulation of Policy in School Councils," *Journal of Education Policy* 5(4): 315–331.

Wehlage, G.G.; Rutter, R.A.; Smith, G.A.; Lesko, N.; and Fernandez, R.R. (1989). *Reducing the Risk: Schools as Communities of Support*. London: Falmer Press.

Weick, K.E. (1976, March). "Educational Organizations as Loosely-Coupled Systems," *Administrative Science Quarterly* 21, pp. 1–16.

Weiss, H.B. (1995). *Raising Our Future: Families, Schools and Communities Joining Together*. Cambridge, Mass.: Harvard Graduate School of Education, Harvard Family Research Project.

Werner, E.E., and Smith, R.S. (1982). *Vulnerable but Invincible: A Study of Resilient Children*. New York: McGraw-Hill.

Weston, W.J. (ed.) (1989). *Education and the American Family: A Research Synthesis*. New York: New York University Press.

White, J. A., and Wehlage E. (1995). "Community Collaboration: If It Is Such a Good Idea, Why Is It So Hard to Do?" *Educational Evaluation and Policy Analysis* 17(1); 23-38.

Wiles, D.K.: Wiles, J.; and Bondi, J. (1981). *Practical Politics for School Administrators*. Boston: Allyn & Bacon.

Wilson, K.E., and Daviss, B. (1994). *Redesigning Education*. New York: Henry Holt & Co.

Wilson, W.J. (1987). *The Truly Disadvantaged: The Inner City, the Underclass, and Public Policy*. Chicago: University of Chicago Press.

Wilson, W.J. (1996). *When Work Disappears: The World of the New Urban Poor*. New York: Alfred A. Knopf.

Wireman, P. (1984). *Urban Neighborhoods, Networks, and Families: New Forms for Old Values*. Lexington, Mass.: Lexington Books.

Wirt, F.M. (1990). "The Missing Link in Instructional Leadership: The Superintendent, Conflict and Maintenance." Project Report, The National Center for School Leadership. Urbana-Champaign: University of Illinois.

Wirt, F.M., and Christovich, L. (1989, February). "Administrators' Perceptions of Policy Influence: Conflict Management Styles and Roles," *Educational Administration Quarterly* 25(1): 5–35.

Wirt, F.M., and Kirst, M.W. (1989). *Schools in Conflict*, second edition. Berkeley: McCutchan.

Wise, A.E. (1988, January). "Legislated Learning Revisited," *Phi Delta Kappan* 69(5): 329–333.

Wise, A.E. (1990). "Student Welfare in the Era of School Reform: Legislated Learning Revisited." In S.B. Bacharach (ed.), *Education Reform: Making Sense of It All*, pp. 400–409. Boston: Allyn & Bacon.

Witkin, B.R. (1984). *Assessing Needs in Educational and Social Programs*. San Francisco: Jossey-Bass.

Witkin, B.R. (1991). "Setting Priorities: Needs Assessment in a Time of Change." In R.V. Carlson and G. Awkerman (eds.), *Educational Planning: Concepts, Strategies, Practices*, pp. 241–266. New York: Longman.

Wong, K.K. (1990). *City Choices: Education and Housing*. Albany: State University of New York Press.

Wong, K.K. (ed.) (1996). *Advances in Educational Policy: Rethinking School Reform in Chicago*, Vol. 2. Greenwich, Conn.: JAI Press.

Wong, K.K., and Rollow, S.G. (1990). "A Case Study of the Recent Chicago School Reform, Part I: The Mobilization Phase," *Administrator's Notebook* 34(5): 1–6.

Worthington, R. (1990, March 4). "Students' Rights to Switch Puts Schools to the Test," *Chicago Tribune*, Sunday, pp. 1, 14.

Wynn, J.; Richman, H.; Rubinstein, R.A.; and Littell, J. (1987, November). *Communities and Adolescents: An Exploration of Reciprocal Supports*. A Report Prepared for the William T. Grant Foundation Commission on Work, Family and Citizenship: Youth and America's Future. University of Chicago: Chapin Hall Center for Children.

Youth and America's Future. (1988). *The Forgotten Half: Pathways to Success for America's Youth and Young Families*. (Final Report of the William T. Grant Foundation Commission on Work, Family and Citizenship). Washington, D.C.: Wm. T. Grant Commission on Work, Family and Citizenship.

Zeigler, L.H.; Jennings, M.K.; and Peak, G.W. (1974). *Governing American Schools: Political Interaction in Local School Districts*. North Scituate, Mass.: Duxbury Press.

Zeigler, H.; Kehoe, E.; and Reisman, J. (1985). *City Managers and School Superintendents: Responses to Community Conflict*. New York: Praeger.

Ziegenfuss, J.T., Jr. (1989). *Designing Organizational Futures*. Springfield, Ill.: Charles C. Thomas Publishers.

COURT CASES

Adler v. Board, 342 U.S. 485 (1952)

Aurora East District v. Cronin, 442 N.E. 2d 511 (1982)

Bethel District v. Fraser, 106 S.Ct. 3159 (1986)

Board of Education of City of Chicago v. VanKast, 625 N.E. 2d 206 (1993)

Board of Education of Kiryas Joel v. Grumet, 114 S. Ct.2481 (1994)

Board of Education of Oklahoma City v. Dowell, 111 S.Ct. 630 (1991)

Bradley v. Richmond, 382 U.S. 103 (1965)

Brown v. Board of Education of Topeka, Kansas, 347 U.S. 483 (1954)

Burlington School Committee v. Dept. of Education of Massachusetts, 105 S.Ct. 1996 (1985)

Child Welfare Society of Flint v. Kennedy District, 189 N.W. 1002 (1922)

City of Louisville v. Commonwealth, 121 S.W. 411 (1909)

Cleveland Board of Education v. LaFleur, 414 U.S. 632 (1972)

Council of Organizations and Others for Education About Parochiad, Inc. v. John Engler, 554 N.W. 2d 903 (1996)

Davis v. Grover, 480 N.W. 2d 460 (1992)

Dothan City Board of Education v. V.M.H., 660 So. 2d 1328 (1995)

Eagle v. Vitale, 370 U.S. 421 (1962)

Edwards V. Aguillard, 482 U.S. 578 (1987)

Epperson v. Arkansas, 393 U.S. 97 (1968)

Fischer v. Snyder, 476 F. 2d 375 (1973)

Florence County School Dist. v. Carter, 510 U.S. 7 (1993)

Franklin V. Gwinett County Public Schools, 112 S.Ct. 1028 (1992)

Freeman v. Pitts, 112 S.Ct. 1430 (1992)

Fumarolo v. Chicago Board of Education, 566 N.E. 2d 1283 (1990)

Gaines v. Anderson, 421 F.Supp. 337 (1976)

Goss v. Lopez, 419 U.S. 565 (1975)

Griffin v. County School Board, 377 U.S. 218 (1964)

Grove City College v. Bell, 104 S.Ct. 1211 (1984)

Hall v. Tawney, 621 F.2d 607 (1980)

Hazelwood District v. Kuhlmeier, 108 S.Ct. 562 (1988)

Honig v. Doe, 108 S.Ct. 592 (1988)

Henrick Hudson District Board of Education v. Rowley, 458 U.S. 176 (1982)

Wallace v. Jaffree, 437 U.S. 38 (1985)
Weiss v. Bruno, 523 P.2d 915 (1974)
Westside Community Schools v. Mergens, 110 S. Ct. 2356 (1990)
Widmar v. Vincent, 454 U.S. 263 (1981)
Wisconsin v. Yoder, 406 U.S. 205 (1972)
Witters v. State Commission for the Blind, 771 P.2d 1119 (1989)
Wright v. Council of City of Emporia, 407 U.S. 451 (1972)
Zobrest v. Catalina Foothills School Dist., 113 S.Ct. 2462 (1993)
Zorach v. Clauson, 343 U.S. 306 (1952)

INDEX